SOCIETY AND GOVERNMENT IN
RICHELIEU AND MAZARIN, 1624–6

SOCIETY AND GOVERNMENT IN FRANCE UNDER RICHELIEU AND MAZARIN, 1624–61

RICHARD BONNEY

Professor of Modern History
University of Leicester

MACMILLAN
PRESS

First published 1988

Published by
THE MACMILLAN PRESS LTD
Houndmills, Basingstoke, Hampshire RG21 2XS
and London
Companies and representatives
throughout the world

Typeset by Wessex Typesetters
(Division of The Eastern Press Ltd)
Frome, Somerset

Printed in Hong Kong

ing in Publication Data
Bonney, Richard
Society and government in France under
Richelieu and Mazarin, 1624–61.
1. France—Politics and government—
1610–1643   2. France—Politics and
government—1643–1715
I. Title
944′.032   DC123
ISBN 0–333–41848–4 (hardcover)
ISBN 0–333–41849–2 (paperback)

For Alexander Bonney

CONTENTS

LIST OF MAPS AND FIGURE

ACKNOWLEDGEMENTS

The tasks of judicious editing and ruthless pruning were rendered painless by the heroic efforts of Dr Margaret Camsell.

The author and publishers gratefully acknowledge the permission granted by the following to quote from sources which may be in copyright. These are specifically:

Bercé	© Librairie Droz S.A., Geneva
Dickmann et al.	© Aschendorffsche Verlagsbuchhandlung, Münster
Grillon	© Éditions Pedone, Paris, and Commission Internationale pour l'Édition des Sources de l'histoire européene, series Monumenta Europeae Historica
Mongrédien	© Éditions Gallimard, Paris, 1961.
Mousnier	© Presses Universitaires de France, Paris
Mousnier, Durand	© Presses Universitaires de France, Paris
Labatut	
Ranum	© Oxford University Press

In addition, the author gratefully acknowledges the permission granted to use three maps and one figure from *Political change in France under Richelieu and Mazarin, 1624–1661* (Oxford University Press, 1978).

RICHARD BONNEY

LIST OF ABBREVIATIONS

MANUSCRIPT SOURCES AT PARIS

AAE France	Archives des Affaires Etrangères, Mémoires et Documents, France
AG	Archives de la Guerre
AN	Archives Nationales
BL	British Library
BN	Bibliothèque Nationale

PRINTED SOURCES

Avenel	*Lettres, instructions diplomatiques et papiers d'état du Cardinal de Richelieu*, ed. D. L. M. Avenel, 8 vols (1853–77).
Bercé	Y-M. Bercé, *Histoire des croquants. Etude des soulèvements populaires au xviiᵉ siècle dans le sud-ouest de la France*, 2 vols (Paris–Geneva, 1974).
Chéruel	*Journal d'Olivier Lefèvre d'Ormesson* . . . , ed. P. A. Chéruel, 2 vols (1860–1).
Chevallier	P. Chevallier, 'La véritable journée des dupes (11 novembre 1630) . . .', *Mémoires de la Société Académique de l'Aube*, cviii (1978), 194–253.
Clément	*Lettres, instructions et mémoires de Colbert* . . . , ed. P. Clément, 10 vols (1861–82).
Courteault	'Journal inédit du Parlement de Paris pendant la Fronde (1 déc 1651–12 avril 1651)', ed. H. Courteault, *Annuaire-Bulletin de la Société de l'Histoire de France [année 1916]*, (1917), 163–315.
Dickmann et al.	*Acta pacis Westphalicae. Serie I. Instruktionen. Frankreich. Schweden. Kaiser*, ed. F. Dickmann et al. (Münster, 1962).
Feillet	A. Feillet, *La misère au temps de la Fronde et Saint-Vincent de Paul* (5th ed. 1866).
Feillet et al.	*Oeuvres de Retz*, ed. A. Feillet et al. (10 vols, 1870–96).

Floquet	*Relation du voyage du Chancelier Séguier en Normandie,* ed. A. M. Floquet (Rouen, 1842).
Grillon	*Les papiers de Richelieu. Section politique intérieure. Correspondance et papiers d'état,* ed. P. Grillon (in progress; 1975–).
Histoire générale de Languedoc	*Histoire générale de Languedoc,* ed. C. Devic and J. Vaissette, cont. E. Roschach, xiv (Toulouse, 1876).
Lair	J. Lair, *Nicolas Foucquet* . . . (2 vols, 1890).
Legrelle	A. Legrelle, 'Les assemblées de la noblesse en Normandie, 1658–9', *Société de l'histoire de Normandie. Mélanges,* 4th ser. (1898), 307–46.
Lublinskaya	*Vnutrenniaia politika frantsuzkogo absoliutizma, 1633–1649 [The internal politics of French absolutism],* ed. A. D. Lublinkskaya (Leningrad, 1966).
Mailfait	H. Mailfait, *Un magistrat de l'ancien régime. Omer Talon, sa vie et ses oeuvres, 1595–1652* (1902).
Michaud and Poujoulat	Omer Talon, *Mémoires,* ed. J. F. Michaud and J. J. F. Poujoulat, 3rd ser. vi (1839).
Mongrédien	G. Mongrédien, *10 novembre 1630. La journée des dupes* (1961).
Mousnier	*Lettres et mémoires adressés au Chancelier Séguier, 1633–1649,* ed. R. E. Mousnier (2 vols 1964).
Mousnier, Durand, Labatut	*Problèmes de stratification sociale. Deux cahiers de la noblesse pour les Etats Généraux de 1649–1651,* ed. R. E. Mousnier, J-P. Labatut and Y. R. Durand (1964).
Porchnev	B. F. Porchnev, *Les soulèvements populaires en France de 1623 à 1648* (Fr. trans., 1963).
Ranum	O. A. Ranum, *Richelieu and the councillors of Louis XIII* . . . (Oxford, 1963).
Thérive	Guy Patin, *Lettres pendant la Fronde,* ed. A. Thérive (1921).

INTRODUCTION

A relatively short volume of texts and commentary can scarcely lay claim to comprehensive coverage of the ministries of Richelieu and Mazarin. It was felt preferable, in a book dedicated to the idea of text-based study, to concentrate in depth on certain key themes. One of the great issues of French history is the transition from so-called 'Renaissance' monarchy to 'absolute' monarchy, the strengthening of royal authority and its institutions. This did not occur as a gradual, linear development. Periods of formative change were interspersed with periods of relative stagnation or even regression. Few historians would doubt that the ministries of Richelieu and Mazarin were one such period of formative change, perhaps the most important in the history of *ancien régime* France. Some have talked of a 'revolution in government', but the cautious student should beware of such a convenient label. Governments do not make revolutions, since the essence of government is almost invariably the maintenance of power and defence of the status quo. Richelieu, Mazarin and the other ministers wanted to conserve and restore what was best in France, not to reform and change it.

The critical student should also ponder what is meant by that much over-worked term 'absolutism'. It is a word of relatively recent derivation, dating from the period of the French Revolution. In its simple formulation of 'absolute power' or 'absolute authority' it was certainly used in the sixteenth and seventeenth centuries. Richelieu, or a source very close to him, commented that 'as long as the Huguenot party subsists in France, the King will not be absolute in his kingdom' (doc. 4). The chief minister was accused by his opponents of seizing 'absolute power' (doc. 18). However, few contemporary commentators would have expected a system of government to be described under such an all-embracing label. Strictly speaking, absolute power is a logical and practical impossibility. In this respect, the great political theorist Jean Bodin commented in 1576:

> If we say that he has absolute power who is not subject to the law, no such prince can anywhere be found, given that all princes in the world are subject to the laws of God and of nature and to many human laws which are common to all peoples.

No 'absolute' ruler in theory enjoyed absolute power in practice. One recent historian states that 'absolutism was always in the making but never made': it was an objective incapable of complete realization. Others see absolutism as no more than an ideological cloak to mask the weakness of royal power in practice. According to such an interpretation, the theoretical power of the king had to be freed from restrictions to offset the limitations on his power in practice.

This comment might suggest a working definition of absolutism such as 'freedom for the monarch in practice from institutional checks on his power.' Even this definition has some drawbacks, however. The kings of Castile were called 'absolute' even though they had to consult the Cortes, the national representative institution. The French kings were called 'absolute' whether or not they summoned the Estates General. There is clearly no single European model of an 'absolute' ruler. One historian has suggested that for 'absolutism' we should read '*relative* absolutism'. This has some semantic disadvantage, but the reality is that some rulers *were* 'more absolute' than others. Even a weak French king such as Henri III might seem an absolute ruler compared to the prince of the Netherlands, as became clear in the negotiations between Anjou, his advisers (including Bodin) and the Dutch in 1580. The existence of elective monarchy, and other concessions to the nobles, led Bodin to doubt whether the king of Poland could be termed a sovereign ruler at all. For Bodin, the fundamental characteristic of sovereignty, under which all other powers were subsumed, was the power to give laws 'unto subjects in general without their consent'.

This book is about the practice, rather than the theory, of government. Any historical theory on the nature of absolutism must ultimately be tested by applying it to the reality of government. The most striking fact about the way government operated under Richelieu and Mazarin is that it was scarcely ever concerned with broad principles and issues, and almost exclusively concerned with pressing realities of a day-to-day kind. The growth of the modern state is to a significant degree the story of the growth of its fiscal power. This is not to argue that other developments, such as the rise of bureaucracy, the police and the army, were not also vitally important. However, these aspects of governmental power require finance. Without 'modern' taxation, that is to say, a regular and heavy fiscal burden, these other developments could not have occurred. The period of Richelieu and Mazarin saw a rapid increase in taxation to pay for France's long foreign war against Spain. This increased fiscal burden was one of the crucial factors in opposition to the regime. Yet there was never enough tax revenue to pay for the multifarious costs of the French monarchy, above all the financing of the war effort. A degree of innovation, both of a fiscal and administrative kind, was forced on reluctant ministers when ordinary sources of revenue and methods of administration had failed. Seventeenth-century statesmen such as Richelieu, Mazarin and their ministers were not high-minded 'absolutists' seeking to apply some blueprint for stronger monarchy on a docile population. They were first and foremost pragmatic politicians, seeking to cling to power, not above exploiting the fruits of office, above all desperate for success. Perhaps only in their desire for success did the interests of Richelieu and Mazarin clearly coincide with those of Louis XIII and Louis XIV.

University of Leicester   RICHARD BONNEY

1 THE CHIEF MINISTER: POLICIES AND CRITICS

The greatest problem faced by any government in early modern Europe was how to mobilise the resources of the state in time of war without arousing excessive discontent among the population at large. The two Cardinal ministers faced this problem throughout their period in office. One fact stands out as of supreme importance: the duration of the war against Spain (1635–59). There were several other significant wars, too.[1] Richelieu's ministry began in the last phase of Louis XIII's struggle against the military power of the Huguenots, which led to further fighting in 1625–6 and 1627–9. In short, there were only two years of real peace during the entire ministries of Richelieu and Mazarin (1660–1).

Because the issue of war or peace was so fundamental to the conduct of orderly government, the extent to which it was debated among the ministers is of great interest to historians. The decision of the French government to resort to force in support of the (Protestant) Grisons' claim in the Valtelline and in opposition to the Spanish-backed Catholic position, had been taken before Richelieu became chief minister on 13 August 1624. The new element, which seems to have taken Richelieu completely by surprise, was the revolt of the Huguenots in 1625: the initial rising led by Soubise in January was followed in February by that of his elder brother, the duc de Rohan, and by the great fortress of La Rochelle in May. The chief minister immediately grasped the financial danger posed to the government by war on two fronts (doc. 1). Should the government reach a compromise settlement with the Huguenots in order to pursue its military objectives in Italy? The issue divided the government and the court (doc. 2). Peace at any price might seem the safest course of action (doc. 3). Richelieu's view, however, was that a compromise peace with the Huguenots was desirable so that an undivided French military

---

[1] Such as the wars over the Valtelline (1624–6) and the Mantuan Succession (1628–31), and those against England (1627–9), Lorraine (1632–3) and the Emperor (1636–48).

1

effort could be mounted in the Valtelline conflict (doc. 4). In the event, peace with the Huguenots came first, in February 1626, before any treaty with Spain.

A new test of the resolution of the French government was not long coming, with the attempt of the Spanish governor of Milan and the duke of Savoy to partition the Mantuan–Montferrat succession on the death of the last Gonzaga duke in direct line in 1627. With the successful siege and capture of La Rochelle in 1627–8, Louis XIII's armies were free to bolster Nevers' position in Montferrat by relieving Casale. This was to be achieved, on a very tight schedule proposed by Richelieu, *before* the complete defeat of the Protestant rebellion in Languedoc (doc. 5); however, there can be no doubt that the Cardinal desired to achieve victory over the Huguenots too (doc. 6).

The capture of Pinerolo by the French forces on 29 March 1630 was a decisive event in the Mantuan war. Even Marie de Médicis, the Queen Mother, recognised that its capture offered France diplomatic advantages (doc. 11). Marillac, the Keeper of the Seals (that is, interim Chancellor) was increasingly influential in the counsels of the Queen Mother and advocated strictly limited intervention because of the risk of protracted war with Spanish power in Italy. He pointed to the threats posed by popular unrest in France, resistance to taxation, and the general indifference, if not outright hostility, to French war aims. Marillac contrasted the financial and administrative consequences of war in Italy with his own (and to some extent, Richelieu's) reforming intentions (docs. 7, 8, 12).

In contrast, Richelieu's view was that Pinerolo offered the prospect of a permanent French capacity for intervention in Italy, making Louis XIII the 'arbiter and master' there. Richelieu recognised the extent of the financial commitment that would result from a protracted conflict with Spanish power in Italy, and that any immediate prospect of reform would be dashed (docs. 9, 10). His repudiation of the treaty with the Emperor Ferdinand II negotiated at Regensburg appeared to open up the prospect of a prolonged war and focused the minds of his critics. In the aftermath of the crisis of the Day of Dupes, the myth was born that while Marillac had sought peace, Richelieu had always sought war (doc. 14); moreover, it was said that he had usurped the king's sovereignty to achieve this aim (doc. 15).

French intervention in Italy ended in 1631, sooner than

Richelieu's critics had feared. However, Louis XIII's retention of the fortress of Pinerolo, in contravention of the official terms of the peace, was regarded by Philip IV of Spain as a legitimate cause for a new war. But when the Spanish council of state debated the possibility of declaring war on France on 13 April 1634, it found that the necessary European coalition to sustain such a war did not exist, and the declaration was postponed. Louis XIII, however, remained profoundly distrustful of Spanish intentions and in a secret memorandum to Richelieu argued the case for a 'vigorous open war against Spain in order to secure a beneficial general peace' (doc. 16). The decision for war was taken on the king's own initiative: Richelieu had outlined the options since 1630; it was the king who had the awesome responsibility in 1630 and again in 1634–5 of drawing the logical conclusion from the advice of his chief minister.

Secret negotiations began with Spain soon after the declaration of war in May 1635, but all such overtures proved abortive in the lifetime of Louis XIII and Richelieu. With the death of the Cardinal (4 December 1642), followed by that of the king (14 May 1643), the Regency of Anne of Austria was proclaimed and Mazarin became chief minister. They were obliged to continue Louis XIII's foreign policy and diplomatic alliances, and had to show caution in their dealings with the Habsburgs: Anne of Austria was the sister of Philip IV and Mazarin was a foreigner by birth. For these reasons, it would have been political suicide to sign a peace with Spain that could later be criticised as detrimental to French interests. This foreign policy carried risks in the new domestic political situation. It was regarded as unusual, even among the ministers themselves, for a Regency government to fight a foreign war – the precedents of 1561 and 1610 were respectively of a time of peace and of a war that was rapidly ended. Many contemporaries were convinced that Mazarin might have had peace if he had acted with more moderation and openness (doc. 17), though this view failed to take account of Spanish intransigence and a natural desire on Philip IV's part to exploit any weakness of the French government during a period of royal minority.

Nevertheless, Mazarin's conduct of government was vilified in the propaganda of the Fronde, known collectively as the *Mazarinades* (doc. 18). Even the *Parlement* of Paris, the most prestigious lawcourt in the land, joined the criticism in 1649 and

3

again in 1652 (docs. 19, 20). Opposition to the foreign policy of the crown was one of the consistent themes of the aristocratic opponents of Richelieu and Mazarin, and formed a clear link between the revolts of the 1630s and the Fronde (see Chapter 4). The nobles also objected to the style of government adopted by Richelieu and Mazarin, their ruthless elimination of ministerial rivals (see Chapter 2) and other controversial aspects of government, such as the rise in expenditure and taxation. Contemporaries also cast doubt on the chief ministers' motives in the advocacy of war. Richelieu, it has recently been shown, systematically built up an immense personal fortune of 22 million *livres*, Mazarin a far greater one of 37 million, probably the largest personal fortune of the old régime. Was all the wealth of the Cardinals derived from legitimate sources by valid gifts of the king? Many thought it was not – this accusation of ministerial corruption forms a perspective on Richelieu's claim to be disinterested (doc. 6), and on his criticisms of Bullion's corruption (see Chapter 2). It also provides a perspective on the arrests of La Vieuville in 1624 and Foucquet in 1661.

1. Richelieu, Memorandum for the King, [beginning of May] 1625

To judge properly what resolution the King should take, it is necessary to look at, and consider maturely, the present state of affairs throughout Christendom . . . I shall not emphasise that Spain, pressed to extremity by us, might enter its forces into France, either from the kingdom itself or from Flanders. It is easy to guard against invasion from Spain with small forces because of the lie of the land. The King has a fresh and powerful army on the frontier of Picardy and Champagne which, without further expense, he could lead in person . . . Rebellions are so common an occurrence in France that while we are considering humiliating others we may receive a worse blow from ourselves than we are able to give our enemies. These rebellions can only come from malcontent great nobles or the Huguenots. From the great nobles there is nothing to fear presently. Some are weak. While others would like to see some sort of disturbance in which they might improve their position, they themselves do not wish to provide the leadership. They well understand that this is not the moment for them to gain maximum advantage.

As for the Huguenots, they are accustomed to advance their cause at

4

the expense of the State, and to seize their opportunity when they see us occupied against those who are our declared enemies. They did so during the siege of Amiens.[2] We must fear that they will do the same on this occasion. Their taking to arms and insolent demands remove all doubt about it. However, it is necessary to see whether or not their power is sufficient to stop the King from following his plans for foreign war. It is certain that they are not powerful enough in themselves to do so; but they could become so by accident, for example if Spain assisted them with money or ships. We already have some knowledge of such plans. By chance they might have some success. A treasonable governor might voluntarily hand over his fortress. This might result in those who are well disposed towards them actually declaring for them, which could compromise our policy.

We must further consider that public affairs are like a human body, which grows, attains maturity and then declines. The essence of political prudence consists in seizing the most advantageous opportunity to implement one's policy. At this moment everybody trembles at the prospect of the armed forces of France. Up to now everything has gone as one would wish. We have not seen the divisions which are normally in the armies of allied powers, although we cannot ignore that the signs are already there in the army in Piedmont.

Although the King has money, as we have said above, and nothing has been lacking in the armies, expenditure is so excessive in France that no-one can be sure that we will always be able to bear such excessive costs. In questions of war one knows how and when they begin, but no-one can foresee the timing or the nature of their ending; in as much as the appetite sometimes increases with eating and military matters are a day-to-day business.

However, I do not think that there is anybody who does not consider that it is necessary to make peace either at home or abroad. It is certain that any man with judgement would say that it is too much to have two businesses at the same time, and that one is sufficient to keep you fully occupied.

. . . As long as the Huguenots have a foothold in France, the King will never be master at home and will never be able to undertake any glorious action abroad. The difficulty is to make a peace with Spain which will be secure, honourable and in which all our allies can have the advantage which they reasonably might desire. Otherwise, however useful it may seem, peace will be extremely damaging . . .

[2] In 1597, during the reign of Henri IV.

It is necessary to see a prompt conclusion to the proposed negotiations on this subject, so that if they do not succeed, His Majesty may give satisfaction to the Huguenots. He will thus be able to create unity for the war against the Spaniards. It is certain that the Spaniards cannot sustain this war for a long time if we are able to attack them powerfully on several fronts. However, if our war effort is feeble, they will be able to carry on easily. This will force us into a lengthy war in which they will have an equal advantage . . .

(Source: Grillon, i. 181–6)

2. Richelieu to the Queen Mother, 16 August 1625

. . . I beg your Majesty to tell the King, while advising him to keep the whole matter completely secret, that since I have been here[3] I have discovered that there are some who wish to pursue war vigorously against the Huguenots without considering whether the timing is convenient or not. There is a cabal of others, who wish to commit the King to a war against Spain, and to sign peace with the Huguenots, without considering whether this is to the advantage of the King or not. There is considerable reason to believe, for reasons which I cannot write but which I shall tell the King and Your Majesty personally, that the man who comes from the ambassador of Spain will be encouraged by such people . . .

(Source: Grillon, i. 205–6)

3. Anonymous memorandum [by Fancan?] on the necessity of peace in the kingdom [September 1625]

. . . There is scarcely a more necessitous King than our own, since he has no demesne, no certain revenues, nor subjects that could be poorer. It is also true to say that there has been a very bad management in the past of the finances of the State. One cannot deny that all this has greatly altered the kingdom; but these disorders on their own have not reduced it into its present state. Civil war alone, and particularly religious war, has

---

[3] At Limours.

6

brought the King, the provinces and all the people in the countryside to the deplorable state they are in at present.

. . . This arises from foreign cabals and our lack of foresight in throwing ourselves into civil wars at a time when the Spaniard triumphs over our neighbours. The sole means of guaranteeing ourselves from this is not to reject the blandishments of his councillors, and above all to decide promptly to heal this sick State from its illness by establishing a firm, lasting peace. Without this, it will be very difficult for the King to re-establish his affairs either within or outside the kingdom. It will also be difficult for the poor people to survive the burden of taxes which they suffer. If there is no peace in the kingdom, it will be necessary for the King and the people to seize the wealth of those seigneurs, office-holders, and merchants who have it. This will be to everyone's disadvantage. Whereas, by a solid peace, a thousand expedients could be found for the conservation of the King, the State and the people.

. . . The greatest benefit that the King could draw from the Assembly of Notables is to make it resolve upon the necessity of peace, which will give His Majesty the opportunity to deal with all matters at leisure and without which there is a serious possibility that France will fall into deplorable confusion.

That all these calamities of the State arise from our wars of religion, none could deny. Nor could anyone doubt that to embark upon even the smallest war, be it against England or La Rochelle (or anywhere else in the kingdom) would lead to our entire ruin. As a result, it seems that the King cannot take wiser advice than to have the necessity of peace agreed upon in the assembly in which the principal members of the three Orders of the State will be present . . .

(Source: Grillon, i. 218–20)

4. Anonymous memorandum [by Richelieu?]: Discourse to see whether, if there is peace with Spain in Italy, it is necessary to have it also at home, 25 November 1625

It is certain that as long as the Huguenot party subsists in France, the King will not be absolute in his kingdom, and he will not be able to establish the order and rule to which his conscience obliges him and which the necessity of his people requires. It is also necessary to destroy the pride of the great nobles, who regard La Rochelle as a citadel in whose shadow they can demonstrate their discontent with impunity. It is besides certain that no one will dare to undertake anything glorious abroad, nor even to oppose foreign ambitions, because the Huguenot party will seek to profit from the situation, as it did in the last war. There is no doubt that the first and principal objective His Majesty must have is to ruin this party. We must also see whether the timing and occasion for doing this are propitious, while we are occupied abroad, since the justification they have given us of their notorious rebellion is great and evident to everyone . . .

The people, towns, and most of the sovereign courts of this Kingdom are strongly of the opinion that we should undertake an immediate war against the Huguenots, and that the destruction of their power is easy. They call those who speak against such views 'bad Catholics', and are encouraged in this view by several discontented personages. It is to be feared that if the war against the Huguenots is halted, people will start thinking along the lines of the Catholic League as in former times on a similar pretext . . .

Reasons for making peace within the Kingdom
Prudence does not permit the undertaking of two wars at the same time. It is not known when the war in Italy will end. However, it would seem that one should settle the civil war, chiefly because the occasion to deal with the Huguenots will return, whereas if one loses the opportunity to deal with the foreigners' ambitions it will not be possible to do so again in a single attempt.

Pacification of the kingdom will allow us to plan the ruin of the Huguenot party by peaceful means. Such a settlement would probably bring about peace with the Spaniards; they have gained some advantage while we have had a civil war on our hands, but will not wish to take us on when we can bring our full forces against them . . .

The armies of the King have just entered Milan from Piedmont and the Valtelline. However, it is to be feared that the Spaniards, who are aware of this, may take the only option open to them, counter-measures on our frontiers. If we make peace within the kingdom, there is nothing to be feared if they invade, and it is likely that they will not undertake this course of action. But if we are well embarked on the siege of La Rochelle, they would certainly do so with impunity, and in such circumstances we would have to abandon the siege . . .

(Source: Grillon, i. 226–9)

5. Address [by Richelieu] to the King, [December] 1628

Sire, in capturing La Rochelle Your Majesty has ended what has been the most glorious undertaking for yourself and the most useful one for your State in your lifetime. Italy, oppressed for the past year by the armies of the King of Spain and the duke of Savoy, waits to receive from your victorious arms the relief of its misfortunes. Your reputation obliges you to take in hand the cause of your neighbours and allies, who are unjustly despoiled of their States. Besides these very considerable reasons, your own interests oblige you also to turn your thoughts and your arms to this issue. I dare to promise you that if you take this resolution and carry it out as required, the outcome of the enterprise will be no less happy for you than that of La Rochelle. I am no prophet, but I can assure Your Majesty that, if no time is lost in carrying out this plan, you will have lifted the siege of Casale and given peace to Italy by the month of May. Returning with your army into Languedoc, you will have reduced it completely to your obedience and given it peace by July. As a result, I hope that Your Majesty will be able to return victoriously to Paris in August . . .

(Source: Grillon, iii. 587–8)

6. Advice given to the King for the good of his affairs after the capture of La Rochelle [13 January 1629]

Now that La Rochelle has been captured, if the King wishes to make himself the most powerful monarch in the world, and the most esteemed prince, he must consider before God, and examine carefully and secretly with his faithful creatures, his personal behaviour and reforms for his State . . .

At all costs the heretical rebellion must be destroyed. Castres, Nîmes, Montauban and all the other places of Languedoc, Rouergue and Guyenne must be taken. [We must act vigorously and obtain the necessary financial measures to do so.] All fortresses not on the frontier must be razed; we should keep only those at river crossings or which serve as a bridle to mutinous great towns. Those which are on the frontier must be properly fortified; in particular, a place should be acquired at

9

Commercy. The people must be discharged from taxes. The *paulette*[4] should not be re-established when it expires in a year's time. The sovereign courts, which lay claim to sovereignty for themselves and regularly oppose matters for the well-being of the kingdom, should be humbled or moderated.

We must act in such a way that the King will be completely obeyed by great and small alike. Bishoprics should be filled with wise and capable people. Alienated royal demesne should be repurchased. Revenues should be increased by half, which can be achieved by innocent means.

There are still other disorders to regulate, but it is sufficient at first to remedy the most important . . .

The King is good, virtuous, secretive, courageous and a lover of glory, but in truth one must say that he is extremely easily aroused, suspicious, jealous, sometimes susceptible to passing aversions on first impressions to the prejudice of the third or fourth meeting; finally, he is subject to a variety of humours and inclinations which it would be easier for him to correct than for me to comment on, since I am so accustomed to publicise his virtues that I can scarcely comment on his faults even to him privately . . .[5] After this, I beg His Majesty to consider in what ways he wishes that I correct myself, in order that I may be more agreeable to him. The same reason which has led me to inform him of the above also obliges me to examine myself and to correct my faults . . .

I had never thought that, by accepting this office . . . I could gain the reputation of being an interested party. On no occasion did I ask for it. On the contrary, I let it be known by a third party, that, if he had the kindness to gratify my brother-in-law, as it is said, I would consider myself greatly obliged.[6] I made it known at the same time that if he had some other plan, I wished him to follow it. All these considerations purge me, in my opinion, of the suspicion of this blemish on my reputation. But although I am innocent, I have the evil humour of the King against me, which leads him to prefer giving benefits to people who are almost unknown to him rather than to the relatives, in-laws or friends of those who have the honour to serve him.

---

[4] The annual payment by an office-holder for the privilege of resigning his office to his heir.

[5] However, Richelieu gives detailed comments on Louis XIII's propensity to be suspicious; his jealousy; his aversions; his need to humour the great nobility; his lack of application, and so on.

[6] Brézé, Richelieu's brother-in-law, was appointed captain of the king's guards on 20 September 1627.

. . . I refused 20 000 *écus*[7] of extraordinary pension, which it pleased the King to offer me, although my expenses are great and I only subsist because of the liberalities of the Queen his mother. Instead of taking an abbey which it pleased him to give me, I left it to the Chancellor, who does not give better service than I do . . .[8] To have borrowed more than a million *livres* to help the Ile de Ré campaign and the siege of La Rochelle – if this is being an interested party, then I have to confess that I am one.

The King gave me [the governorship of] Le Havre, but His Majesty well knows, I am sure, that it is not worth a *sou* in revenue. I leave to everyone to judge what interest there is in placing oneself on ill terms with all the great nobles and particularly Monsieur who could become my master to France's misfortune . . .

I must ask if I am an interested party because I have maintained 30 guards at my expense for two years, to protect me from the hate of my enemies. The sole consideration of the State placed these at my charge. I can further truthfully say that since I was called to the King's affairs, I have spent four times more than I did before, without having increased my revenue.

Great princes normally for reasons of their grandeur and well-being allow those who hold the most important offices of their State and have their confidence to make an honest fortune. Such princes allow their servants to leave office after receiving due recognition of their services, which displays the magnificence of their masters. Such considerations led the Emperor Charles V in his testament to counsel his son to take care for the affairs of those who managed his. The King by his generosity has made me wealthier than I am worth: since I have had the honour to serve him, he has given me six abbeys worth [   ].[9] When I entered the service of the Queen Mother, I only had 25 000 *livres* in revenue from benefices; due to the misfortune of my family there was only about the same from land. Everything I hold beyond this, which is not a little, I hold from the liberality and grace of Their Majesties in which I am extraordinarily content as I have good reason to be.

For some time the disgrace which has arisen has led me to wish to retire from affairs. At this time, however, it is only my ill health which forces me to beg their Majesties that I should be discharged from the burden of affairs while remaining close to their persons, from whom I shall never separate myself . . .

(Source: Grillon, iv. 24–47)

[7] 60 000 *livres*.
[8] Chancellor d'Aligre was in disgrace.
[9] Blank in text.

7. Marillac to Richelieu, 15 February 1629

. . . At Paris we hear rumours of the King's plan for an invasion of Italy, and I look upon this with confidence since God guides you. It seems to me that if it pleases God that either from fear of the King's armies, or from their actual passage into Italy, you relieve the siege of Casale, this will have a glorious consequence and will add greatly to the King's reputation. If he then turns immediately upon the rebels, it will fill the province of Languedoc with astonishment and greatly advance the reunion of his kingdom and the establishment of his authority there. This seems the design of God and the reason for His blessing His Majesty's actions. A flourishing army which has already gone beyond the Alps will easily be led on further . . .

I confess that great attractions may be found in such counsels. But one must consider that carrying the King's arms into Italy further than is necessary engages one without seeing clearly or assuredly the outcome; that rebels are left free to fortify themselves in France; that factions will gain second wind; and that the Habsburg armies of Germany or Flanders could perhaps enter Picardy or Champagne. I do not know if we have God's blessings for such designs, and it seems to me that all this has to be weighed up very carefully. I do not doubt that you will bear in mind all these necessary considerations.

Moreover, the management of affairs obliges me to tell you that we are doing a great number of things from which the people receive great affliction. The office-holders and merchants are greatly tormented. Necessity requires all this and we cannot avoid it. The justice of the King's arms and the progress of his plans makes these miseries tolerated patiently. It seems to me that it is principally owing to, and to the glory of, a good government to think in terms of alleviating the consequences of its decisions, and drawing up beneficial rulings for the good of the State, which can only be carried out in peacetime. Many people consider another war unnecessary. I do not know whether they will patiently put up with everything which we are forced to do. In order to survive, we have to impose new taxes and other burdens to an intolerable extent. At the moment we have to do many things which would not be accepted at other times. I thought, my lord, that I ought to point this out to you in order to honour and follow all the resolutions which it pleases you to take. On this I pray to God to give you by his grace a very happy and very long life. I am,

My lord,

Your very hur ble, very affectionate and grateful servant,

De Marillac.   (Source: Grillon, iv. 103–4)

8. Marillac to Richelieu, 21 February 1629

. . . Here at Paris everyone is talking about war or peace according to their whim. We wait avidly for news of the resolution which the King will take. His loving subjects are apprehensive at the prospect of seeing the King leave his kingdom. In your regard we rest fully on whatever it pleases you to resolve with His Majesty . . .

(Source: Grillon, iv. 112)

9. Memorandum [of Richelieu] for the King, 13 April 1630

Pinerolo is taken. It is impossible fully to describe the importance of this conquest. We must envisage what could happen as a result of this success . . . The question consists in examining whether it is better to buy a peace by giving up Pinerolo or to conserve it in a long war which will oblige us to keep a strong army in Piedmont, another in Savoy with the King present in person, and a third powerful army in Champagne. If we wish to make peace, we can do so with glory, not shame; but there is reason to doubt the security of Italy for the future.

If we make war, it will be undertaken safely for the conquest of Savoy and the conservation of Pinerolo; but there is reason to suspect that we may be attacked in Champagne and we may fear the length of the war. It must be seen, moreover, if the finances are sufficient to sustain the war and if the interior of the kingdom will remain pacified . . .

The first point, concerning the risk and difficulties of the war, must be decided principally by the judgement of the King. The fear of an internal disturbance depends on Monsieur's[10] attitude. No war can be fought if he is not reconciled with the King. As to whether or not money is sufficient, that depends on Monsieur the finance minister, who must reckon for this army's subsistence that we must have every three months 600 000 *écus*,[11] for which we have received up to now 1.2 million,[12] which will not last us until the end of June. He will know that on such occasions we cannot subsist by assignments but must have cash. The armies of Italy, Savoy and Champagne cost at least 500 000 *livres* a month. More than 2 million is needed.

[10] Gaston d'Orléans, Louis XIII's younger brother.
[11] 1.8 million *livres*.
[12] 3.6 million *livres*.

If my opinion is asked for, the place which I am at[13] prevents me from giving it. But I must state frankly that either there must be a genuine and firm reconciliation between Monsieur, the King and Queen to win over his supporters, so that there rests no suspicion on one side or the other, or we must make peace over Pinerolo, because otherwise we will achieve nothing. If one resolves on peace, it must be made promptly, without wasting a moment, whilst the affairs of the King are in good repute. If, on the other hand, one resolves on war, Savoy must be attacked without delay and the soonest this is done will still result in too long a delay. If the King resolves on war, we must quit all thought of peace, of economies and of rulings within the Kingdom. If on the other hand, we want peace, we must quit all thoughts of Italy for the future . . .

(Source: Grillon, v. 208–13)

10. Advice of Cardinal de Richelieu following that of the Queen Mother and Marillac, Keeper of the Seals [Mid-May 1630]

All the arguments put forward by Monsieur the Keeper of the Seals show clearly that peace is desirable; I have always wanted it for these reasons, and have not omitted anything to secure it . . . The reasons of Monsieur the Keeper of the Seals also show that one cannot make war without great disadvantages; this is true not merely in the present case but in all others, war being one of the scourges with which it has pleased God to afflict men.

But this is not a reason to make peace on conditions which are weak, base or shameful, since this exposes us to inconveniences which are much greater than those of the present war.

The aversion of the people for the present war is not a considerable motive to bring us to such a peace, since they often feel like this and complain about necessary evils as well as those which could be avoided. They are as ignorant of what is useful to a State as they are sensitive and prompt to complain of the misfortunes they suffer in the hope of avoiding greater ones.

Whoever makes peace on shameful conditions will not conserve it for a long time, but will lose reputation for ever, and will expose himself in the future to wars of long duration. It is certain that no-one will be afraid to attack us in view of our lack of consistency and firmness when we hold all

[13] Pinerolo.

the advantages – this situation will not return again. Foreigners will judge our alliance useless because of our irresolution. They will seek security from Spain, whose tyrannous rule they will accept to protect themselves from the designs of the Spaniard, against whom they judge us incapable of giving protection . . .

(Source: Grillon, v. 259–61)

11. Queen Mother to Richelieu, 21 May 1630

My cousin. I was very pleased to learn from your last letter of Mazarini's visit.[14] However, I only wish for peace on advantageous conditions for the King, Monsieur my son, and appreciate that otherwise it will be the road to a new war . . .

(Source: Grillon, v. 273)

12. Memorandum of Marillac to Richelieu, 24 July 1630

These inconveniences[15] are principally the expense, which will be very great, and yet essential: great disaster and shame could result from any deficiency. Reason and experience lead us to fear that matters handled at a distance away from the direct oversight of the King and the Cardinal will not be accomplished properly according to the orders that have been given. Great expenditure will necessarily mean that the State will be in need, accentuating the misery of the people, which is already acute. There are already difficulties in recovering the taxes to pay for all these expenses; new expedients must be adopted, which will go beyond the forms of justice, and will alienate the principal inhabitants of our towns. Intrigues, rebellions and frequent riots will result in the towns. The pretentions of the *Parlements* and sovereign courts will increase, opposed as they are to all new fiscal measures and inclined to prevent the examination of new edicts. Finally, the malice and artifice of malevolent people will grow. Such people are numerous among all social groups. One of the worst consequences of such ill will is that it excites hostility to the actions of His Majesty and his council.

I can scarcely bring myself to admit it – but I must not hide the fact – that, for whatever reason, many people up and down the kingdom

---

[14] Mazarin was the Papal emissary who helped negotiate a truce at Casale.
[15] Of the Mantuan War.

criticise this war. Such people do not talk to those who understand affairs of state. Anyone to whom one explains affairs of state is capable of understanding them. However, there is a general disgust and bad opinion in the kingdom which diminishes the esteem and reverence due to the King. In my opinion this is the greatest evil that can arise.

. . . For all these reasons, it is necessary for the King to be near the heart of his kingdom, to deal with matters of State and all the issues that I have raised. His Majesty's council should be near his person, and well attended, and His Majesty must been seen by his subjects, because his dignity and authority is more important than anything else – this helps the reputation of affairs, and restrains the *Parlements*, the provinces and the great nobles of the kingdom . . .

It is also necessary to comment that the present location of the King and his council[16] prevents them from dealing with affairs necessary for the longer term. I am obliged to say that I fear great necessities and great inconveniences arising from a shortage of funds in the longer term . . .

(Source: Grillon, v. 429–31)

13. Augier and De Vic, English residents, to the English government on the events of the Day of Dupes, 11 November 1630[17]

Yesterday there was held a great and long council at Luxembourg house, the King being present, especially in point of ratifying or refusing the Treaty of Ratisbonne,[18] which is now that the citadel of Casale is revictualled and the town and the castle with other places adjoining restored to the Duke of Mantua, they seem here to neglect and to insist upon the cassation[19] of certain articles in that treaty wherein they do utterly disavow their ministers[20] as having transgressed their commission, and this is credibly thought to have been the resultat[21] of yesterday's council . . .

As we were shutting up this letter, we have received a note through a

---

[16] St. Jean-de-Maurienne.
[17] Spelling modernised.
[18] Regensburg.
[19] That is, repudiation.
[20] Brûlart and Père Joseph, the French plenipotentiaries.
[21] Decision.

very good hand containing that the Cardinal was certainly disgraced and Madame de Combalet[22] already retired from the Court to the Carmelites . . .

(Source: Chevallier, pp. 218–27)

14. Apology for the sieur Marillac Keeper of the Seals of France against a pamphlet published under the title of 'Interviews at the Champs-Elysées' [n.d.: 1631]

. . . He vowed not to enrich himself either directly or indirectly from gifts from the King, which vow God gave him the grace to carry out and to refuse great gratifications and many occasions of great profit . . . [As Keeper of the Seals he never signed a decree] without properly understanding it, and nearly always he read it himself. It is well known that he annoyed many important people on this point . . .

The Cardinal wanted war and feared peace, in which laws, order and justice would have their ordinary course and he would no longer have the pretext of being so preoccupied himself, and the mind of the King so preoccupied, on the matter of war expenses and the consequences of these expenses.

The Keeper of the Seals on the contrary wanted peace and did all he could to arrive at it by honourable and assured means. He saw the needs of the church and the faith, the great misery of the people, the disorder of justice, the novelties that one was forced to adopt all the time to obtain money, the hazards run by the King given his health, the frequent riots of the populace and the universal discontent – that was why he desired peace.

(Source: BN Ms. fr. 17 486)

15. Gaston d'Orléans to Louis XIII, 30 May 1631

For a long time, Cardinal de Richelieu has had a well-formed plan to make himself ruler of the land under the title of first minister. For a while he is prepared to allow you to retain the crown. However, he seeks to make you dependent on him and having rid himself of both you and me,

---

[22] Richelieu's niece.

17

he plans to gain supreme power. To achieve this objective, he has deemed it necessary to have control in three areas. Firstly, the resources of the kingdom; secondly, your authority; finally, your person, that of the Queen my mother, and that of myself.

As to the first . . . he has nothing more to achieve, since he controls all the resources of the kingdom. He commands the fortresses, the troops and the artillery since he has dismissed the officer of the crown who had this function.[23] He controls the navy. Financial administration is carried out by one of his clients.[24] He has gathered together most of the money in circulation and has placed it under guard in his fortresses. He has gained the power to distribute benefits, to accord graces, to inflict punishments. In short, he has instilled the notion that all decisions whether for good or evil depend on his whim.

As to the second . . . he is already complete master of your conduct, not merely by the absolute confidence that you have in him, but also because he has so isolated you that at present the Queen my Mother cannot approach you, and no institution acts around you except under his direction. Thus all the sounds you hear are merely echoes of his voice, so that it is true to say, my lord, that despite your great abilities as yet you have not been able to avoid your wishes and your actions falling into dependence on him.

As to the third, it is self-evident that he holds your person in his power surreptitiously, while he holds the Queen Mother in captivity. He has attempted to arrest me. Having failed to do so, he is seeking all possible means to destroy me, as you will realise by the rest of this letter . . . He has made you believe that the Queen, M. the Comte de Soissons and myself are his enemies; that we are seeking to murder him and that all the great nobles are leagued against him. He alleges that all this is a consequence of the faithful service he renders you. . . . If he wishes to dismiss your ministers or your servants, he accuses them either of conspiring with me, or else of lacking sufficient courage to serve you at times of crisis.[25] On other occasions, he has alleged that your servants have been insufficiently secretive in carrying out your commands. Having dismissed your servants, he chooses others with the same faults who are his clients.

Moreover, there is no chance for those who hope to approach you to do so other than through his favour or by being in his dependence, nor for

[23] This refers to the dismissal of Sully as *grand maître de l'artillerie*.

[24] This refers to d'Effiat, whom Richelieu appointed as finance minister on 9 June 1626.

[25] This was Richelieu's criticism of Marillac.

those to do so who are out of his favour for not having wished to widen the rift between Your Majesty and myself – a rift which he initiated and continues to foster by carefully planned schemes to increase his influence.

The wasting of your income, as a result of which he has reduced your subjects to the direst of conditions, is a further consideration. This cannot be accounted for simply by bad administration and by war expenditure. (Nevertheless, the Italian campaign, which has cost more than 50 million *livres*, was undertaken solely for his pride, his ambition and his own interests and to the detriment of France). Chiefly, it arises from his obvious wish to impoverish the state by loans, taxes and excessive expenses, and to increase his power by amassing all the money in circulation and thus making himself all powerful . . .

I have only told you what I have seen. There is scarcely a third of your peasants who eat ordinary bread; another third live on oat bread alone; the last third are not only reduced to begging but languish in such a lamentable condition that some actually die of starvation while the rest live like wild beasts surviving only on acorns, plants and such things. The least pitiful of this last group are those who eat only the husks of the grain dipped in the blood they collect from the gutters by butchers' shops. I have seen poverty such as this with my own eyes in many places since I left Paris.

(Source: Mongrédien, pp. 215–18)

16. Louis XIII to Richelieu, 4 August 1634

My cousin,
Since you made it known that you wished that I send you the reasons that I gave you orally the other day which might bring us to a rupture with Spain, I have written them in my hand. No living soul has seen them. I send them in this packet. Forgive me if they are not written elegantly: I have never studied eloquence except in the army and among soldiers. I write no more except to assure you of my affection which will rest with you until death, and continue my prayers to God that He will always keep you in his Holy care.

At Chantilly, this 4th day of August 1634.   Louis.

Reasons for making war.
    1. One cannot doubt the design of the Spaniards to attack France

whenever they are able to do so. . . . I consider it preferable to attack them presently rather than to wait for them to attack us.

2. . . . The people and the great nobles of the Low Countries are extremely discontented with Spanish domination and inclined to revolt.

3. They will never have as many affairs on all sides as they have presently.

4. They will never be so weak in men and money.

5. We ought not to fear a rising in the kingdom, since the Huguenots are cowed . . .

6. The Dutch are in good spirits and strong in troops. But it is to be feared that if they see that we wish to attack the Spaniards openly the party of the Truce will recommence its intrigues and indeed sign a Truce . . .

7. If Sweden and her allies see us break with Spain, this will give them great courage and will heal the divisions among them . . .

8. Even if neither Sweden nor the Dutch Republic makes a treaty and their wars continue, as seems most likely, we are required always to keep a strong army which does nothing but consume our finances and drain our money. When we have need of it, we will no longer have it. But, by making war, we will be discharged of the subsidies that we give the Dutch Republic and Sweden. We will increase our territory at a cost of only a million *livres* a year more.

9. I think that when we attack them strongly in their own country, together with the Dutch, they will have difficulty defending themselves. Their country will become the battlefield and not France. My brother will think of returning to this Kingdom, which must be avoided, not because he can do any harm, but because the troops he will bring with him may hurt the poor people. If there is any choice, we must have an external and not an internal war.

10. If I thought that there was any chance of a general peace I would not draw these conclusions. On the contrary, I conclude, and am of the opinion, that we must have a strong open war against the Spaniards in order to arrive finally at a beneficial general peace and not otherwise.

Written at Chantilly, 4th August 1634.

(Source: Dickmann et al., i. 18–20)

17. Extract from the memoirs of Omer Talon, advocate-general in the *Parlement* of Paris, 1648

. . . Monsieur the Cardinal Mazarin was greatly disliked as a foreigner. He was accused of having refused to sign peace on very advantageous conditions. (Monsieur de Longueville and Monsieur d'Avaux[26] had said this loudly.) Besides which, he was accused of having transported the wealth of the kingdom to Italy. He made no friends, because in all the gifts which he made there was always something which diminished their value. He did not understand the conduct of domestic policy. When he asked advice, a natural distrust possessed him; he did not know which view to accept, and frequently made mistakes since he did not know how to take the best opinion. His spirit was timid, and he thought he could deceive everyone by reason. Not only did he want to draw up all the foreign dispatches himself; even on other matters he dictated to Monsieur the Chancellor the words that he should utter. He wanted to sign in person decrees of the council and public declarations, making much of this and not recognising that among Frenchmen all postures and words are useless if they are not maintained by authority. Thus he was not loved in the Palais-Royal. Even the Queen herself, who deferred absolutely to his counsels, complained every day of his cowardice and lack of courage; in the *Parlement* of Paris he was despised; among the populace he was hated . . .

(Source: Michaud and Poujoulat, p. 272)

18. Request of the three estates presented to Messieurs of the *Parlement* [of Paris] in 1648 against Cardinal Mazarin [a *Mazarinade*]

The three estates of the governorship of the Ile-de-France, together with the bourgeois and inhabitants of the good town of Paris . . . state that since the death of King Louis XIII of happy memory, the princes, great lords and office-holders, together with the whole kingdom, have suffered enormous injustices and intolerable evils from the person who seized absolute power close to the King under the new name of first minister of the State. They protest loudly that they will no longer suffer an

---

[26] French plenipotentiaries at the Westphalian peace negotiations.

individual raising himself up onto the king's shoulders, to everyone else's oppression. Nevertheless, because of their excessive generosity, a foreigner named Jules Mazarin arrived and installed himself in this sovereign ministry, to which he had not been elevated by birth, by any notable service rendered to this state, or by any other merit. It is known that he is Sicilian in origin and a natural subject of the King of Spain, of very sordid birth.[27] For a time he was a servant in several parts of Rome, and participated in the most abominable debauchery in that land. He brought himself forward by knavery, tricks and intrigues and arrived in France where by the same methods he introduced himself to those who governed,[28] who advanced him to serve as their spy, and used him for their own intrigues. In time, he made himself a very powerful influence on the Queen's personality and in her counsels, treating disdainfully all the great nobles of the kingdom, so that no person at court, and no influence in internal or external policy was recognised other than his own. This was greatly to the scandal of the royal household and the whole of France, and a matter of derision to foreign nations. For the last six years he has caused more harm, destruction and devastation to the kingdom than had the cruellest enemies arrived as a conquering army . . .

What is worse, he has pillaged and ravished the King's finances, and has reduced His Majesty to extreme poverty, and all his subjects to a misery worse than death. Not only has he exhausted all the ready cash in the kingdom by cash expenses which amount each year to 50 or 60 million *livres*; worse still, he has consumed three years of the King's revenue in advance. In order to muddle and confuse for ever the order of financial affairs, he has authorised and increased this accursed breed of tax contractors, for the most part former lackeys and grooms, who use their new position to oppress the kingdom of France. They have established loan contracts anticipating the revenues of the *taille*,[29] and levy it by means of fusiliers who are like so many unchained demons. They have created unbearable new taxes and a great number of new office-holders of all types . . .

He has not provided the frontier places with men or munitions, nor has he paid the costs of the navy and the artillery, which are four years in arrears. He has not made gifts to people of virtue and merit, or given

---

[27] This was untrue; he was born in the Abruzzi, the son of a client of the powerful Colonna family and a Papal administrator.

[28] Richelieu.

[29] The main direct tax in France.

recompense to those who have squandered their wealth and shed their blood for the King's service. On the contrary, he has allowed nearly all the King's armies to perish from hunger and necessity, since they have only received two monthly payments a year for the last five years. More than 120 000 soldiers have died from misery, necessity and horrible poverty. It is certain, and may be proven by irreproachable witnesses, that he has divided up great sums of money with those whom he has authorised[30] and has . . . had it transported by letters of change or as silver plate and precious stones, under pretext of prosecuting the war in Italy, and conquering certain places such as Piombino and Portolongone. It is well known, however, that he has allowed the garrisons to starve, being presently due to them eight payments, and that he has neglected the repair of the fortifications so that they could not resist even a feeble attack by the enemy. Moreover, to continue the war and as a pretext for his tyranny and his thefts, he has delayed the possibility of a peace treaty when France could have had an advantageous one . . . There is reason to suppose that he has had secret understandings with the enemies of France and the State in the hope that they will provide him with refuge if the enemies of his tyrannical rule in France chase him out of the kingdom . . . What is more, as a foreigner and natural subject of the King of Spain,[31] he is incapable of exercising any office in France by the laws of the kingdom and ordinances of the kings, who have often exiled Italians, notably by the celebrated decree of the *Parlement* in 1617 following the death of the Maréchal d'Ancre . . .

(Source: Michaud and Pojoulat, pp. 316–18. AAE France 861, fo. 405)

19. Remonstrances of the *Parlement* of Paris, 21 January 1649

The interests of those who attempt to usurp sovereign authority are always contrary to the true interests of the sovereign. We have seen under his ministry[32] a conduct of politics that is foreign to us and completely opposed to our customs. The true interests of the state have been abandoned or betrayed. The war has been continued; peace delayed; the people exhausted; the finances of the king dissipated or misappropriated; everything which is most considerable in the Kingdom

---

[30] The financiers.
[31] Mazarin was a naturalised Frenchman after 1639.
[32] Mazarin's.

has been either corrupted or oppressed in order to subject all Frenchmen to the power of a single foreigner. Finally, the state has been brought to such a pass that it is almost ruined unless God intervenes powerfully to assist it.

Who can doubt that Cardinal Mazarin has always wanted to continue the war and to prevent peace, in order to make himself necessary and to have a pretext to levy great sums of money so that he may enrich himself? Who has not discovered several occasions when he has prevented the success of our armies in order to keep matters on a knife-edge? Witness our armies which have been lost due to lack of subsistence at the siege of Lérida, the feeble assistance sent too late to Naples, the siege of Cremona and the loss of Courtrai, and other actions of this type.

As for the peace negotiations . . . he has never wanted to allow anyone but his confidant[33] into the secret of the matter, although the duc de Longueville and the other deputies are of such known probity that they cannot be suspect. He preferred to lose our allies[34] than to make peace. If there had not been a lack of loyalty, this would be a criminal error . . . It is more than evident that he has betrayed our true interests in a matter of such importance, and that his prevarication would alone merit the penalty of execution . . . One may reasonably impute from his conduct the motive of wishing one day to partition the kingdom of France with the Spaniard . . .

As for the abuse and depredation of the King's finances, sovereigns who are legitimate tutors of their people regard their wealth as the wealth of others to be used and conserved as they would conserve their own wealth: they never use it without necessity and without moderation. But usurpers of sovereign authority regard the wealth of the people as their prey, and are avid for its substance, and the last drop of its blood is the only limit of their greed . . . There are few people in the countryside who still have a bed on which to sleep, fewer still who still have sufficient bread to nourish them for their work . . .

(Source: Michaud and Poujoulat, pp. 323–28. BN Ms. fr. 3854, fos. 20–32)

[33] Servien, later finance minister.
[34] The Dutch, who signed a separate peace with Spain in January 1648.

20. Remonstrances of the *Parlement* of Paris to Louis XIV, 23 March 1652

. . . Cardinal Mazarin has shown, by seeking to continue the war, that he does not care about the future: he has employed all his efforts in this, exhausting the supplies of soldiers and money in France, without considering that if these two things dried up, then he would be forced to consent to a shameful peace. He has been unwilling to give in to the public hatred that has arisen against him because he lost the occasion of concluding a treaty that was honourable and advantageous to France, as had been settled and was on the point of being signed at Münster. This was broken by Cardinal Mazarin, who could not turn away from his own private interests, and who never wished to consent to peace. Cardinal Mazarin has always imagined that he would find his security in these troubles, which maintain him in great lustre and make him seem important, since he has seized control of the command of the armed forces.

We now see that he has caused such disorder that we are in both a foreign and a civil war, and we have lost several places which were left to us in treaties which he has broken. The Spaniards owe Cardinal Mazarin an obligation in that not only has he rendered to them conquests which he thought were his, but even some which were captured in the reign of the late King your father . . .

Cardinal Mazarin has not envisaged a situation in which finances, which are the sinews of war, would be lacking, and that it would be impossible for him to maintain seven or eight armies on land and sea and pay the garrisons of a great number of conquered places . . . Either a lack of money was to be feared . . . or, following the failure to pay the troops, that your provinces would be exposed to the licence of the soldiery, who in the last three years have treated them with all sorts of hostile and barbaric actions.

Who can doubt that Cardinal Mazarin wanted to have the sole direction of the war, and that this is not the true cause of all the evils which we have suffered and which have become insupportable? . . . When Cardinal Mazarin considers what happened over thirty years ago to a person of his nation, who was much less criminal than himself, he will judge the danger into which he has fallen . . .[35]

(Source: AAE France 882, fos. 98–108)

[35] Concini, assassinated in 1617.

2 THE MINISTERIAL TEAM

The dominance of the central government by a chief minister encompassed several distinct phases: a period of personal rule by Louis XIII (15 December 1621–14 May 1643), a period of Regency (18 May 1643–7 September 1651), and a period when Louis XIV was declared to have come of age but did not govern (7 September 1651–9 March 1661). It ended only when Louis XIV expressed the wish, on the death of Mazarin, to rule without a chief minister. Clearly the real power enjoyed by the chief minister varied considerably between one period and another and within each period significant changes could occur. Previous powerful influences upon the government had tried to exploit the position of royal favourite to dominate the ministers. Concino Concini, the favourite of Marie de Médicis, had tried to do this from 1610 until 1617. Luynes, the favourite of Louis XIII, had achieved this from 1617 until 1621: his ascendancy had been so all-encompassing that he had held the posts both of Constable of France and Keeper of the Seals.

The death of Luynes in December 1621, and the king's assertion of personal rule, left a power vacuum. This was filled at first by Schomberg, the finance minister. He was ousted in January 1623 by Chancellor Brûlart de Sillery and his son Puysieulx, the foreign minister, who agreed on La Vieuville's appointment simply as a device to get rid of Schomberg. The new finance minister was frequently in conflict with the other ministers until he succeeded in ousting the Brûlarts in February 1624. La Vieuville's position as *de facto* chief minister, foreign minister and finance minister was in turn vulnerable. Louis XIII's dissatisfaction with his ministers over the previous three years is evident from his remarks following the arrest of La Vieuville on 12 August 1624 (doc. 21), and is understandable given the extent of ministerial rivalry. There seems to have been evidence of La Vieuville's corruption (doc. 22). The fact remains that he was ousted in a political coup by Richelieu, who likened him to a drunkard who could not walk a step without stumbling. La Vieuville was accused of having tried to arrogate too much power to himself. He had also made serious mistakes in foreign policy.

Richelieu gained power gradually. He entered the king's council on 29 April 1624, as a result of pressure from Marie de Médicis. He was appointed chief minister on 13 August 1624, following the arrest of La Vieuville. He justified his ascendancy in the council on the grounds that cardinals had precedence over other dignitaries of the crown such as the Chancellor, the head of justice, and the Constable, the head of the army. In retrospect, the support of the Queen Mother, and Louis XIII's need to conciliate her in September 1622 by agreeing to Richelieu's appointment as cardinal, were crucial factors in his rise to power. However, a largely theoretical precedence in the council still had to be turned into the real exercise of power and survive the trauma of disagreement, both in the council and at court over the issues of foreign policy: this was to be Richelieu's central task between 1624 and 1630.

It was clear that the growing complexity of government business required improved organisation in the king's council. The chief minister could not deal with private requests (doc. 23) and detailed business, not least because of Richelieu's poor health (doc. 26), a problem that dogged his ministerial career and gave hope to his enemies. The first, tentative, steps towards two long-term developments of fundamental importance were taken in the early years of the ministry: specialisation of council business and growth of ministerial power. The first was already evident in a proposal in 1625, which also envisaged a reduction in the size of the council and an improved quality of appointments as councillor (doc. 24). The council subsequently fluctuated greatly in size. The division of the council into three main sections – a council of state, council of finance and council of justice (called *conseil privé*) – was a feature of the ministries of Richelieu and Mazarin. Chancellor Séguier later depicted the council as a model of efficiency (doc. 176). The situation was not quite as idyllic as he suggested, but there can be little doubt that the large increase in council business under Richelieu and Mazarin was handled relatively effectively.

It seems almost paradoxical that ministerial power could develop at the same time as the power of the council itself, but this seems to have occurred. Each of the four secretaries of state continued to administer some of the French provinces, as had been the case in the sixteenth century. The year 1626 saw the beginnings of a war ministry under Beauclerc and the restoration of a single secretaryship of state for foreign affairs (doc. 25). Richelieu's crucial patronage role in obtaining offices for his clients, and channelling the clients of others into his service, is clear from the appointment of Bouthillier (docs. 28, 29). After 1626, d'Effiat was a more forceful finance minister than his predecessors. He emphasised foresight, diligence, and above all the ability to impress the financiers in order to 'conserve credit' (doc. 27) – these were to be themes to which later finance ministers frequently returned. The crisis of the Mantuan war saw Richelieu and d'Effiat personally supervising armies abroad, with a consequential physical separation of authority: modern government had by no means arrived (docs. 30, 31).

The crisis of the Day of Dupes (11 November 1630) revealed the stark choice for Richelieu: service to the king and the Queen Mother had become incompatible (docs. 32, 33). Marie de Médicis and her cabal thought that they had persuaded the king to dismiss Richelieu. They were 'duped' because the king had made no decision, misled them, or changed his mind. Since the decision was a personal one by Louis XIII, the outcome of the crisis of Richelieu's ministry was unpredictable. Richelieu seems to have retained majority support among the ministers (even though this support was not a critical factor on the Day of Dupes). Marillac was thus isolated and became the first victim of the Day of Dupes: on 12 November, the Seals were removed from his custody and he was arrested. Richelieu was left in undisputed control of the king's council, filling vacancies with his appointees, and forging a ministerial team in his own mould. Disputes and disagreements in the king's council did not come to an end in November 1630. What changed, however, was the whole atmosphere in which the choices in foreign and domestic policy were debated. No-one seriously challenged the view that Spain, the Emperor and the duke of Lorraine were allied against France and that a general war was inevitable. Richelieu and the other ministers could present proposals to the king in the confident expectation that he would accept their advice. Tensions within the system of government remained, however, because serious financial difficulties arose with the French declaration of war against Spain in 1635 (doc. 34).

In essence, the first French campaign of the war ended in failure. Richelieu is said to have been 'astonished' at this failure despite 'many millions' spent on the war effort. He accused Bullion and Bouthillier, the joint finance ministers, of unwarranted delays in the transfer of funds (doc. 35). They feared a general bankruptcy, which would force France out of the war on disadvantageous terms (doc. 36). Bullion asserted that war expenditure was too high and was prepared to appeal directly to the king to gain support for his viewpoint (doc. 37). Such independence, combined with accusations of corruption, made Richelieu increasingly suspicious of Bullion. In 1638, he extracted undertakings that he would reform his conduct of financial administration (doc. 38). Richelieu began to feel that popular resistance to taxation could become a serious issue, particularly if the finance ministers' narrow preoccupation with short-term fiscal issues blinded them to the longer-term need for the king to be seen to keep his undertakings to his subjects (doc. 39). A revolt comparable to that of the Catalans against the king of Spain was to be feared (doc. 43). Bullion in turn stressed the need to enforce the levy of taxes by effective royal commissioners (doc. 40). He seems to have anticipated revenues, which brought the risk of bankruptcy (doc. 41). The collapse of two leading financiers shortly after Bullion's death in December 1640 indeed threatened such a general bankruptcy (doc. 42).

Despite the severe financial and fiscal pressures caused by the war, and despite all Richelieu's criticism of his ministers, the team held firm from 1636 to 1642. The death of Richelieu on 4 December 1642 removed a powerful patron. Mazarin was brought into the king's council the following day, but he was only one of a triumvirate – the other two ministers being Chavigny and Sublet des Noyers – who controlled policy after the death of Richelieu. Richelieu had needed merely to influence the king against La Vieuville to secure his rise to power, but Mazarin had the much more complicated task of reassuring a king whose health was rapidly failing, while retaining the support of the future Regent, Anne of Austria. A measure of Mazarin's success is seen in the fortunes of his two rivals. Sublet des Noyers was dismissed by Louis XIII after a dispute over the war estimates (doc. 44: though he may also have sided too early with the future Regent). Chavigny was demoted by Anne of Austria because he appeared to remain loyal to the king's wish that a regency council be set up after his death (doc. 45). Whereas Richelieu had never been the favourite of Louis XIII, and this had been a source of weakness, Mazarin was clearly favourite of Anne of Austria. His continuance as chief minister appeared the best guarantee not only of her Regency, but of her son's future accession to absolute power. Later, during the criticism of the Fronde, Mazarin convinced Anne of the parallel between his own cause and that of Strafford in England. Once Charles I had sacrificed Strafford, so the argument ran, the monarchy itself did not long survive (doc. 67). Concessions thus could not be made to the opposition, because these merely served to encourage faction. The crown must retain its prerogative of choosing and dismissing ministers at will, the crucial issue irrespective of the qualities – or faults – of the chief minister. Criticism of ministerial corruption in general, and not simply of Mazarin's corruption, came to the fore during the Fronde, when it was argued that a purge of ministers would yield much-needed money and restore the government's popularity (doc. 56). There was some truth that ministers, and even the Chancellor, looked after their family interests (doc. 46): the distinction between public and private interest was not drawn sufficiently clearly.

The Regency of Anne of Austria was proclaimed officially in the *Parlement* of Paris on 18 May 1643, and at the same time the limitations on the Regent's powers imposed by the last will and testament of Louis XIII were removed. Anne was thus made president of the council and given those powers of appointment and patronage which her husband had sought to deny her. Almost inevitably, this accretion of power to the Regent made Cardinal Mazarin, her favourite, chief minister, and the delicate checks and balances within the proposed regency council were removed at a stroke. By the end of the year, most commentators agreed that d'Hémery, though only controller-general of finance, was all-powerful in financial affairs, and indeed the second minister in the government after Mazarin. He was especially trusted by the Cardinal, and had been his client since 1635. Whereas Bullion and Bouthillier had borrowed as an expedient to cover a budgetary deficit, d'Hémery elevated the search for credit to the level of a financial principle. Revenues were systematically anticipated on an unprecedented scale (doc. 47), and with hindsight it is clear that bankruptcy was inevitable. D'Hémery was dismissed, and bankruptcy declared, in July 1648. The previous year there had been discussion as to whether bankruptcy should be declared by the government and manipulated in its interests. The criticism of the government associated with the onset of the Fronde in the spring of 1648 ensured that bankruptcy was chiefly caused by a collapse of confidence among the financiers.

The bankruptcy of 1648 paralysed the government without permanently removing the burden of debt. In an atmosphere of heightened political tension, it was difficult to recruit a finance minister of stature, so much so that d'Hémery had to be recalled in November 1649, partly on the spurious argument that since he had caused the problem, he would presumably know how to solve it. Before his recall, the interim financial administration was too weak to provide firm leadership (doc. 48). The financiers were able to get their own way, and there was little that the government could do except strike back at them at a later date through retrospective taxation (doc. 49). The crown had been forced to concede reductions in taxation in 1648, which aggravated its financial problems (docs. 50, 51). While Mazarin was firmly in charge of the government, it seemed that political recovery was possible. The arrest of the princes in 1650, and their unconditional release by Mazarin in February 1651 (see Chapter 4), dashed this prospect. Mazarin's position in France was no longer tenable, since Condé in particular was bent on revenge. Mazarin chose to go into exile, but this threatened the whole system of government. His clients, such as Le Tellier, the war minister, were vulnerable (doc. 52). In the competition for power, each minister had to look after his own interests and the government lost its collective purpose (doc. 53). Sectional groups, such as financiers who considered the prospect of La Vieuville's appointment to be to their advantage, pressed for a change of finance minister (doc. 55).

The crisis with the princes broke in July 1651 over Mazarin's continuing secret influence over the government (doc. 57). His main supporters in the ministry, Servien, Le Tellier and Lionne, were dismissed later in the month (doc. 58), but Le Tellier was the only one of the three to hold a secretaryship of state, and this office was not filled by a new appointment so that his recall would not later be impeded (doc. 59). In exile, Mazarin was virtually bankrupt (doc. 54), and powerless to assist Anne of Austria against Condé's revolt. However, he received a substantial payment from La Vieuville for his appointment as finance minister (doc. 60), although some commentators recognised that this was likely to prove highly unpopular (doc. 61). The news of the new appointment did not become official until the declaration of the king's majority in September 1651 (doc. 62). Mazarin was thus able to finance his invasion of France in December 1651. He disclaimed all intention of re-entering the ministry (doc. 63), but stated that he would have failed in his duty not to have opposed Condé's rebellion (doc. 64). The task then fell to his ministerial clients such as Le Tellier to establish the propaganda framework for his return, for example projecting Mazarin to the citizens of Paris as the champion of the *rentiers*, those who held state-funded annuities (docs. 65, 66).

With the end of the Fronde, and the death of La Vieuville, who had threatened to become a powerful political force in his own right, Mazarin was once more the undisputed dispenser of political patronage. Collective financial leadership was ruled out as a recipe for instability (doc. 69). Mazarin chose two clients of proven loyalty during the Fronde as joint finance ministers, the young and ambitious Foucquet, who argued the case for reform (doc. 68), and the aging Servien, who denied that the finance minister need concern himself with detail (doc. 70). It was a decision which appeared to consolidate Mazarin's power as head of the government, allowing him complete freedom of action to supervise the details of war administration on the northern French frontier, sending back general letters to Paris requesting provisions and funds for the army. What Mazarin wanted was a team which would produce military victory against Spain; his clients as ministers were to do his bidding and leave him the reality of power.

At first, the new ministerial team established in February 1653 seemed to work reasonably well. The new finance ministers adopted a conservative stance, retaining financiers of ability (albeit corrupt) and emphasising the need to restore the government's credit-worthiness (doc. 71). They were hostile to the encroachments of the war minister on their powers (doc. 72). They stressed the disastrous revenue implications of billeting troops on the French provinces (docs. 73, 74). They were alert to the problems of the financiers (doc. 75). When borrowing became too expensive on the private market, this gave the ministers problems. They were forced to connive in Mazarin's disastrous increase in the number of intendants of finance (doc. 76): Mazarin wanted rich clients to hold this office, both to raise an immediate capital sum from the sale of the office, and later to obtain loans from a pliant inner group of officials (doc. 77).

However, the chain of command established by Mazarin to ensure his personal control suffered from crucial weaknesses. It fragmented authority in financial policy, and in order to work it required a high degree of co-operation between the two finance ministers, which was most unlikely given the great differences in their age, experience and temperament. Throughout 1653 and 1654, Servien was unquestionably the senior finance minister, although the precise division of responsibility with Foucquet is not clear. By December 1654, however, the disputes between the two men had become serious. Mazarin held Servien responsible for the continuing financial difficulties of the French crown and the failure to secure full co-operation with the financiers. Much to his chagrin (doc. 78), Servien was thus demoted, and given charge of expenditure, while Foucquet was given the much more difficult task of procuring funds (doc. 79). From 1655, whatever the theory of a joint finance ministry, Foucquet was the real finance minister.

The new arrangements proved no more satisfactory than the old. On at least three occasions Mazarin seriously contemplated dismissing Foucquet. This evidence was later used at Foucquet's trial in an attempt to prove that Mazarin had regarded his finance minister as corrupt. Foucquet retorted that there had been an almost permanent conspiracy to oust him from power (doc. 82). The background of intrigue can scarcely have assisted the cause of sound financial administration in the 1650s, even if it consolidated Mazarin's grip on the government. The defensive tone of Foucquet's letters to the chief minister are vivid testimony to his problems (docs. 80, 83, 84). From early on in his ministry, he made private loans to the government which helped ensure his survival in office (doc. 81). When a general bankruptcy threatened in 1658 (doc. 85), he responded with further loans (docs. 86, 87). These seem to have been made without clear records being kept: most of the chief minister's orders had been given orally. Hence Foucquet's growing alarm at the criticisms made by Colbert, the administrator of Mazarin's vast personal fortune (doc. 88). Foucquet began to talk the language of reform (doc. 91), but not soon enough for Colbert, who condemned previous finance ministers' 'maxim of confusion' and their pursuit of an illusory credit-worthiness of the government (doc. 89). Foucquet patched up the quarrel with Colbert, at least on the surface (doc. 90).

However, the death of Mazarin in March 1661 left him vulnerable to Colbert's intrigues. On his death-bed, Mazarin had held a private interview with the king. The full account of what passed between them is not known, because 'certain intrigues' caused Louis XIV to break off his dictation of the chief minister's maxims (doc. 92). **Whether Mazarin warned the king of Foucquet's ambition is uncertain.** Foucquet's control of financial policy was restricted by the need to inform the king, and by Colbert's appointment as intendant of finance in charge of the register of revenues and expenses. Foucquet may have hoped that his severest critic would be implicated in his financial policies: but at a stroke, the weapons at Colbert's disposal, and the power base from which to strike at his rival, were vastly strengthened. The arrest of Foucquet on 5 September 1661 (doc. 94) was followed shortly afterwards by other measures bringing Mazarin's system to an end, above all by the establishment of a new council, called the royal council of finance, following the abolition of the post of finance minister (doc. 93). The king had thus assumed personal control of his finances, and consolidated the personal rule that he had declared on Mazarin's death.

21. What the King said to the Council after the disgrace of La Vieuville, Mid-August 1624

... I have been unfortunate enough to have had self-interested and impassioned men running my affairs. They asked to discuss my business but instead talked to me about their own interests. They kept pressing unreasonable demands on me, which I refused to accept.

Now I am no longer in this position.

You will see what I will do to reform my State.

In the past, people used to say my personality was severe. This was because the Constable,[1] Puysieulx[2] and La Vieuville[3] made me like that, since they vented their spleen on me. They made me believe that there was good reason for me to be grateful to them.

They gave the impression that I was mean. At the same time they told me privately that the necessities of my State did not permit me to make gifts. They thus sought to escape responsibility for matters against which they advised me ...

La Vieuville complained that I mistrusted him, and that it was impossible to serve me. I mistrusted him because I did not esteem his brain. I saw that he defended his own interests and passions. I saw

---

[1] Lesdiguières.

[2] Foreign secretary.

[3] Finance minister from 23 January 1623 until his arrest on 12 August 1624.

through him from the start. Had this not been so, I would have trusted him.

It is said that I do not love my great nobles. The Constable, Puysieulx and La Vieuville discouraged me from being too friendly towards them, for fear that they gained credit to their own disadvantage. It will be seen whether or not I love my nobles . . .

(Source: Grillon, i. 104)

22. Charges against the sieur de La Vieuville [1624]

There is evidence in the trial of Beaumarchais[4] that all money orders, debts and arrears of salaries and pensions which he had listed at half value in his accounts for 1620 were in fact purchased in 1623 during the administration of the sieur de La Vieuville, his relative. The sieur de La Vieuville gave him a fund to carry forward this expenditure contrary to the true account which had been finalised by the previous administrator[5] in the year 1622.

There is also evidence that this 1622 account was destroyed and that in its place the sieur de La Vieuville had another one drawn up in 1623 in which more than 2 million *livres* of false expenses were added . . .

It is thus clear that he has diverted the King's money and given funds to his father-in-law to use in false expenses – in purchases of old money orders, bad debts and old arrears of salaries where he himself was beneficiary [?].[6] The *chambre de justice* recognised that the sieur de La Vieuville was guilty of complicity in all the crimes of Beaumarchais, and issued a decree against him . . .

(Source: AAE France 779, fo. 15)

23. Ruling for Messieurs the Secretaries of State, 11 February 1625

The King has to take into consideration the fact that a great number of persons are at court to pursue their claims and other interests, in which they consume a great amount of time and constantly visit his ministers.

[4] Formerly chief treasurer.
[5] Henri de Schomberg, comte de Nanteuil, finance minister from September 1619 to January 1623.
[6] Word missing in original.

35

Their visits to the ministers are frequently pointless since the ministers cannot know the wishes of His Majesty on these individual requests and thus cannot give satisfaction. His Majesty wishes to deal with this inconvenience and establish a firm ruling, by the means of which reasonable pretensions and just demands are promptly dealt with, and claims which cannot be accorded are speedily rejected. This will save time and trouble for everyone. Henceforth individuals of whatever status who wish for something from His Majesty, should address themselves to his secretaries of state, according to the nature of their business and the different provinces from which they originate.[7] The secretaries of state will hear the individual requests and receive their memoranda, which are to contain a succinct summary of their pretensions and demands. Each secretary will act according to the functions of his office, so that nothing is forgotten, and there is no confusion. Once the business of the secretaries is separated in this way, it will be dispatched more promptly . . .

His Majesty intends that when his ministers are approached on matters which should be dealt with by the secretaries of State, they should refer the matter to them in order that they are dealt with according to the rules established above . . .

(Source: Grillon, i. 160–1)

24. Project for the establishment of the Council, February 1625

Among the matters in the kingdom which seem to require reform, the form of the establishment of the King's councils is one of the most important, not simply because of the poor choice made of those who are admitted, but also because of the confused number of those who are introduced almost daily. A vast number of people have letters patent as councillor of State and draw the emoluments from this position although they are not suited for it either by birth or merit. This brings confusion and overburdens the King's finances.

Everyone knows that the Council of the Prince is the soul of the State and good councillors the guiding spirits of the Kingdom. This is why there is no issue on which the sovereign must be more circumspect than in the establishment of a good order in his councils, and above all in not giving the title except to persons of eminent birth or of eminent capacity.

---

[7] Each secretary had a responsibility for a certain number of the French provinces. See doc. 25.

It is to the Prince's honour that only persons of such condition carry the title . . .

When the list is drawn up of those whom His Majesty wishes to honour with this title, it will be necessary to ascertain exactly in what area they should serve the King. Some may be good at one thing but quite unsuitable for another. Thus His Majesty must ensure that individuals are moved, in order to make them more expert in their functions, which will be good both for them and for the King's business.

After the death of Charles IX,[8] Queen Cathérine de Médicis divided the King's Council into three sections to overcome the confusion there, which was similar to that now. One section dealt with affairs of state over which the Cardinal of Bourbon presided; another dealt with justice and the third with financial affairs. The King could follow this example and establish three separate councils, each composed of eight persons with a president. Monseigneur the Cardinal de Richelieu or the second minister in his absence could preside over a council of dispatches, assisted by the secretaries of state on matters concerning their departments, and such other ecclesiastical personages, and members of the nobility and the robe which it pleases His Majesty to summon.

In so far as legal men are rarely capable of managing high affairs of state, and that for this reason Chancellors in the past were only concerned with legal matters, the King, for great considerations concerning the public welfare,[9] should discharge Monsieur the Chancellor and the Keeper of the Seals from the inner councils,[10] so that in future they will only participate in the judicial Council with other councillors from the sovereign courts, ecclesiastics and nobles, who will also be chosen by His Majesty for this task. The Masters of Requests will report to them cases concerning private lawsuits, which will speed up the expediting of documents and cause much relief to those who pursue lawsuits before the Council. If the Chancellor as head of justice is not diverted by other tasks, justice will be rendered more promptly to all His Majesty's subjects.

In the council of finance, where economies and the King's revenue are discussed, Monsieur the finance minister[11] will preside, assisted by the

---

[8] 1574.

[9] Chancellor Aligre was not disgraced until January 1626, but this appears to suggest doubts about his support for Richelieu.

[10] *Conseils de cabinet.*

[11] Between August 1624 and February 1626 there were two finance ministers, Bochart de Champigny and Marillac.

controller-general,[12] the intendants of finance and four other persons experienced in financial affairs. This number will be more than sufficient, bearing in mind that it is important that few people know the true state of the Prince's finances.

Every Thursday, Monsieur the Keeper of the Seals and Monsieur the finance minister should hold a council composed of the councils of justice and finance together, to lease out publicly the revenue farms, determine which offices are returned to the King, and reply to the grievances[13] of the provinces. The Masters of Requests should also attend and will make their reports in cases concerning His Majesty's rights. Accounts finalised in the council and the implementation of leases of the revenue farms will be retained and judged in cases where the King's affairs are concerned and not otherwise. All other disputes will be sent to those *Cours des Aides* which have verified the relevant edicts and leases of the revenue farms.

Those who preside in these councils will sign the decrees together with those who present them.[14] In the absence of the presidents, the senior councillor will assume the presidency.

In order to avoid confusion, everyone will remain in the council to which he is nominated by His Majesty, without those of one section of the council claiming the right to enter another. This is the practice in Spain. To help ensure this, the King will announce a form of dress: those of the Privy Council will wear long cloaks down to the ankle, those of the Council of Justice a long robe, and those in the Council of Finance cloaks with sleeves, as in the *Chambre des Comptes*.

Above all, His Majesty must guard against increasing the number of councillors: otherwise, people will solicit for places, and serious consequences will result. Nobody should be promoted except if a vacancy arises from death or because someone is sent on an ambassadorship.

The inner council will remain the King, the Queen Mother and the ministers of state.

(Source: Grillon, i. 172–4)

---

[12] Bochart de Champigny also held this office.
[13] *Cahiers*.
[14] Those who presented them were called *rapporteurs*.

25. Ruling between the Secretaries of State, 11 March 1626

The King considers it useful and expedient for his affairs that the dispatches concerning all the foreign countries should be in the hands of a single secretary of state, who will deal with the correspondence. His Majesty has thus resolved to change the departments according to which the secretaries have operated, in order to give the three other Secretaries honourable employment, and so that all four can work on good terms and in friendship according to the dignity of their offices. The King orders that henceforth the sr. de Loménie or the sr. de la Ville aux Clercs, his son, who has been established in the expectancy of his office, will have His Majesty's household, Paris, the Ile de France, Orléans, Berry, Soissons, and the *Parlement* of Navarre; that the sr. d'Herbault will have all the foreign provinces,[15] and in addition within the kingdom, Languedoc, Guyenne, Brouage, Aunis, La Rochelle and the general affairs of the Huguenots; that the sr. d'Ocquerre will have Auvergne, Bourbonnais, Nivernois, Burgundy, Champagne, Brie, Picardy, Normandy, Brittany, the three bishoprics of Metz, Toul and Verdun, Lorraine and the marine of Ponant; and that the sr. de Beauclerc will have war following the ruling of 1619 for the kingdom internally, but also completely for abroad,[16] the *taillon* and the artillery without any other of the secretaries of state having any part. In addition, he will have Poitou, Marche, Limousin, Lyonnais, Dauphiné, Provence and the marine of Levant. And with regard to fortifications, each will draw up the accounts for those in his department.

[Written below in the King's hand]. I wish the present ruling to be followed. LOUIS.

(Source: Grillon, i. 300–1)

---

[15] That is, as a unified secretary of state for foreign affairs.
[16] That is, as a unified secretary of state for war.

26. Letters patent of the King discharging Cardinal de Richelieu from 'visits and solicitations of individuals' to reserve for him cognisance in the 'general and most important' affairs in order to conserve his health, Blois, 26 June 1626

... His Majesty does not wish in any way to deprive himself of [Richelieu's] service, since events have shown that he has usefully and successfully contributed to the great events of the last two years . . . to the contentment and glory of His Majesty and the well-being of the state. He therefore has discharged him from all affairs, concerning both external and internal affairs, wishing nevertheless that he takes as much cognisance of foreign affairs and the general and most important affairs of the state as possible without prejudicing his health. While his indisposition continues he may not deal with other matters. No-one may accuse him of lack of application, since His Majesty expressly instructs him to act in this way so that he can continue to work without prejudicing his health. Because the King wishes to conserve his minister's health, he discharges him from the visits and solicitations of individuals. His intention is that individuals should address themselves to other Ministers and secretaries of state, who will present these matters to the King. When he is in the King's presence, the Sieur Cardinal will give his opinion on such matters. His Majesty hopes for a long time yet to benefit from his labours for the good of his affairs and wishes to relieve him from the requests and importunities of individuals . . .

(Source: Grillon, i. 368)

27. [Memorandum of d'Effiat on the qualities needed in a finance minister. Written c. February 1628 when he thought he was on his death bed.]

Foresight, diligence and vigilance for revenues in order not to be surprised by ordinary and extraordinary expenditure.

Inventiveness, persuasiveness, civility, honesty in order to encourage men to enter contracts and provide the King with money.

The ability to keep one's word in order to gain, and conserve, credit.

The skill to expedite the affairs of the financiers, give them preferential treatment, and reward them honestly. This in order not to be short of money in moments of necessity.

The capacity to be resolute in the councils and subordinate councils to settle money matters, and to have the decisions carried out.

Intelligence, in order not to be outwitted.

Courage, so as to be vigorous in refusing some matters whilst carrying out other matters which are justified for the King's service . . .

(Source: AAE France 795, fo. 185)

28. Bouthillier, secretary of state, to Cardinal de Richelieu, 13 October 1628

My lord,
I write these lines in haste while waiting for the Queen [Mother] to write both to the King and to you on the subject of the office of secretary of state with which it has pleased His Majesty to honour me. Since on this occasion I cannot find words sufficiently worthy to express your excessive kindness towards me and the infinite obligations which I have towards you . . .

(Source: Gillon, iii. 527)

29. Queen Mother to Richelieu, 16 October 1628

My cousin. I am sure that you have not yet told the King Monsieur my son the pleasure which you have correctly perceived that I would have of the choice which it has pleased him to make of Bouthillier, who is in my service,[17] to fill the charge of Secretary of State of the late Sieur d'Ocquerre. I ask you to present to him the letter which I write to thank him for agreeing to send me the provisions of the office, in order that Bouthillier receives them from my hands. Everyone will thus realise that the King's consideration for me brought him to agree to appoint him, in the belief that he would serve him in this office with the same fidelity with which he has served me. I do not doubt that you would wish to be his surety, since you gave me the same assurance more than ten years ago. You are the author of everything which has happened to him since this time . . .

(Source: Grillon, iii. 531)

---

[17] He was secretary of Marie's *commandements* from 1618.

30. Marillac, Keeper of the Seals, to Richelieu, 17 July 1630

. . . We are dealing with affairs here[18] and at every moment Messieurs the intendants of finance, chief treasurers,[19] and treasurers of casual revenues[20] have need of us. You have nothing more important to deal with than finance and munitions,[21] and I confess to you that I tremble with fear that there will be some shortfall. I have never felt anything more strongly than this: when I held this office[22] I never felt it as acutely as now . . .

(Source: Grillon, v. 405)

31. Marillac to Richelieu, 15 August 1630

. . . I fear greatly a lack of money and have abstained from writing, leaving it to Messieurs the intendants of finance. But, from what I hear, they have received no order from Monsieur the finance minister since he left . . .[23] Necessity made us resolve to borrow the million *livres*, as you were informed, but problems in Paris have caused Monsieur the finance minister not to sign the decree. The financiers created difficulties about lending without the order of the man who must reimburse them. I consider it very important that the sieur finance minister provides some clarification, because I believe that he has all the necessary information . . .

(Source: Grillon, v. 522–3)

32. Richelieu to the Queen Mother, 11 November 1630

Madame,
Knowing the misfortune of being disgraced by you, I would not dare to

---

[18] At Grenoble.

[19] *Trésoriers de l'Epargne.*

[20] *Parties casuelles,* that is to say revenues from office-holding.

[21] Richelieu had been appointed lieutenant-general in the army of Italy on 24 December 1629.

[22] Finance minister, that is to say, from August 1624 until June 1626, in sole charge after February 1626.

[23] For the army of Piedmont. D'Effiat had been appointed lieutenant-general in the army of Italy in the summer of 1630.

write to you if I did not hope that it would be a means of escaping from it. This letter begs you, Madame, to agree to restore me to your good grace. I assure you, Madame, that I have never had the intention of doing anything which could be disagreeable to you. What Your Majesty found to say against my actions arose because of my misfortune in having to please others so as to conserve my position. I did not consider what might displease you. I hope with an extreme passion to render Your Majesty the respect and service which I owe her. For this purpose, knowing that Your Majesty does not wish me to visit you personally, I have withdrawn to my abbey, ready to leave France, if my absence alone will bring you contentment. Whatever happens, I will be content, Madame, provided that you forget the past, pardon me my misfortune and recognise that I have not omitted anything for you to regard me all my life as your servant . . .

(Source: Grillon, v. 642–3. The only note corrected in Richelieu's hand during the Day of Dupes)

33. [Richelieu] to the King, 12 November 1630

It is impossible for me not to convey to His Majesty the extreme satisfaction which I had yesterday at the honour of seeing him. His sentiments were full of generosity, particularly since they were based on reason and just considerations of the good and safety of His State. I beg him not to hesitate to communicate them to his creatures, who will study them and make them succeed to his contentment and advantage. I wish for your glory more than any servant has wished it for his master, and I will never omit anything which can contribute towards it. The singular demonstration which it pleased you to show me yesterday of your good will pierced my heart. I feel myself so extraordinarily obliged that I can scarcely express it. I entreat Your Majesty in the name of God not to do yourself any harm by melancholy, and I hope that by God's goodness you will be perfectly happy. For my part, I shall never be content except in making it better known to Your Majesty that I am the most faithful creature, the most committed subject, and the most zealous servant that any king and master has in the world. I will live and die in this position, being a hundred times more Your Majesty's servant than I am my own . . .

(Source: Grillon, v. 644)

34. Bullion, finance minister, to Richelieu, 31 December 1635

. . . We have to collect nearly 20 million *livres* this month and next month.[24] Whatever mildness or rigour we adopt, the debtors[25] evince good will but whatever they do they are unable to receive the money. . . .

If the shortage of money continues, as there is strong reason to suspect because of the cessation of commerce[26] and the transportation of money abroad (immense sums have been transported abroad over the last three years), then I consider that we will have to decide to manufacture copper coins[27] to provide the provinces of Champagne, Picardy, Normany and others with the means to facilitate trade and the payment of troops. Otherwise we will continue to be short of money. The salt farmers,[28] who are the worst off, state that more than 3 or 4 million *livres* is owed them by the people who cannot pay because of the shortage of coin . . .

(Source: AAE France 816, fos. 199–200)

35. Richelieu to Bullion and Bouthillier, finance ministers, 7 February 1636

. . . To conclude, I request Messieurs the finance ministers henceforth to expedite matters that have been resolved without any delay. I can assure them that it is quite impossible for affairs to succeed otherwise, whatever care is taken. I tell them this without seeking a quarrel but with great displeasure and resentment at seeing that matters are not proceeding as the King's service and the good of the state require, and all this because of lack of diligence . . .

(Source: Avenel, v. 965)

36. Bullion and Bouthillier to Richelieu, 22 February 1636

. . . The principal difficulty before us is whether we should make prisoners of all the tax contractors. The entire council of finance and

[24] From a forced loan on the towns.
[25] I.e. financiers.
[26] With Spain.
[27] Called *douzaines*.
[28] That is to say, the revenue farmers of the *gabelles de France*.

especially Messieurs the chief treasurers are protesting about the complete ruin of financial affairs with regard to the tax contractors. If we put pressure on them, then most of them would go bankrupt. It would seem appropriate that it please Your Eminence to have a council held in your presence where you take the trouble to hear them all. Afterwards Your Eminence and His Majesty could take the necessary decision, which we will have carried out immediately. We need a declaration to reduce the value of money and request Your Eminence to write a word to the Chancellor about it so that he may have the matter expedited . . .

(Source: AAE France 820, fo. 131v.)

37. Bullion to Louis XIII, 9 May 1636

. . . When expenses are so excessive and on so many fronts, Your Majesty who has cognisance of his affairs knows better than anyone that if there are no funds it is impossible for us to render the obedience due to you. If we were in an abundance as in the past, when there was often more than 14 million *livres* in cash at the Treasury, it would be easy to obey you . . . but as for cash, Your Majesty will see the difficulties and embarrassments which occur daily in trying to get in money, which has never been as difficult to obtain as it now is . . .

(Source: AAE France 820, fos. 258v., 259v.)

38. Ruling which the King wishes to be observed inviolably in his finances, 19 July 1638

No member of the council is to receive more than the sums in the King's lists; nor may he claim any recompense to be paid extraordinarily or by a secret cash payment.

No tax contract is to be expedited except by secretaries of state nominated by His Majesty.

No list of secret payments called 'secret payments by roll' is to be drawn up if it contains gifts to individuals.

As for secret payments which are expedited in the council for the profits of the tax contractors, Messieurs the Chancellor and finance ministers are to retain one copy, which they are to show to His Majesty whenever it pleases him to command it or to anyone else to whom he sees fit.

Leases of the revenue farms are to be drawn up in the council as has been done in the past without turning away those who seek to increase the rents on the farms, on penalty of incurring the King's displeasure. No remissions will be accorded to revenue farmers and tax contractors without Messieurs the Chancellor and finance ministers having first received orders from His Majesty himself . . .

Messieurs de Chavigny and des Noyers alone will be empowered to sign the secret payments which His Majesty commands, that is to say the sieur de Chavigny will sign those expedited for pensions and affairs of state and the sieur des Noyers the secret expenses for war, whether within the kingdom or beyond.

His Majesty wishes and intends that the ruling for the direction of his finances of January 1629, which was very advantageous to his service, and was announced in his presence at the *Parlement* of Paris, shall be carried out punctually by his councillors.

I will obey the present ruling and will carry it out with all my power. Paris, 19 July 1638. Bullion.

(Source: Ranum, pp. 197–8. AAE France 830, fo. 261)

39. Richelieu to Bullion and Bouthillier, 21 August 1638

Messieurs of the council will please accept that if they do not take care in the future with regard to new taxes which they establish in frontier towns – considering, for example, whether or not they are impoverished, and what assurances the King has given – they will drive them to despair so that great inconveniences could result . . . The King loses the reputation of his word; the inhabitants their enthusiasm and affection; towns, and consequently the kingdom, their security; and all of this for the satisfaction of a Barbier[29] or another tax contractor . . . I have often heard Monsieur de Bullion state that it is only the finance ministers' word which finds them money. If this is so . . . Messieurs of the council must equally recognise that nothing is as necessary as that the King retain the hearts of his subjects by keeping his word . . .

(Source: Avenel, vi. 98–100)

40. Bullion to Richelieu, 2 March 1639

. . . I am obliged to tell Your Eminence that since the Treasury funds are

[29] Louis le Barbier, a prominent financier.

employed for the subsistence of the troops, it is impossible to provide the expenses for the campaign. We even lack cash for the subsistence. For general expenses of the state the most that we can do is find 32 or 33 millions . . . It is impossible to collect the subsistence except by the diligence of the commissioners of His Majesty,[30] who are not doing their duty . . .

(Source: AAE France 833, fo. 59)

41. Bullion to Richelieu, 24 March 1639

. . . The tax contractors are very disobedient in their payments. The *taille* for last year and the present year is not coming in as it should. This creates disorder and this lack of funds removes our credit. It is necessary to take measures on the subsistence for next winter quarter because the shortfall in the *taille* brings inconveniences which it is impossible to remedy . . .

(Source: AAE France 833, fo. 74v.)

42. Bouthillier, finance minister, to Richelieu, 17 August 1641

Your Eminence would not believe to what extent the bankruptcies of Barbier and Sabathier,[31] and the apparently reasonable remedies that we have taken prejudice affairs . . . Our tax contractors scarcely find any credit any more, and they are afraid that soon one will no longer say 'scarcely', because the money-changers, who are really notorious usurers, are afraid that their usuries and excessive interest will be discovered by the commissioners that we have appointed to establish the possessions and debts of those who are insolvent. They fear that we are preparing an investigation against them, which would be justified according to good morals and the observance of law. But we are constrained to tolerate them; they do bad things at Rome in order to avoid worse ones . . .

(Source: AAE France 839, fo. 173v.–174r.)

[30] A ruling of 24 July 1638 envisaged sending out intendants into each *généralité* with the task of levying the subsistence for the troops.
[31] Legal action by Louis le Barbier's private creditors had to be blocked by the council of finance in January and March 1641. Similar action was taken on 6 April 1641 at the request of François Sabathier, a more considerable financier.

43. Richelieu to Bouthillier and Séguier, 16 October 1641

If Messieurs of the council continue to allow tax farmers and tax contractors the freedom to treat the King's subjects according to their unruly appetite, then it is certain that a disorder similar to that in Spain will happen in France . . .

(Source: Avenel, vi. 881)

44. Extract from the journal of Olivier Lefèvre d'Ormesson, 12 April 1643

Monsieur des Noyers had been attacked by the King strongly on two or three occasions. Last Friday, he at last resolved to demand a release from service after a dispute between himself and the King on the matter of the war. The King told him that it seemed that he saw contradicting him as part of his task. Monsieur des Noyers replied that since his service was not agreeable to him, he asked to be allowed to withdraw. The King replied that he had never refused to release people from service, at which Monsieur des Noyers thanked him and withdrew . . . It is said that this disgrace will harm the Jesuits, who are the councillors of Monsieur des Noyers . . . He was sent away because he thought much of himself and had had absolute disposition of more than 30 million *livres* a year without rendering any account under Monsieur Cardinal de Richelieu, and wished to continue in the same manner and render no account to the King . . . The King has spoken well of Monsieur Le Tellier, saying that he was capable of higher employment . . .[32]

(Source: Chéruel, p. 23)

45. Extract from the journal of Olivier Lefèvre d'Ormesson, end of April 1643

[Declaration of Louis XIII 'touching the government of the Kingdom after his death' 20 April 1643]. On this I say only that everyone mocks

---

[32] Le Tellier received letters patent as war minister on 13 April 1643, but was unable to buy a secretaryship of state until 22 October 1645, after the death of Sublet des Noyers.

48

the precautions which Messieurs the four ministers[33] have taken in this declaration to avoid their disgrace.

(Source: Chéruel, p. 32)

46. Bragelongne, intendant at Orléans, to Séguier, 28 October 1645

[Levy of the *taille* at Brinon, Séguier's parish].

. . . I can prove to you that the inhabitants have had no increase in the *taille* since a reduction from 10 000 *livres* to 6 500 *livres* in the assessments of 1644 following your letter. Their statements which render suspect my affection for your service are untrue. They have made false accusations to induce you by extraordinary action to give them more than they deserve. If you were properly informed of the state of their affairs, you would not wish to favour them with your full protection . . .

(Source: Mousnier, ii. 742–3)

47. Extract from the memoirs of Omer Talon, advocate-general in the *Parlement* of Paris, 1648

King Louis XIII died in the month of May 1643. The Queen was declared Regent. She recalled all those who had been exiled, and those who had been in disfavour during the ministry of Cardinal de Richelieu she considered with compassion, since she had herself felt similar misfortune, although as a Queen she could survive such difficulty.

Through the death of the King, the administration of finance changed hands. This was not just by the promotion of two new finance ministers, Messieurs de Bailleul and d'Avaux,[34] because the first of these had no intelligence or application for affairs of this type and the second was immediately sent to Münster to work on the peace treaty. The real change, however, was that when Monsieur Bouthillier was replaced as finance minister, M. d'Emery[35] was made controller-general. He had great influence with Cardinal Mazarin, who became first and absolute

---

[33] Mazarin, Séguier, Bouthillier and Chavigny. The testament of Louis XIII was annulled in the *Parlement* of Paris on 18 May 1643. Bouthillier and Chavigny both lost office under the Regency.

[34] Appointed joint finance ministers on 13 June 1643.

[35] Particelli d'Hémery, sole controller-general after 8 November 1643.

minister: the sieur d'Hémery became all powerful in the direction of financial affairs, in the conduct of which he showed no moderation.

From the beginning of his administration, he spared no money to acquire the friendship and goodwill of those whom he considered useful people to serve him, and those who could harm him. Besides, the Queen contented everybody with money. Those who returned from exile demanded the restoration of their offices and governorships. Those who held them did not want to relinquish them. The treasury was opened up in an attempt to settle these differences . . .

[*Additional comments.*]

Monsieur the Cardinal de Richelieu having died on 4 December 1642 and the King on 14 May 1643, everybody believed that the change of government would bring about some great transformation in affairs, and that the ruin of Cardinal de Richelieu's household would bring about that of his family, his relatives, and his financiers who possessed all the wealth of the State. This did not happen, because Monsieur the Cardinal Mazarin was called to the ministry, and openly and loudly protected the family and the remnants of Monsieur the Cardinal de Richelieu, to whose memory he was obliged because of his Cardinal's hat . . .

Monsieur d'Hémery, who was made controller-general, and subsequently finance minister,[36] was infinitely talented at gratifying those who could help his fortune, or whose authority he feared, principally those of the *Parlement*, whose anger and justice he dreaded. He despised any sort of order in financial affairs, either in revenues or expenditure. In order to have ready cash, he drew up loan contracts on the revenues of the *taille*, and paid 15 per cent interest to those who advanced money. He did the same on the revenue farms. Thus it was that in 1648 he anticipated the revenues of the years 1650 and 1651, and brought matters to such a pass that having engaged the King's finances by more than 100 million *livres* to the tax contractors and financiers, he could not make the state subsist except by cuts on the payment of salaries to office-holders and *rentiers* . . . Most of the wealth of Paris was founded on the large interest payments paid by the King. Merchants had for the most part abandoned their normal trade in order to place their money in this infamous financial activity . . .

(Source: Michaud and Pojoulat, pp. 270–2; 299–300)

---

[36] On 17 July 1647.

48. Le Tellier to Mazarin, 2 July 1649

... In truth so much terror of the misfortunes with which France is menaced has arisen in the spirits of men, by false predictions or exaggerated truths, that those who have the money will not bring themselves to lend it. Rather, they employ all their industry to hide it in order to guard against the accidents which they fear. Thus the richest people in this town[37] cannot use their credit, and remain poverty-stricken among their great wealth, because of the interruption in the commerce of money ... Messieurs the directors of finance[38] are unable to approve the proposal to mint new *sous* because it would be too ruinous to the state and they consider that the extraordinary financial tribunal would completely prevent the re-establishment of credit ...

(Source: AAE France 864, fos. 385, 387v.)

49. Le Tellier to Mazarin, 4 July 1649

The sieur Launay Gravé, La Rallière and their associates in the farm of the entries into Paris obtained very great advantages from Messieurs the directors when they advanced the first payment for the German troops. At their example, all those who make loans treat the King in the same way, so that his revenues (which are already greatly diminished by last year's declarations) are further reduced by reimbursing the farmers and receivers-general for part of the loans they have already made, by deducting also the interest charge of those who levy the *taille* in the provinces, and by interest payments for those who advance loans from one payment date to an earlier one. I can assure Your Eminence that there remain only 20 million *livres* net to the King for the expenses of the state. I have seen this myself in the investigation that I have undertaken with Messieurs the directors since I have been here.[39] I know that there are expedients for the King to regain the advantages which the financiers take of the present necessity of his finances. Subsequently, we may well regain from them what they exacted in the present disadvantageous conjuncture. But when we carry out this act of justice, they will plead a lack of faith on our part and their clamours will discredit those who serve His Majesty in the administration of finance ...

(Source: AAE France 864, fo. 392)

[37] Paris.
[38] Aligre and Barillon de Morangis, appointed on 9 July 1648 following the dismissal of d'Hémery. They were left in control after the resignation of La Meilleraye as finance minister on 14 April 1649.
[39] At Paris.

50. Aligre and Barillon de Morangis, directors of finance, to Mazarin, n.d., *c.* 4 July 1649

. . . We are working at drawing up a list of the revenue of the Kingdom, what is consumed, what is assigned, and what remains . . . There is no means of providing for so many expenses from the ordinary revenue of the state, since this is diminished by the reductions given to the people, and the re-establishment of salaries and rights of the office-holders. In addition, four provinces, encouraged by the *Parlements*, refuse to pay anything in the current year and for the past . . .

We hope to encourage some individuals to make loans on what little revenue remains to us for this year and the next few years. We consider it nevertheless very difficult to achieve this until affairs are entirely re-established, the people reduced to obedience and the King's authority better recognised than it is at the moment. In the present state of public credit, no-one wants to persuade the financiers and others to make loans to us . . .

(Source: AAE France 864, fo. 408)

51. Le Tellier to Mazarin, 15 July 1650

. . . Monsieur the Maréchal de l'Hôpital said that he had the word of Messieurs the first president,[40] and presidents de Mesmes and de Mesgringy that they would find the necessary money for these military expenses. Monsieur the finance minister[41] replied that he did not believe that anyone would want to lend money when they learnt that it was for the King, but that if these gentlemen wished to find people in their private capacity then doubtless this would succeed. Monsieur the Maréchal de l'Hôpital also says that he has people offering to lend 400 000 *livres* provided that they are assigned 500 000 *livres* as reimbursement and 100 000 *livres* of old debts are accepted, with which Monsieur the finance minister is in agreement.

(Source: AAE France 871, fo. 207)

[40] Of the *Parlement* of Paris, Mathieu Molé.
[41] Longueil des Maisons, who was appointed on 24 May 1650.

52. Anonymous correspondent to Mazarin, 23 February 1651

It is said that his[42] downfall is delayed a little because those who claim the right to succeed him cannot reach agreement among themselves . . . I know on good authority that the sacrifice of Monsieur Le Tellier is one of the conditions of the reconciliation of the Princes with the Queen.

(Source: AAE France 874, fos. 110–11)

53. Anonymous correspondent to Mazarin, 14 April 1651

. . . Monsieur Le Tellier is back in favour, and has been to see Monsieur d'Orléans, as did Monsieur Servien yesterday. Everybody is astonished at this, since the wheel has suddenly turned full circle . . . The designs against him[43] are not at an end but matters are rather confused . . . There are new cabals everywhere at the Queen's and at the princes' residences. The ministers have different objectives. Everyone is wary of his colleague. It is evident that the Queen only trusts those who are clients of Monsieur the Cardinal. It is easy to judge that he must return or the whole council will be overturned.

(Source: AAE France 874, fo. 243)

54. Colbert, intendant of the Cardinal's household, to Mazarin, 14 April 1651

. . . The wealth of Your Eminence consists in property, possessions and debts. Your property and possessions are the revenue of benefices, residences, furnishings, emoluments, pensions and the loans made for the King's service, part of which have been assigned on revenues . . . The property and possessions of Your Eminence are rendered almost worthless because of the seizure of his benefices ordered by the *Parlement* of Paris . . . The emoluments and pensions can only be paid on the Queen's orders, since Monsieur the finance minister has very little intention of doing it.

(Source: AAE France 874, fos. 247–9)

---

[42] Le Tellier's.
[43] Le Tellier.

55. Anonymous memorandum to Mazarin, 6 May 1651

The finance minister[44] has had a great scare in the last few days. There is a strong faction against him added to which there are new proposals from the financiers. What could save him from the cabal of the marquis de La Vieuville is that this fellow has stupidly fallen into the trap of promising those financiers who are prepared to assist him, or who want him as finance minister, that he will stay as finance minister for four years. They offer the King an advance of four million *livres* in cash in order to allow the state to subsist for a certain amount of time provided that they take over all his revenues. In addition to meeting all the expenses of the state, they offer to acquit all the loans which have been made up to now and to repurchase alienated royal demesne. But in these proposals there are many inconveniences. They would have the effect of returning to loan contracts on the *taille* and to overturn the whole council without any certainty of success. This is the reason why Doublet,[45] the principal instigator and speech-maker for them, has not received a favourable reply. But he had the satisfaction of his proposal being properly examined for a long time and on this matter a great council was held at the palais d'Orléans . . .[46]

(Source: AAE France 875, fos. 15v.–16r.)

56. Anonymous memorandum to Mazarin, 28 May 1651

The finance minister is no longer tottering. His position has been strengthened. The duc d'Orléans has said that he has regained the Queen's favour, providing money for Monsieur the Cardinal. The support of Monsieur Le Tellier and Monsieur de Chavigny has assisted him. He has also the support of Monsieur de la Rochefoucauld in Monsieur the prince's circle. But today there was a breach, Monsieur the prince[47] spoke against him at the Chancellor's on the matter of 50 000 *livres* which the finance minister refused for the expenses of the king's household . . .

---

[44] Longueil des Maisons.
[45] Jean Doublet, the spokesman of financiers who did not directly handle royal revenues as did the receivers-general and revenue farmers.
[46] On 27 and 30 April.
[47] Condé.

Money is so rare in the King's coffers that the Queen is forced to demand 20 000 *livres* from each of the ministers, the princes for their part holding the clearest revenues of the King. In the extremity which we are in, we must at last come to the only extraordinary means left to the King, which is to hold a strong extraordinary financial tribunal.[48] If the Queen was counselled by persons who were prepared to be involved financially in this, this could be quickly achieved and 10 million *livres* could be obtained in six months . . . [There should be an investigation] of those who have been in charge of financial administration over the last twenty years. One would find all the wealth of France in the hands of Monsieur Bouthillier, Monsieur de la Meilleraye, Monsieur Tubeuf, the widows of Monsieur d'Effiat, Monsieur de Bullion, Monsieur d'Hémery and the widow of Bretonvilliers.[49] Lambert, a clerk in the Treasury, should also be included, since he has gained 5 million in five years. Everything – justice and the royal ordinances – and everybody – the office-holders and the people – are against these sorts of people. Those who dispose of the king's finances do not take the risks of financiers, who are all ruined. Only sixty years ago it was common practice to prosecute those who managed the king's finances.[50] The evidence against them is the abundance of their wealth. Under the ordinances, peculation is a capital offence. No time could be more propitious for an investigation. No action can be envisaged which is more justified and more useful to the King than this. It must necessarily be achieved, whatever protection is claimed by those who have managed the King's finances. If the King does not establish this tribunal, the Estates General will make its protests to the King . . .

(Source: AAE France 875, fo. 106 ff.)

57. Anonymous memorandum to Mazarin, 8 July 1651

[The princes are resolved] not to return to the King's council while Messieurs Le Tellier, de Servien and de Lionne are still there, since these gentlemen, the masters of affairs, are supporters of Cardinal Mazarin and encourage Her Majesty in her hope of seeing his return. When Monsieur the prince or the prince de Conty suggest something in the

---

[48] *Chambre de justice.*
[49] Clerk of the council.
[50] Called *ordonnateurs.*

council, the Queen always asks for time to consider the matter, in order to communicate it to Cardinal Mazarin and have his opinion. She does nothing without his participating in the decision.

(Source: AAE France 876, fo. 70)

58. Anonymous memorandum to Mazarin, 15 July 1651

Monsieur the prince has not had his hopes fulfilled, since the decree[51] will merely provide for remonstrances for the exiling of these gentlemen.[52] But it was agreed that Her Majesty would be requested to give Monsieur the prince the necessary security so that he could return to court . . . Her Majesty would also be requested to send a declaration to the court confirming the assurances that she has given that she would not recall Monsieur the Cardinal . . .

(Source: AAE France 876, fo. 110)

59. Brienne to Mazarin, 21 July 1651

[The Queen] has commanded me to carry out the office of Monsieur Le Tellier and I have agreed so that she does not have to appoint anyone else to it, as was the intention of several people who doubtless hoped to render his return more difficult by placing an obstacle in his path. It seemed to me that justice, the interest of the offices, and the friendship between us obliged me to take it . . .

(Source: AAE France 876, fo. 121v.–122r.)

60. Anonymous memorandum to Mazarin, 28 July 1651

. . . The change of finance minister is rumoured.[53] It is said that Monsieur de La Vieuville has given you 400 000 *livres* for it and 100 000 to Madame the princess palatine . . . This plan of changing the finance minister is very good for you, for the kingdom, and for the Queen,

[51] Of the *Parlement* of Paris.
[52] Le Tellier, Servien and Lionne.
[53] La Vieuville did not replace Longueil des Maisons officially until 8 September 1651.

because the present one does nothing for you unless he is forced to. If the funds to assist you are mismanaged, the consequences will be your total ruin and the ruin of the Queen.

(Source: AAE France 876, fo. 182)

61. Millet, a client of Mazarin, to Mazarin, 29 July 1651

[Reports rumours of La Vieuville's nomination]. We believe that this is a story invented to damage Your Eminence with the public, seeking to demonstrate your wish to govern from Cologne as if you were at Paris, and that Your Eminence wishes to establish a council at your whim. [The Maréchaux d'Estrées and La Ferté Seneterre argue that] although this change may be necessary, its timing must be delayed until the end of the year when funds begin to arrive. At the moment they are all consumed . . . The financiers have refused to co-operate. The munitions contractors have even gone to the Palais Royal to protest that they will all resign. The finance minister has similarly offered to resign. The Queen has been counselled to pacify this strike and to assure them . . . that she has no design to change anything with regard to financial administration. Moreover, the cabal of Longueil in the *Parlement*[54] has joined with that of Monsieur the prince . . .

(Source: AAE France 876, fos. 185v.–186r.)

62. Colbert to Mazarin, 8 September 1651

Yesterday in the Council the King spoke to His Royal Highness[55] about the establishment of the council, naming the persons who are to be in it. His Royal Highness did not approve of this, and left stating that he would not return . . .

(Source: AAE France 876, fo. 391)

63. Mazarin to Louis XIV, at Bouillon, 23 December 1651

. . . For ten months I have suffered with constancy my reputation being

---

[54] Longueil des Maisons also held the office of president there.
[55] Gaston.

torn to pieces, and being deprived of all the wealth which belongs to me because of the liberality of Your Majesties. I had committed my wealth in great loans to assist your affairs and your service at a time of pressing need, when the exhaustion of royal finances and the delays of the formal procedures would have led to their collapse . . . [I have been called] a thief and a pirate, a disturber of the public, enemy of the state and the scourge of Christendom . . .

The love that I have for France has taken such deep roots over many years that no ill treatment is capable of shaking it . . . I have had as principal objective to obtain a general peace, knowing that this is the surest means of defeating the factions which have arisen against Your Majesty and extinguishing the fire presently raging in the Kingdom . . . It is true, Sire, that I cannot deny that my friends and those who accompany me are called *Mazarins*, and carry with pleasure a name which many seek to render odious . . . but I have not seen anyone carrying this name lack loyalty to Your Majesty and take the side of the Spaniards and other enemies of your crown . . .

I do not wish to be involved in future in any way in the management of affairs. On this point, if Your Majesty had a sufficiently high opinion of me as to order me to take up affairs, this would be the only point on which I am capable of disobedience towards Your Majesty . . . Your Majesty does not lack a suitable number of able ministers, whose application and commitment are better rewarded than mine in that they have gained public approbation. If they wish any assistance and information from me from the time when I was in affairs, then I shall give it willingly and sincerely, rather than return to the position which they occupy . . .

(Source: AAE France 879, fo. 187ff.)

64. Mazarin to Anne of Austria, 23 December 1651

[Writes in similar terms as to Louis XIV but adds:] I have avoided defending myself by manifestos when my reputation has been cruelly torn to pieces, and have prevented my friends who know my innocence from publishing those which they have prepared, so that there would be nothing with which to reproach me . . .

I did not consider that I could be a true Frenchman, or a true servant of Your Majesties, if I shamefully stood by with folded arms in the present state of affairs . . .

(Source: AAE France 879, fos. 193, 194v.)

65. Le Tellier to Mazarin, 11 January 1652

... [The decree of the *Parlement*][56] has no example and was given without any cause. Her Majesty wishes it to be suspended. In the meantime she takes Your Eminence under her safeguard and protection . . . When I had the honour to see the Queen at midday, I found her in a contrary sentiment and insisting that the decree be annulled. This is also the opinion of Messieurs de Châteauneuf and de Villeroy, who do not consider it fitting for the King's dignity or propriety that the decree should subsist. They add that it is to be feared that some wild men among the *dévots* might undertake something[57] under pretext of this decree . . .

The repayment of your debts is more difficult because Monsieur the finance minister leads us to understand that the state cannot survive with their full payment while the civil and foreign wars last. This leads one to fear a riot in the city.

This fear led us to consider the matter yesterday in the council, where the Queen expressed her wish that the *rentes* be paid and Monsieur the Keeper of the Seals[58] pointed out the inconveniences that could arise if they were stopped. Monsieur the finance minister persisted in saying that it was absolutely impossible to pay them, and proposed as remedy to write to the mayor advising him that the King was obliged to issue this decree not to divert payment of the *rentes* but to prevent individuals who hold assignments on the same revenues for the years 1649, 1650 and 1651 from profiting on them . . . It is considered preferable to issue the decree before Your Eminence's arrival, so that it should not be thought at Paris that it had been issued after your return . . . If some settlement can be made on this, it will be you who will gain all the glory and advantage: this is the opinion of all Your Eminence's servants . . .

(Source: AAE France 881, fo. 70ff.)

66. Mazarin to Le Tellier, 18 January 1652

I consider the decision taken by Monsieur the finance minister dangerous, since it could provide powerful assistance to Monsieur the duc d'Orléans to obtain the alliance he wants with the city of Paris and the *Parlement*. It would have been better to have delayed this matter a

---

[56] Of 29 December 1651 against Mazarin.
[57] An assassination attempt.
[58] Molé, appointed on 8 September 1651.

month or two, during which time, if the *Parlement* and the city remained in the obedience they owe the King, then we could have examined the issue of the *rentes* and found expedients commensurate to the state of the King's finances, the current attitude of the *Parlement* and the city. If these two bodies in the meantime had joined with the princes, we could have blamed them for the cessation of the payment of the *rentes*. This would have created great difficulties for them which would not easily have been solved. Thus my opinion is that if the decree of the council for the revocation of the assignments subsists, Monsieur the finance minister should order the first revenues he draws from the provincial receipts to be transported to Paris, so that the payment of *rentes* is not delayed . . .

(Source: AAE France 887, fo. 23)

67. Draft letters patent for Mazarin, 12 August 1652

[Louis XIV notes the requests for Mazarin's exile and the 'aversion which my people have for his ministry, which has been decried by people who wish to make it odious . . .' He continues:] I was born to render justice to my subjects. I am King for this purpose. I wish to do this. I owe justice to my cousin Cardinal Mazarin as much as to anybody. He is my subject and my servant. He has received both qualities as a grace from my late father of glorious memory, as a result of several great and notable services. This is what inclined me to heed his request that he should withdraw voluntarily from my kingdom, to cede to the violence of the rebellions which threatened as a result of his presence, and to divert the plans of those who, under pretext of his ministry during the Regency of the Queen my honoured lady mother, attempted to attack the law of majority and delay its declaration . . . [Mazarin was condemned by decrees of the *Parlement* of Paris] as if he was guilty of atrocious crimes which rendered him unworthy of the nomination which the late King my father made of him in his testament . . .

After the declaration of my majority, he had recourse to my judgement, in requiring me to take cognisance of those of his actions which were accused by others of being crimes, as justice obliges me to do. He felt this necessary because arms had been taken up against my service, and treaties had been entered into with enemies of the state under conditions of not laying down arms until the conclusion of a general peace . . . I have found no precise accusation against him, although he is accused of malversation in the administration of my affairs . . . They contain only a denunciation full of passion, hatred, menace, cruelty and desire for vengeance against him. They are written in a style foreign to the gravity of justice and the manner with which remonstrances should be addressed . . . from the pen of a man[59] who previously sold himself to the Spaniards to write injuriously against the honour of Cardinal de Richelieu . . . [The declaration against Mazarin issued on 6 September 1651 was only conceded by the Regent because she feared] the diminution of my authority and the undermining of the fundamental laws of my royalty . . . owing to threats to extend the period of my minority and remove her from the Regency . . . [The King denounces] the claim to authority which some members of my *Parlement* assert without due title, claiming that the sovereign intendancy of the government of the state is in their hands when the Kings are not of age to rule, whereas no law of this Kingdom has ever shown the slightest trace of this injurious right . . . The recent example of the terrible consequences of the willingness of the late King of England, my brother-in-law and my good friend, to consent to the wishes of his Parliament against one of his principal ministers[60] must confirm me in my view . . .

(Source: AAE France 884, fo. 57ff.)

68. Foucquet, procurator-general of the *Parlement* of Paris, to Mazarin, 2 January 1653

. . . Since maladministration of the royal finances is one of the principal reasons for the discredit of public affairs, the death of Monsieur the finance minister,[61] and the necessity of filling his place, obliges me to explain to Your Eminence . . . the importance of choosing persons of known integrity, credit with the public, and inviolable probity. In the work I have undertaken in investigating the means of ending the present abuses and to prevent greater ones in the future,[62] I have found that everything depends on the will of the finance ministers. It would not be disadvantageous for the King and Your Eminence to employ me. I have examined the ways to succeed. My office is not incompatible with this

---

[59] Mathieu de Morgues.

[60] Strafford.

[61] La Vieuville died earlier that day.

[62] Foucquet had served as procurator-general in the abortive *chambre de justice* set up in 1648.

position[63] ... I have served for 18 years in the council as master of requests, and on many occasions have shown affection and loyalty for your service ...

(Source: AAE France 892, fo. 39)

69. Le Tillier, intendant of finance, to Mazarin, 21 January 1653

... The King's finances are at present in such a great lethargy that if something is not done soon by your prudent counsels, all good men will begin to despair of the safety of the state, which can only be restored if financial affairs are re-established. The three affairs which His Majesty principally recommended to the care of the directors of finance[64] were to find enough money to give satisfaction to the holders of annuities, to pay the Swiss, and to oblige the munitions contractors to provide enough bread for the subsistence of the garrisons and the king's armies. You know better than any one, my lord, in what manner the munitions contractors honour their contract. They have a reasonable fear that the successor of Monsieur de La Vieuville will not continue their lease, because its price astonished all good men, since the assignments given for their reimbursement included extraordinary double interest charges ... As for the Swiss, they are dissatisfied but wait patiently for Your Eminence's return,[65] hoping that you will protect their interest. The *rentiers* hoped for things from the return of the King to Paris ... However, we are now in the fourth week when no payment has been made at the town hall. The revenue farms on which the payments are assigned are abandoned and without farmers. This produces such an effect that, joined with the ill will and speeches of trouble-makers and malcontents who are still too numerous, Paris is on the eve of some great sedition ...

There is a rumour here that Your Eminence has the plan of establishing a council of finance ... It has always been recognised in France that such councils are the ruination of affairs and have never

---

[63] At the time of Longueil des Maisons' appointment, it had been argued that it was difficult to maintain ministerial secrecy if the finance minister also held office in the *Parlement*.

[64] Aligre and Barillon de Morangis, appointed on the death of La Vieuville on 2 January.

[65] Mazarin returned to Paris on 3 February.

lasted more than six weeks. A number of people bring as many different opinions for reasons of self-interest, envy or a spirit of contradiction. Such a number may be suitable for issuing general rulings. But for the summary discussion of individuals' affairs, proposals for extraordinary taxes, and contracting loans of money, secrecy and speed are very necessary . . .

(Source: AAE France 892, fos. 137–9)

70. Servien, minister of state, to Mazarin, 25 January 1653

. . . It is a great misfortune for me frequently to see tasks which are more burdensome than this one[66] succeed in my hands only to be told that the care of the royal finances is too laborious for me. This is tantamount to saying that I am not judged capable of anything important, since there is no office where less work is required. It requires foresight, firmness and probity rather than industriousness. No other proof of this is needed than the example of Monsieur de Bullion, who did it very well in his time although he never paid attention to the detail, scarcely did any work, and lacked one of the principal attributes, which is probity. Monsieur d'Effiat similarly did not have much application and worked very little. Monsieur d'Hémery and Monsieur des Maisons gave more of their time to intrigues at court and the entertainment of ladies at banquets, at gambling and other pleasures rather than at the work on affairs, for which they relied on subordinates. To tell you the truth we must conclude that a man who is incapable of being finance minister is incapable for all time of holding any great office in the Kingdom, where necessarily more work and assiduousness must be brought to bear than in this office . . . [He notes his rivalry with Le Tellier, whose family boasts that 'we have at last excluded Monsieur Servien from the finance ministry'].

(Source: AAE France 891, fo. 54. AAE France 892, fo. 148)

71. Servien and Foucquet, finance ministers, to Mazarin, 19 September 1653

[Discuss munitions contaract for bread for the army in Champagne and Picardy.] Although those who have made these offers assure us that they

[66] The office of finance minister.

have good partners, we do not consider them as suitable for this task as those who are presently charged with it, who are active and far-sighted. They want to make money for themselves, but they are also capable of looking after the King's business, which inclines us (unless Your Eminence has contrary views) to prefer them if they make reasonable terms, rather than making a dangerous experiment of bringing in new men who may be incapable of making money for themselves or looking after the King's business . . .

We take the liberty to tell Your Eminence that it is very important not to take an action of authority in financial affairs which is not founded in justice. We have observed that this conduct brings the financiers back to us and re-establishes the King's credit so that we see the purses of private individuals opening up to us (which the debasement of the coinage also greatly assists).

This reason has obliged us to delay until now a settlement of the matter of the revenue farm of the entries of Paris. It is true that the farmers who hold the lease are difficult and uncompromising, but His Eminence will observe that the harsh treatment received by farmers who hold a lease issued in due form discourages other tax-contractors . . .

(Source: AAE France 892, fo. 352ff.)

72. Servien and Foucquet to Mazarin, 25 September 1653

. . . If orders continue to be sent to billet troops in the provinces and to pay for them on the *taille*, as has been done up to now, it will be impossible for us to guarantee the winter quarter. If we take funds of the *taille*, the financiers will demand a reduction to compensate for the revenues which have been diverted. What is worse, they will stop the payment of their loans on this pretext. His Eminence should please consider that this has never been done except during great confusions of the Kingdom, when the King's taxes could not be received through the ordinary means. There is no point in having finance ministers if Messieurs the secretaries of state issue orders for funds . . .

(Source: AAE France 892, fo. 380v.)

73. Servien to Mazarin, 2 October 1653

. . . We are sending Your Eminence a summary list of the amounts which we have paid in cash. From this you will see the efforts which it has been necessary to make in a year in which the revenues have been anticipated, and in which the best revenue farms and receipts have been without any order, abandoned to the discretion of the troops and the generals who have used them as they pleased . . .

(Source: AAE France 892, fo. 402v.–403r.)

74. Servien and Foucquet to Mazarin, 24 November 1653

. . . We have been content to give cash to the munitions contractors to provide the bread rations for the army for the rest of this month. Your Eminence may be assured that while the army still holds together bread will not be lacking. When we do not have ready cash, we are able to borrow. At the moment we find plenty of people who freely provide their money simply on our word, which we have not failed to keep up to the present. This is what has given us the means of carrying out our orders at the required dates. Your Eminence would be astonished if he saw the list of all the cash payments we have made since we have been in office . . .[67] We have already informed Your Eminence that it is impossible to force the financiers to make payments which they have promised if they bring us orders from Messieurs the secretaries of state permitting governors and troops to keep the proceeds from the *taille*. If this practice continues, therefore, it will be impossible to answer for the King's revenues or to carry out the contracts which have been drawn up, because the financiers require cash from us for payments made by the communities on the authority of letters under the King's private seal of which we have no knowledge. The prejudice this causes is such that not only are all the King's revenues consumed by this, but the generals of the army, governors of the provinces and governors of the fortresses abuse this practice and take it upon themselves to give orders concerning the King's revenues, and seize control of them . . .

(Source: AAE France 892, fo. 444ff.)

75. Servien and Foucquet to Mazarin, 19 June 1654

Our principal care is to find cash promptly, in which we encounter great difficulty, both because of the great advances which we have made before

---

[67] Servien and Foucquet were appointed as joint finance ministers on 8 February 1653.

the departure of the King (the detail of which we have shown Your Eminence) and the sterility of the season, which makes money rare and expensive even among individuals. Tomorrow morning we hope to finish off the matter of the payers of the *rentes*, and escape from this as advantageously as possible ... It is quite impossible to avoid anticipating next year's revenues of the *taille*, which we will attempt to replace according to opportunity and any extraordinary measures that we have to hand.

Since we cannot discharge Guyenne from the billeting of troops, as had been promised, the person who has contracted the loan on the revenues of this province demands with great insistence that their expense should at least be regulated, and that they should be made to conduct themselves with discipline . . . [Subsequently the financier had returned to them to say] that if this were not promptly remedied . . . he would not be able to honour his contract. We humbly request Your Eminence to deal with this matter as diligently as possible, not only because of the threatened ruin of the loan which he has made this year, but because of the impossibility of finding another financier to enter such a contract next year . . .

(Source: AAE France 893/1, fos. 74–5)

76. Servien to Mazarin, 4 July 1654

I take this opportunity to present to Your Eminence the growing necessity for money, which increases every day. The present interest rate between individuals is 15 per cent. This places us in great difficulty and obliges us to ask Your Eminence very humbly to assist us with his credit on occasions which present themselves for producing money. [Proposed increase in the number of intendants of finance to 12:] I think that it is necessary to expedite promptly the provisions of Monsieur Paget[68] together with the letter of assurance which he demands similar to those given to the other intendants. Without this, no-one will be found to pay anything for these offices. No-one apart from him has offered to buy one. A rich and intelligent person whom I approached on the same matter would not even consider doing so. Perhaps when the matter is better known more purchasers will be found. We have an extreme need of the sum which it will raise, to send part of it to Catalan front and the other part for the payment of the guards . . .

(Source: AAE France 893/2, fo. 121)

---

[68] As intendant of finance.

77. Servien and Foucquet to Mazarin, 19 July 1654

. . . We take this occasion to ask Your Eminence to ensure, as we have very humbly requested him, that we are sent the orders of the King at the same time as you order us to incur expenditure. It is impossible for us to satisfy all these orders for payment. . . . It is not as easy to find money as it is to sign an order. Formerly when we provided in advance for some payment which was necessary for the war, Your Eminence notified us that it would be best to wait for the King's orders. We are obliged to tell Your Eminence in confidence and with much regret that we have never encountered so much difficulty in finding money. All the financiers carefully avoid concluding contracts with us for fear of having to lend money because of the difficulties in finding it now that it is so rare and so expensive . . . We are taking all the measures we can to find money promptly. Among these is the expedient of creating two more intendants of finance . . .

(Source: AAE France 893/2, fos. 166v.–168)

78. Servien to Mazarin, 22 December 1654

When I entered the administration of finance, I was not unaware of the enormity of the burden after a long war which had consumed, or brought about the alienation of, the principal and clearest revenues of the Kingdom. I had hoped (and I think that it was also Your Eminence's belief) that there being two finance ministers, it would be an easier burden to carry, and that the co-operation which Monsieur the procurator-general[69] promised would be such that we would act as one person, remedying the obstacles and delays which usually arise in such offices when responsibilities are divided. No-one could then have imagined that this division would have been disagreeable to Monsieur the procurator-general, who was only 37 years old at the time and had another very considerable office, or that he would have difficulty in suffering as colleague in the finance ministry a man of my age[70] and long services. All my friends wanted to dissuade me from accepting the office on this condition, which seemed to demonstrate that Your Eminence did not have the same confidence in me that he had had in Messieurs de La

---

[69] Foucquet.
[70] Servien was 60 in 1653.

Vieuville, des Maisons and d'Hémery. They considered it to some extent prejudicial to my reputation to be joined by a man so much younger than myself. Besides this, they knew the humour of Monsieur the procurator-general and that of Monsieur his brother,[71] their general conduct and constant intrigues to get what they want, and they all foresaw what has now happened . . . His original plan is now fully revealed, since he was not content with his function if he could not remove mine, and he considered himself doing nothing if he was in second place. The advantage of primacy cost me so dear that it was not worthy of envy . . . We do not need to look elsewhere to find the cause of the coldness of the tax-contractors, and their closing of their purses contrary to the disposition they showed Monsieur Hervart[72] and myself earlier that they would open them, and make us considerable loans . . . I will blindly submit to the resolutions which it may please Your Eminence to take . . . I ask only as a favour that you moderate the shame which I receive in the public eye. I know that many people who cannot be contented by the finance minister in the present necessities are against me. It would be unreasonable to be exposed to their discontent since this arises from the care which I have taken to do my duty. The first rule of a true finance minister is to prefer the interests of his master and the public to those of individuals . . .

(Source: AAE France 893/2, fo. 383v.ff. and AAE France 893/3, fo. 457)

79. Ruling for the functions of Messieurs Servien and Foucquet, finance ministers, 24 December 1654

His Majesty intends and orders that henceforth . . . and for the duration of the war, the sieur Servien will take care to order the funds of all expenses concerning the war, royal households and all others of whatever kind . . . The sieur Foucquet will have the revenue farmers and tax-contractors account to him, allowing as expenses everything they have paid as a result of quittances and treasury bills expedited on the orders of the finance ministers. He will finalise also all the tax- and loan-contracts, and will examine all the proposals which are presented, ensuring that the necessary edicts, declarations and decrees are drawn

---

[71] The abbé Basile Foucquet.
[72] Intendant of finance.

up and registered. The sieur Servien will sign without difficulty the lists, accounts, leases on the revenue farms, decrees and other documents which are required after they have been signed by the sieur Foucquet. Each of the sieurs finance ministers . . . will carry out the function of his office . . . without doing the other's except in the absence or legitimate impediment of the other minister . . .

(Source: AN E 272b, fo. 565. BN Ms. fr. 4222, fo. 195. AAE France 893/2, fo. 410)

80. Foucquet to Mazarin, 5 September 1655

It seems from the letter of Your Eminence that you are not satisfied with the care with which I seek money, and suggest that I have promised something which I have not been able to fulfil. Your Eminence is very humbly requested to believe that I will never fail to honour what I promise, and that is perhaps why I am not always willing to promise everything he demands, because I prefer to do more and promise less . . .

(Source: AAE France 894, fo. 296)

81. Foucquet to Mazarin, 12 June 1656

I have a great displeasure in learning from Your Eminence's letters of the necessity which the army suffers because of lack of money. However, greater efforts cannot be made at this time of year, and Your Eminence should consider that the extraordinary sources having been exhausted, and the sovereign courts being accustomed to resist the King's authority, it is impossible to gain assistance except from voluntary loans from financiers . . . I am well aware of the difficulties which Your Eminence is encountering and with good heart I employ all my private money and my personal credit to help out as much as I can. My brother will give Your Eminence an account in a few days time. In the meantime, I request you to be persuaded that I would give my life willingly for your service but that there are some things which are not in my power . . .

(Source: AAE France 900, fo. 78v.–79r.)

82. Foucquet to Mazarin, 12 September 1656

I was very surprised at the things my brother told me on the part of Your Eminence. I could easily defend myself if you had done me the grace of telling me them before my departure . . . It is true that I told Messieurs Talon and Bignon,[73] after discussing with them the edict of the demesne about which I was asking for their support, that it was necessary for everyone to help obtain extraordinary measures because the King's revenues did not suffice, there being no money in the Treasury and it not being evident where it could be found . . .

What disturbs me most is that Your Eminence asserts that I am not concerned with your fortune . . . It seems to me that my past conduct, exposing my family and my friends to certain [financial] ruin, the loyalty with which I have acted in the offices to which you have appointed me, and the affection with which I have spoken within the *Parlement* against Cardinal de Retz and on behalf of Your Eminence were certain proof of my loyalty . . . Your Eminence will please recall that when you spoke on financial affairs to Monsieur Servien and myself, I did not state that there were no means of maintaining the expenses of the next winter quarter and other expenses of the state. It is certain that the measures taken at present are not just and that the plans would be very different, both for revenues and expenses, in peace-time from what they are in war . . .

(Source: AAE France 900, fo. 354f.)

83. Foucquet to Mazarin, 26 June 1657

I have felt extreme pain on learning from several quarters of the continual complaints that Your Eminence makes of the lack of money and the bad administration of finance . . . I have asked you many times not to allow things to hinder credit by making it impossible for us to serve usefully. It is unreasonable that as soon as the King is away from Paris I am exposed to all the ill offices of my enemies and those who are envious of me . . . Besides the calumnies to a man such as myself who likes to keep his reputation, the true evil done to me is the loss of credit. It is an abuse to believe that we can survive without consuming at least one year's revenue in advance, so that on this basis I had no doubts about contracting loans on the *taille* of several *généralités*, while leaving some of them clear . . .

(Source: AAE France 902, fo. 119f.)

---

[73] The advocate- and procurator-general in the *Parlement* of Paris.

84. Foucquet to Mazarin, 5 July 1657

I am greatly obliged to Your Eminence for having deigned to enter into the detail of the matters which I had the honour to write to you about, which I would never have undertaken had it been for my personal interest: it is not just that Your Eminence, in the place where you are,[74] occupied in sustaining all the burden of the affairs of the Kingdom and in protecting it from the enemies' forces should have been distracted by things of such small consideration . . . I will make all possible efforts to ensure that Your Eminence is satisfied with my conduct, I hope to be able to continue to provide the sums when you want them, provided that the expenses do not exceed the limits that Your Eminence put on them in the memorandum you gave me for this coming winter. You must also continue to give me your protection and allow me freedom to gain funds while providing you with whatever sort of account you want. But I humbly request Your Eminence not to abandon me, and to decide promptly on the things that I advise you are necessary . . .

(Source: AAE France 902, fo. 132)

85. Foucquet to Mazarin, 14 July 1658

. . . It is necessary for Your Eminence to understand that the troubles which there have been everywhere have prevented the financiers from receiving their money. My illness has made some of those who are greatly committed in loans reflect on their certain ruin if there were a change of finance minister. The illness of the King, which has followed, has also had the same effect, so that everyone is on his guard and many are powerless to make any loans. The great bankruptcies which there have been have also contributed to this. So that when Your Eminence tells me that it is necessary to delay the reimbursements due to the financiers, this cannot be done without a general bankruptcy because they neither wish to do this nor can they do it. They reimburse themselves very slowly because the revenues are not coming in . . . We must gradually let the commerce of money re-establish itself and take money where we can find it. The taxes on the financiers proceed very slowly, and apart from a dozen men who are under our thumb, we cannot take any violent actions, nor attack several at the same time . . . I repeat again, that despite all the arguments of those who do not understand financial affairs, and who criticise the great gains of the

---

[74] La Fère.

financiers, that of twenty affairs which are contracted, it is a matter of chance if one succeeds. The reasons are clear and certain, but too long to explain here . . .

(Source: Lair, i. 445–6. AAE France 905, fo. 262f.)

86. Foucquet to Mazarin, 28 July 1658

Since my illness[75] I have engaged myself for more than 400 000 *livres* in addition to my other loans, which I have borrowed from de La Bazinière[76] and the Monnerot brothers.[77] In doing this, perhaps I have done something imprudent, but at least I am satisfied that at present my spirit is in conformity to my humour . . .

(Source: Lair, i. 446–7. AAE France 905 fos. 204–205)

87. Foucquet to Mazarin, 22 July 1659

. . . My principal application is to find money for the inevitable expenses for the King's departure.[78] I have had great difficulty in doing this, and I found myself obliged to engage myself still further beyond my existing debts. However, I shall never spare myself when it is for the satisfaction and service of Your Eminence, to whom all my wealth and credit is entirely devoted. . . .

(Source: AAE France 907, fo. 228v.)

88. Foucquet to Mazarin, 3 September 1659

. . . When Your Eminence sees the state of my affairs, and what I have provided in loans although I have been reimbursed for virtually nothing, you will doubtless be astonished at the ease with which I have risked everything of mine. I would be satisfied if I could please Your Eminence in risking everything of mine in order to assist you at times of difficulty. But there are some people who serve you[79] who appear very zealous and prompt to censure my actions, but who do not do as much as I do, nor do

---

[75] Since 30 June.
[76] Macé II Bertrand de la Bazinière, one of the chief treasurers since 1646.
[77] The brothers Nicolas and Pierre Monnerot, prominent financiers.
[78] To Guyenne, Languedoc and then to the signature of the Peace of the Pyrenees.
[79] A reference to Colbert.

they have indemnities and assurances taken out against them . . . I must once more tell Your Eminence that there is no moment to lose in order to draw up the ruling of finance for the first years of the peace . . .

(Source: AAE France 908, fos. 23–31v.)

89. Memorandum of Colbert to Mazarin, 1 October 1659

Your Eminence having ordered me to tell him what I could find out about the present state of the finances, in order to satisfy your orders, I am able to tell you that they are still governed in the same way. Everything is dealt with between the finance minister and the sieur Bruant, his clerk, with some small participation of the chief treasurer. This, the most important issue of state, was formerly governed by a council of direction and the finance ministers simply signed on their own the King's ordinances for sums payable by the chief treasurer to different accountants for matters concerning their offices. In various ways it has come to pass that nobody knows what is going on . . .

It is public knowledge and known by everyone that the finance minister has great establishments, not only for himself, but also for all his relatives and friends of long standing; not only for all his clerks, but also for all the persons of quality in the kingdom and others whose favour he wanted to acquire, either in order to conserve his establishments or to increase them . . .

It is necessary to recognise the maxims by which financial affairs have been governed and regulated for the last thirty years or so . . . Those who have managed the King's finances have established as the maxim of their administration that the state could survive only in confusion. It was pointless to think of the future, it was necessary only to think of the present . . . Revenues would increase, and this would allow for an increase in expenditure. It was necessary to alienate the King's revenues, by creating offices and issuing *rentes* . . . Financiers should be given large profits in order to establish credit-worthiness among them, so that 8 or 10 million *livres* could be drawn from them in a few days. This great credit was regarded as the security of the state and established its reputation abroad. If the financiers gained great wealth, means of taxing them could always be found, so that part of it was repaid . . .

By the maxim of confusion, finance ministers persuaded themselves, one after another, that they would make themselves indispensable for the office, since it would be impossible to penetrate the confusion which they

73

had established. The fear of falling into some great disaster through the cessation of financial affairs would always oblige the first minister to maintain them in the office, however much he wished to remove them . . . They made their fortunes as they wanted, and their only difficulty was in hiding the acquisitions and the expenses which they made without the knowledge of the King or the chief minister.

The sole objection that has been made every time that there was a discussion of reforming financial affairs was that it was necessary to survive during the period of reform. Since the King had anticipated his revenues, either bankruptcy was necessary (and this causes the ruin of states, which can only survive by credit) or else it was impossible [to survive in the interim period] . . . It is easy to see that these reasons are false. Firstly, the ordinary revenues of the King are anticipated only by financiers, the richest of whom has only 10 000 *livres* of patrimony, and had less in 1650. All these loans are really only loans of part of the illicit gains of the financiers from the King.

This so-called credit is absolutely false. Credit is finding money and paying low interest charges. He who pays the lowest interest rate has the most credit. One can scarcely say that a man has credit when he borrows money at an interest rate of 20, 30 or 40 per cent . . . This demonstrates clearly that the King does not have any credit and that people contract with him in the belief that he will have to declare bankruptcy . . .

[A *chambre de justice* should be held after Mazarin's return to Paris after the peace negotiations.]

(Source: Clément, i. 164–183)

90. Foucquet to Mazarin, 6 January 1660

. . . I have seen Monsieur Colbert, who took the trouble to come to see me. I told him that I thought I was obliged to defend myself to Your Eminence against many of the things of which I was aware that he charged me. I was certain that in my place he would have done the same. But this did not prevent me from having much esteem for him, and that I might even have obligation to him in many other matters. I was certain if my intentions had been better known to him he would not have criticised my conduct. Since he and I had the same master we ought to have his service in mind, each of us in our own office.[80] I told him I would always willingly receive his opinion when he gave it. I would defer to it when I

---

[80] Foucquet implies that Colbert's principal concern should be with Mazarin's personal finances, not the finances of the crown.

could, or else that I would give him my reasons for not doing so. I wished for his friendship. Together we would work at carrying out Your Eminence's orders. He spoke very civilly to me and I hope that Your Eminence is satisfied with my conduct, since I have no other aim than to please you . . .

(Source: AAE France 910, fos. 1–3v.)

91. Foucquet to Mazarin, 2 April 1660

. . . Those who are not charged with financial affairs and talk continually of liberty of commerce and the discharge of taxes which are imposed on goods and merchandise, appear to be convincing. In fact, they are talking about things which are ruinous in practice and contrary to the good of the state . . . The whole secret is to distribute taxes as fairly as possible. If they are all reduced everywhere, we lose the best and most assured revenues of the kingdom. If taxes are reduced simply in one area, that area benefits, but everywhere else is ruined. Thus one opens a door that cannot easily be shut. Anyone who speaks on the matter does so according to his interest or the knowledge he has of a particular town or a province, often because he is from the locality himself. But those who look at the problem overall must have a different viewpoint. The people must be discharged from the *taille* as much as is possible, and the revenue farms must be increased by all possible means. Once this is done, this achievement must not be lost. Loans are less prejudicial than exemptions, because they can be abandoned, and the people pay their taxes whatever. But once exemptions are accorded, there is no going back on them without infinite difficulty . . .

(Source: Lair, i. 505–6. AAE France 910, fos. 151v.–152v.)

92. Memorandum of Louis XIV, 9 March 1661

The King dictated this to sieur Rose, secretary in his office, and re-read the articles . . .

Monsieur the Cardinal felt that he was approaching his end, and desired to rid himself of all affairs of the world in order to allow himself to think on the afterlife. He gave me the last moments of his life from love for the good of my state and my particular glory. And in this sentiment he left me several very important views, among which are those that follow. I gathered these together as best I could.

Firstly, to maintain the Church in all its rights, immunities and privileges, without permitting it to be weakened under any pretext since I am its eldest son. I was obliged to do this in conscience. I also should take care that those to whom I gave benefices had the capacity, piety and other required qualities for filling these offices worthily . . .

The nobility was my right arm. I should support it and treat it with confidence and generosity in all respects.

As for the magistrature, it was just to honour its members, but it was very important to prevent them from taking liberties, and to oblige them to remain within the limits of their duty. They should concern themselves exclusively with rendering justice equitably to my subjects where I have given them the authority.

The duties of a good King obliged me to alleviate my people, not only with regard to the *taille*, but also all other taxes, in so far as permitted by the necessary and indispensable expenses for the conservation of the state. The populace drew their security from this.

I had around me servants who were very capable and entirely loyal. It was up to me to determine the task for which each was most suitable, and to employ each according to his ability.

I should take guard that everyone was aware that I was the master; that favours could be expected from me alone; and above all not to distribute favours except to those who merited them by their service, by their ability, and their attachment to my person alone.

I should take care that members of my council worked well together, for fear that their divisions might prejudice my service. I should listen to their opinions on all matters; always ascertain which was the best course of action among their different views; take the decision myself, and after that, defend it vigorously, not allowing the slightest attack on my authority.

If any of those who are employed in my affairs were unwise enough to undertake anything without my orders, it was absolutely necessary to get rid of them, as unworthy of my service.

I should suffer no scandal at court, and tolerate no loose living. I was obliged to God to do this, and it was a question of my honour in the world at large. It was necessary that everyone should know that I was severe on this matter and would make no exceptions.

(Because of certain intrigues, the King ceased to dictate the rest of this memorandum.)

(Source: Clément, i. 535–6)

93. Ruling for the establishment of the royal council of finance, 15 September 1661

Since it pleased God to give peace to his people,[81] the King, having considered carefully the poor state of his finances, and the reasons for it, and wishing to prevent this in the future, has resolved upon the present ruling and declaration of his intentions.

His Majesty has suppressed for ever the commission of finance minister[82] and all the functions attached to it.

His Majesty recognises that he can give no greater demonstration of love for his people than to take upon himself the care of the administration of his finances, to prevent the abuses that have arisen in the past. His Majesty is resolved that he will be assisted by a council of persons of known ability and probity, by whose advice he will act in the administration of all matters which were previously resolved and carried out by the finance minister alone.

This council will be called the royal council of finance, and will be formed of a president[83] under the authority and in the presence of His Majesty, when Monsieur the Chancellor is not in the council, and three councillors, of whom one will be an intendant of finance.[84] His Majesty reserves the right to call Monsieur the Chancellor to it when he judges it suitable, in which case he will hold the rank and presidency due to his dignity as the head of all the King's councils.

His Majesty reserves to himself alone the signature of all ordinances concerning the expenses for accountants and the secret expenses,[85] whether for secret affairs or interest payments . . . [The detailed ruling follows].

(Source: Clément, i. 749. AN E 1713, fo. 173)

94. Foucquet to Le Tellier, undated [after his arrest]

. . . All those who during the minority and during the wars carried arms against His Majesty, excited troubles on his state, wished to remove his

---

[81] The Peace of the Pyrenees was signed on 7 November 1659.

[82] *Surintendant des finances.*

[83] Its nominal president was the Maréchal de Villeroy, the King's childhood governor, who was no more than a figurehead.

[84] Colbert was appointed intendant of finance on the death of Mazarin, and it was he who held real power in the council.

[85] *Comptants.*

crown, assisted in the councils of factious individuals . . . all such individuals are left in peace, enjoying their wealth, their offices, their governorships . . . [But Foucquet, who had] rendered services which were as great and perhaps more important than any other individual, without exception [had been arrested]. . . . I may well have committed faults. I do not excuse them at all. I did what was necessary. It was by this means that I maintained affairs and without it, I could not have done so. [As for Mazarin:] he blamed it all, yet permitted it all. He disapproved of everything. Then, once he had been convinced of the impossibility of succeeding without this course of action, he approved of everything. One could obtain no certain rule with Monsieur the Cardinal on matters of money. He never gave precise orders. [After Mazarin's death, Foucquet asked Louis XIV to pardon him]. The King very obligingly told me that he pardoned me for everything and gave me his word . . . His word must have some authority, since it was given to a subject in time of peace, without his being forced to give it . . . I cannot understand why this change was necessary when affairs were going well and everything was in a good state . . .

(Source: BL Add. MSS 39673, fo. 73)

3 ADMINISTRATIVE INNOVATION AND THE REACTION OF THE OFFICE-HOLDERS

The French administrative system had developed in a piecemeal way, and important political forces ensured the continuation of regional diversity. Certain provinces had been acquired relatively late by the French monarchy – Normandy, Guyenne, Burgundy, Provence and Brittany were gained only in the fifteenth century – and had retained some of their former customs and privileges. By the seventeenth century, the estates (or representative institutions) of Guyenne were in abeyance, while those of Normandy and Provence were under threat or succumbed during Richelieu's ministry (Map 1). However, the provincial estates of one province acquired much earlier – Languedoc – remained strong, despite an attempt by the government in 1632 to ensure greater compliance by imposing the edict of Béziers. The estates of Languedoc regained their full independence in 1649, when the government needed to retain the loyalty of institutions during the Fronde. The Chancellor commented that all the *pays d'états* might seek comparable concessions (doc. 157). The government greatly feared local alliances between institutions such as the provincial estates and the regional lawcourts or *Parlements*. These rarely occurred, since rivalry between them was the norm. The first signs of such alliances had to be snuffed out, at times when there was opposition to the money grant by the provincial estates (doc. 178). By 1659, the ministers saw an increase in the grants by the estates as a matter of crucial importance. Failure to achieve it would result in a further decline of revenues from the *pays d'états* with the restoration of peace (doc. 180).

All provinces with estates had a different fiscal regime from the rest of France, both in the nature of the taxes levied and the methods and officials by which they were collected. Thus, for example, the ruling of August 1642, which established the

Map 1   *The provinces of France*

Stippled areas are those with provincial estates in 1661 and after.

intendants' fiscal powers, did not apply to Provence or the other *pays d'états*, where the intendants' fiscal role was limited (doc. 127). Where, as in Languedoc, Brittany and Burgundy, the estates retained the right to vote taxes, they secured effective control over the fiscal process. Perhaps understandably, French finance ministers tended to regard the privileges of the *pays d'états* as an obstacle to good financial management. As early as 1605, Sully declared his intention of having the *taille*, the chief direct tax, collected in the same way throughout France: this implied the reduction or abolition of the privileges of the *pays d'états*. The attack was resumed in the years 1628–32, probably under the inspiration of Marillac. He had served as finance minister before he became Keeper of the Seals, that is, acting Chancellor, in 1626. Marillac stated categorically that the king wished to establish uniformity in his kingdom (doc. 100).

Between 1628 and 1630 orders were issued which created *élections* in Dauphiné, Burgundy, Languedoc and Provence. These *élections* were lesser finance courts which supervised the direct taxes. They were the norm in the rest of France (hence the term *pays d'élections*), but their introduction into the outlying provinces might seem to spell the end of the estates' fiscal control. Whether it did so is a matter of dispute between historians. The commitment of the other ministers to Marillac's policy is by no means clear. The creation of *élections* was not necessarily an administrative reform, since there were grave criticisms of their effectiveness in the *pays d'élections*. Above all, the measure seems to have been a fiscal device: it could be prevented by a province if satisfactory compensation was offered to the government to replace the revenues expected from the sale of offices in the new finance courts. This is what happened in Provence, Languedoc and Burgundy. Only in Dauphiné, where the social groups represented in the estates were too divided among themselves to make an offer, were *élections* permanently established as a result of this initiative.

Ministers were for the most part political pragmatists rather than administrative reformers. They were cautious at the prospect of great political upheaval caused by the attempt to remove the privileges of the estates, above all in time of war (doc. 179). Ministers thus tended to recognise the strength of regional institutions in France, which were committed to the causes of provincial autonomy, low taxation and fiscal conservatism. This induced caution in the ministers' dealings not only with the *pays d'états*, but with all the provinces. This tendency to avoid fiscal experimentation saw only one true exception in the period: the sales tax of 1640–3, a tax on the circulation of goods which was introduced on the Dutch model in a real attempt to alter the regressive tax structure in France. Richelieu gave it a cautious welcome, but condemned the excesses of the financiers in its levy (docs. 115, 116). Bouthillier, the finance minister, warned of the difficulty in establishing the tax if whole provinces gained exemption (doc. 118). Richelieu agreed with this view (doc. 121), but in practice the opposition to the tax, which was seen simply as an additional fiscal burden, became too great. It had to be withdrawn in February 1643 (doc. 266).

Other practical considerations reinforced the caution of ministers. The proliferation of the sale of offices in the sixteenth and the first half of the seventeenth century had had particularly serious consequences for judicial, and especially financial, administration. Almost everyone involved in government and administration was the private owner of his office. These offices could not be abolished, and the owners reimbursed, because this would place too heavy a burden on the king's already badly strained finances. The offices could not be abolished without compensation, because this would be tantamount to an attack on private property. On the other hand, the existence of a vast number of semi-autonomous office-holders ruled out an efficient system of direct administration (a seventeenth-century Inland Revenue or *régie*), since the crown had no direct control over the activities of its financial officials (doc. 96). If the king wanted a new and unpopular tax to be levied, it was by no means certain that his accountants or financial office-holders, men with property interests in the locality, would be co-operative.

In 1634, the government clearly suspected the *élus*, the officials who served in the *élections*, as the chief source of abuse in the levy of the *taille* (doc. 105). By 1640 it was placing the blame squarely for tax inequity on the local interests of the *élus* as property-owners (doc. 114). There were also other grave difficulties with local officials (docs. 119, 123); receivers-general of finance who had fallen into arrears in transferring funds to Paris had to be dismissed and replaced by clerks of the financiers (doc. 126). The collapse of the traditional revenue-raising system in wartime was a precipitant for fundamental administrative change. By June 1642, the government had to provide replacement funds for financiers unable to obtain reimbursement for their loans from the revenues of the provinces (doc. 122). Had it not agreed to this measure, the financiers would have gone bankrupt. The transfer of fiscal powers to the intendants in August 1642 was thus an administrative response to a fiscal imperative. A short-term crisis had been provoked by a long-term administrative malaise.

The administrative structure of seventeenth-century France was

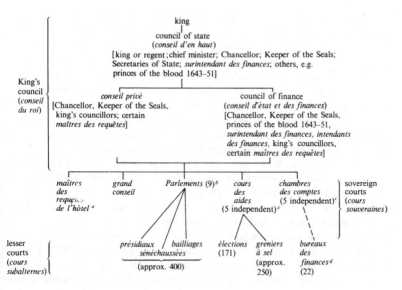

Fig. 1 *The King's council and the judicial and financial courts, 1624–61*

ᵃ The *Parlement* of Paris (e.g. on 17 Aug. 1648) denied the *maîtres des requêtes de l'hôtel* the status of a sovereign court. A number of *maîtres des requêtes* were allowed to sit in the *Parlement*. In 1669, the *Parlement* tried to limit this number to four.

ᵇ Ten after the establishment of the *Parlement* at Metz in 1633.

ᶜ Three of these courts were amalgamated as a *cour des comptes* (Aix, Montpellier, and Pau). Two *cours des aides* (Dijon, Vienne) were linked with *Parlements* (Dijon and Grenoble, respectively) in 1630 and 1658).

ᵈ The *bureaux des finances* claimed to be sovereign courts, but Chancellor Séguier denied them this status in 1653. They claimed also to be superior to the *élections*, but this claim was not recognised except in the years 1640–2.

very complex and defies any convenient depiction in tabular form (Figure 1). Between 1624 and 1661 the central government developed a much clearer sense of its own identity and purpose. There was a growing distinction between membership of the council and membership of sovereign courts such as the *Parlements*, a distinction of executive power. However junior the member of the council, he participated to a certain extent in the decision-making process. The members of the sovereign courts did not. They could, and did, respond to government decisions,

especially new fiscal measures, which they might seek to block –
sometimes arousing the king's fury or that of his council (docs. 98,
109, 110). Conflict between the government and the sovereign
courts was inevitable since the courts had quite different political
aspirations and interests. These were made manifest during the
Fronde, especially in the years 1648–9, but they were expressed in
a less acute form throughout the ministries of Richelieu and
Mazarin. The crown preferred to have the support of the sovereign
courts for new legislation because this facilitated its enforcement
and the compliance of the population as a whole (doc. 99).

Such support was not always achieved. The provincial
sovereign courts – especially the *Parlements* – wanted local power.
They wanted to determine what taxes should be levied, and to
decide how and by whom the money should be raised. The
government argued that authority over certain taxes, such as the
taille, was not included in a *Parlement*'s powers (doc. 164). At a
special session of the *Parlement* of Paris in February 1641, Louis
XIII prohibited it from intervening in affairs of state, and also
limited its powers of issuing remonstrances. Its powers were again
curtailed at the end of the Fronde at Paris in October 1652
(doc. 168). The authority of the council of state over the *Parlement*
of Paris was confirmed at the request of the Chancellor (doc. 176)
in October 1656. These incidents serve to demonstrate that the
sovereign courts had previously assumed an overtly political role.
Why they did so is not always easy to establish, since it is rare to
find a record of debates. The debates within the *Parlement* of Paris
survive in part for 1652, however. They show that in this, the crisis
year of the Fronde, discussion had little to do with judicial
administration and chiefly concerned issues of high politics in a
period of civil war (doc. 165).

Members of the sovereign courts were dedicated to the
maintenance of law and order, although their response to the
governments of Richelieu and Mazarin was not always consistent.
They eschewed faction, especially aristocratic-led faction, even if
they also showed a fierce resistance to the blandishments of the
ministers (doc. 167). However, at the height of the Fronde, some
members of the *Parlements* at Bordeaux and Paris, respectively in
January and July 1652, were either enticed or coerced into
following the lead of Condé and Gaston (docs. 230, 166). The
provincial *Parlements* claimed that they defended the customary
constitution of the province, which was under attack as a result of

misguided ministerial policy. They defended their own interests at the same time. Their definition of the customary constitution was a reflection of a narrowly sectional viewpoint: the members of the courts had gained entry through purchase. The defence of the interests of office-holders was a central preoccupation. Some of them (notably in the *Parlement* of Aix-en-Provence) had a tradition of opposition which lasted throughout the ministries of Richelieu and Mazarin. The creation of what amounted to a rival *Parlement* serving six months of the year (called the *semestre*) provoked armed revolt at Aix and Rouen in 1649 (doc. 156). However, the threat to the government posed by a sovereign court was usually offset by its own internal dissension.

At a national level, the great weakness of the sovereign courts, which was illustrated by the failure of the Fronde, was their inability to co-operate. The *Parlement* of Paris made only half-hearted attempts to explain its actions to its provincial counterparts (doc. 155). It acted with considerable caution even during the siege of the capital in 1649. Thereafter, it ended its lukewarm association with the *Parlements* of Aix and Rouen. Toulouse showed some interest in union with Paris (doc. 162), but this was never brought about. A close political union with Paris was not wanted in the provinces, because this would have restricted the freedom of the courts to bargain with the government and gain local concessions. Almost all the local treaties during the Fronde were negotiated independently. The *Parlement* of Paris had little influence on events in the provinces and took none of the credit for any settlements which emerged.

The failure of the sovereign courts to co-operate might cast doubt on their capacity to formulate a common programme of measures which they – though not the ministers – regarded as reforms. The constructive proposals of the Fronde seem largely the work of the sovereign courts at Paris. Some of their members had very clear views on the shortcomings of government policy, especially in its financial aspects (doc. 139). The proposals of the Chambre St Louis, which was a meeting of the representatives of the four sovereign courts at Paris (doc. 141), and the remonstrances of the *Chambre des Comptes* (doc. 153) mark the apogee of constructive proposals emanating from the office-holders. There was undeniably a genuinely reforming spirit among the office-holders in the summer of 1648; but there was equally clearly a motive of vested interest. The finance ministers had meted out different treatment to the *Parlement* of Paris; only d'Hémery had been so crass as to make a union of the courts at Paris inevitable (docs. 113, 117, 139). The issue uniting them was the renewal of the annual right (*droit annuel* or *paulette*), the annual payment by an office-holder for the privilege of resigning his office to his heir. The government traditionally tried to divide and rule when this privilege was renewed, though its capacity for doing so was restricted by the parlous state of the royal finances (doc. 101). Renewal in 1648 had been made conditional on members of the courts, with the exception of the *Parlement* of Paris, foregoing four years' salary. Once the crucial salary concessions denied in April 1648 were granted to the sovereign courts in October, compromise became possible because the office-holders' vital financial interest had been conceded.

At first, this seemed out of the question because of the courts' continued involvement in high politics, especially in criticism of the chief minister's policies, and the conduct of financial administration. A government threat of force in October 1648 (doc. 152), was transformed into reality in January 1649, with the blockade of Paris (doc. 154). However, after the peace of Rueil in March 1649, the commitment of the *Parlement* and the other sovereign courts in Paris to the issues of government reform and lower taxation waned considerably (doc. 157). There were still some signs of a revival of concern in the 1650s (doc. 175), but no longer any wish to bring support for reform to the point of civil war. The office-holders settled for regular payment of their salaries and annuities. They abandoned the arena of high politics for reasons of corporate interest. There was also some recognition that they had been preoccupied exclusively with medium to long-term reform measures, and had paid insufficient attention to the short-term needs of government in time of war: perhaps reform was illusory, while faction and the government's need for revenue were the reality (doc. 167).

In 1648 the office-holders had wanted to turn back the clock, to reverse administrative innovation under Richelieu and Mazarin. With hindsight, the rise in royal expenditure and taxation appear ineluctable. The office-holders' fury at the personification of these changes, the provincial intendants and the financiers, proved unrealistic. The government could not dispense with them in time of war, and after 1659 it refused to do so in time of peace. Contemporaries saw only that there was a pressing need to attack financial corruption both for its own sake and to demonstrate the effectiveness of government (doc. 95). Hopes of a thorough-going investigation by a *chambre de justice* in 1648 (doc. 146) proved misguided. The royal declaration of bankruptcy in the summer of 1648 destroyed the credit of the financiers, many of whom were left holding worthless promises of reimbursement (doc. 173), though some were treated more favourably than others (doc. 163). In the aftermath of bankruptcy, the government priority was the restoration of credit, not the investigation of corruption: this was Foucquet's mission in the 1650s. Perhaps in the early years of Richelieu's ministry, at the time of the Assembly of Notables of 1626–7, the government had possessed a clear reforming purpose (doc. 97). Such a purpose was clearly lost in the harsh world of war administration after 1635. Not until the return of peace in 1659 could this reforming purpose be seriously revived (doc. 182).

The one administrative innovation worthy of the name reform in the period of Richelieu and Mazarin was the introduction of the provincial intendants, and their transformation into an administrative system. The Chancellor or Keeper of the Seals (as acting Chancellor) appointed royal commissioners: the intendant was thus an official controlled by the government (doc. 102). The first step towards creating a *system* of intendants – as distinct from using the intendants on a random basis according to local requirements – was a commission issued throughout the *pays d'élections* in 1634 for the reform of the *taille* (doc. 103). The commissioners of each *généralité*[1] (Map 2) also received a commission outlining their fiscal role and detailed instructions to proceed summarily in cases of manifest inequity (docs. 104, 105). They were to summon local men as witnesses against the office-holders such as the *trésoriers de France* and the *élus* (doc. 108). The *trésoriers* thought this investigation risked undermining their functions (doc. 106), but emerged unscathed since the commission was temporary in nature, while the forces of bureaucratic inertia were strong (doc. 107).

In the later 1630s, intendants were appointed regularly to the provinces, but their fiscal role was only intermittent. Of course, they helped maintain public order, which was threatened by oppressive taxation and the licence of the troops (doc. 111). They could even propose tax reductions for their provinces (doc. 112).

---

[1] The basic administrative unit for taxation purposes.

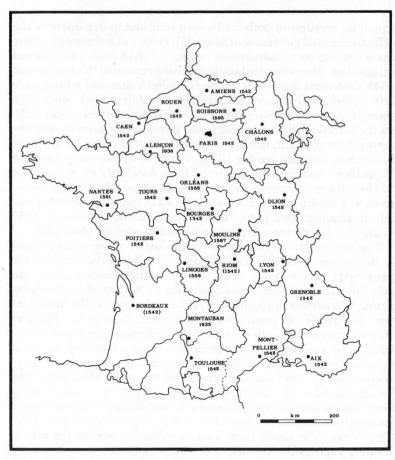

Map 2   *The généralités of France at the time of Richelieu and Mazarin*

The date indicates the year in which the *généralité* was established. *Bureaux des finances* were established at Agen and Issoire in 1542 and subsequently transferred to Bordeaux and Riom respectively.

Further measures were required. The government ordered individual intendants to preside over the *élus* at the assessments of the *taille* in an attempt to halt local corruption (doc. 120). These powers were conferred on the intendants throughout the *pays d'élections* in the ruling of August 1642 (docs. 123, 124). Not only were the intendants' fiscal powers specified; their rights were

88

clarified where they met resistance by local office-holders. They could, and did, carry out the assessments of the *taille* notwithstanding local opposition (doc. 125). The *trésoriers* denounced the ruling, which removed their 'principal function', and argued that far from controlling corruption, the intendants had less experience, and were thus less effective, than themselves (docs. 128, 143). The *trésoriers* received considerable support for their views from the sovereign courts at Paris in 1648 (doc. 144).

The 1640s was a troubled decade for relations between the intendants and the sovereign courts, even in the *pays d'états* where their fiscal powers had not been increased by the new ruling (docs. 131, 133). The intendants' justice was free. Their case work tended to grow as a result, though there were accusations that their clerks made handsome profits for themselves (docs. 129, 134). The intendants' capacity for establishing their own jurisdiction was somewhat increased by the right of subdelegation, that is to say, the power to appoint subordinates. This was envisaged in the ruling of 1642, although in some cases it had to be approved by the council, since it could be argued that it was a power emanating from the king's sovereignty (doc. 136). In the *pays d'élections*, the intendants' subordinates were often chosen among the *élus*, which caused problems (doc. 130) because of their continuing hostility to the ruling of 1642 (doc. 135). The intendants had clerks to help supervise the enforcement of taxes through billeting fusiliers (doc. 137). Though the intendants took a firm line against tax rebellion, they could exercise magnanimity by releasing prisoners held on the orders of the financiers (doc. 138). The weakness of their approach to tax supervision was that parishes which paid their taxes regularly continued to be exploited ruthlessly (doc. 132). Those which failed to pay their taxes frequently gained remission, because the tax arrears had become so large they were impossible to pay.

The summoning of the Chambre Saint-Louis in 1648 threw the intendants on the defensive. They now felt the need to justify their past conduct, to emphasise their moderation and earlier attempts to secure fiscal concessions for their province (doc. 140). The *Parlement* of Paris insisted on the recall of the intendants within its geographical area. The ministers tried to advance arguments for retaining the intendants, but had to concede the substantive point (docs. 142, 145). The intendants preferred to be recalled on ministerial order, before such a declaration was conceded (doc. 147). Others warned of the popular expectation of a substantial remission of taxes (doc. 148). Provinces such as Languedoc and Provence, which were outside the jurisdiction of the *Parlement* of Paris, were not included in the recall of intendants (docs. 149, 150). Even so, some of the provincial *Parlements* wanted to see no more intendants, however restricted their powers (doc. 151). With the removal of the intendants from most of the *pays d'élections*, the ruling of 1642 was in effect abolished and the *trésoriers* and *élus* restored to their former position in charge of the *taille*. They immediately fell into dispute over who held ultimate authority in the assessments, despite the overwhelming need to stand together in order to oppose the reintroduction of the intendants (doc. 158). Talks aimed at a compromise broke down, graphically illustrating the division among the office-holders during the Fronde (doc. 160). Intendants were reintroduced under different titles (doc. 159), such as intendant of finance or master of requests on circuit-tour (doc. 161).

With the collapse of the Fronde by 1652–3, intendants were imposed systematically throughout the provinces in all but name – they were now called 'commissioners deputed by His Majesty' (*commissaires départis*). The hostility of the *trésoriers* to these royal commissioners leaves no doubt that they received similar fiscal powers to those of the intendants after 1642 (docs. 169, 170). The *trésoriers* were put firmly in their place by the council. When a provincial *Parlement* in turn tried to oppose one of the restored intendants, it too was brought into line (docs. 171, 172). Whether the fundamental purpose of the intendants was to deal with the troops – the view of the finance ministers (doc. 174) – or to deal with the assessment of the *taille* – the view of the war minister (doc. 177) – was of scarcely any significance, since the two issues were closely related. After the Fronde, the troops were present in the provinces, levying taxes at will. It was scarcely surprising that the ministers were concerned at the exhaustion of the countryside, and that they should turn to the towns for additional financial assistance (doc. 183). By 1659, however, the strains of the long war were beginning to tell. Intendants, too, wanted a quieter life. There was even suspicion that they might champion provincial interest, instead of acting as docile instruments of ministerial authority (doc. 181). The suspicion was unfounded. The intendant remained in essence the servant of the ministers and the central government. **Less confrontation between centre and locality was desirable, and attainable in the new circumstances of peace which removed some of the crushing fiscal pressure on the provinces. This was to be one of the achievements of Colbert's ministry.**

95. Advice on the proceedings against financiers, [September] 1624

. . . The good conduct of affairs is a matter of timing, and it is unwise to take on too many problems at the same time. Since we have several foreign matters on hand at present,[2] it might be argued that these proceedings are inappropriate, since the greatest need is for money, and the financiers possess all that there is in France.

On the other hand, it is necessary to consider that the people, burdened with taxes to the extremity, would be alleviated by bleeding such persons. Reputation maintains the actions of the prince and his government. Action is now expected on this issue. If it is suspected at the outset that we are backtracking, the king's council will no longer be taken seriously, and it will be said that the King has been diverted from his original intention by various considerations . . . Financiers will then feel free to steal more brazenly than before. This example will demonstrate that there is no risk of punishment. Many will then embark on whatever they want to do, even in matters affecting the State, in hope of impunity.

But if thieves are punished, the people and the communities will be content to remain within the rules of duty for fear of punishment. We are assured of money for current needs. Proceedings can be so quickly taken that these people[3] will not have the opportunity to stop their business and show their ill will by their deeds . . .

The establishment of a *chambre de justice* is necessary to condemn the guilty parties.[4] The fear of such a *chambre* is equally necessary to make the financiers tax themselves or submit to the taxes imposed by the council. However, I consider that it is necessary to have the establishment of the *chambre* published without delay and to get royal commissioners to investigate as necessary, seizing papers and so on. This could be done by a commission which would state that while waiting for the establishment

---

[2] An allusion to the Valtelline war.

[3] Financiers.

[4] The *chambre de justice* was established in October 1624 and levied fines of 10.8 million *livres* on the financiers before it was abolished in May 1625.

of the *chambre*, His Majesty is constrained to use such a procedure in the knowledge that financiers, their agents and intermediaries are diverting papers and evidence which they foresee might be used against them. Such a proceeding will give such a great alarm to those who feel themselves to be guilty that they will come to His Majesty's feet to redeem their lives by money . . .

(Source: Grillon, i. 116–18)

96. [Report of d'Effiat, finance minister] on the state of the King's affairs at 1st June 1626 [written 1628]

. . . Everyone knows that the confusion of finance is such that it was no longer possible to investigate the accounts. The accountants[5] as a result were masters of their funds. Whatever the King might have hoped to undertake, he would not have known how to avail himself of their funds, because of the advantage they had gained from this confusion. They drew up expenses and diverted funds for their profit as they saw fit. The forms of the State do not permit the King to administer the revenues directly, it being necessary for office-holders to give their receipts. When we sought to avail ourselves of money which had arrived, it was found that instead of them owing us money, we owed them money. All that we could obtain were loans which they made on the King's own revenues, the interests of which were so great that they consumed the capital. They always said that they would have to take their reimbursement on subsequent years' revenues, there being no funds in the present year. When we investigated their accounts, however, we found that they had not finalised accounts for five or six years. The finance ministers, seeing a mountain of paperwork, had so much business that they could not find the time to peruse it all, since they were pressed by expenses without the funds to sustain them . . .

All the treasurers demanded money, yet their final accounts showed that they owed money to the crown. To sum up, I have finalised more than 400 accounts of accountants, revenue farmers and tax contractors, including ten accounts of the Treasury. None are still open. All expenses have been finalised except those for the current month. All the accounts have brought in some money to the Treasury. The accountants are now

[5] *Comptables*, a term applied to any financier or financial official who administered a fund from the collection of taxes.

better organised so that instead of there being few people capable of conducting financial affairs, I can say that it is easy to continue them. If God gives us peace, and constancy continues in the generous affection of those who have the principal direction of the King's affairs, it will be easy in the future to bring about an increase of 10 million *livres* in the king's revenue within five years by savings, repurchases and other proposals. These great changes can only be made in a period of stability, with protection for those carrying out the policy. It is necessary on all occasions for ministers to confront the great powers in the State, either the sovereign courts or the great families. They also have to deal with those who propose new financial expedients, who seek honour and recognition from their labours . . .

(Source: Grillon, i. 346–9)

97. Proposals which must be made on the part of the King to the Assembly of Notables in 1626 [end of 1626]

I. On the reduction of the expenses of the State and the increase in revenues.
It will be observed that according to the ruling which was drawn up in 1624, ordinary expenditure, which will be reduced considerably, exceeded ordinary revenue by more than 10 million *livres*. As the accounts of the financial officials demonstrate, the King owes 52 million *livres* . . . Firstly, it is necessary to examine the royal debts and to provide means of getting rid of those that can be paid off. Secondly, the King wishes to relieve his people instead of increasing the charges which they carry, and as a result, it is essential to reduce expenses . . .

IX. On the ruling on the taille.
The King wishes that the Assembly find some sure and effective means for the equalising[6] of the *taille* so that the poor people who carry the greatest burden are alleviated.

X. Concerning the order which must be established to hold grain at a good price.
The King wishes that the Assembly gives him advice on measures to establish an order that grain is always at a reasonable price so that the poor people may subsist without the great hardship they have sometimes suffered.

---

[6] *Régalement.*

XII. On the reduction of State expenses.
The expenses of the State are so excessive that it is impossible to maintain them without having recourse to extraordinary taxes. Messieurs of the Assembly are asked to compare the accounts for 1608 with those for 1624, and to reduce the list of salaries and pensions which are less necessary in the accounts for 1627, to such a point that it is as near as can be to the level of 1608, it being more appropriate to diminish gratifications than to continue them to the oppression of the people.

XIV. Concerning finance.
i) The disorder caused by the abuse of the King's finances is one of the greatest evils which can afflict the State, and which it is necessary to remedy. For this purpose, the intention of the King is to treat favourably his financial office-holders who acquit their tasks faithfully and with integrity. His Majesty also wishes to punish those who commit abuses according to the rigour of the ordinances, in order to prevent repetition of past disorders. For this reason, it is suggested that it might be appropriate to renew the ordinances on the subject of peculation and financial malversation.

XVI. Concerning the ruling on great matters of State.
The King having, for the relief of his subjects, and the maintenance of his authority, abolished and suppressed the offices of Constable and Admiral of France,[7] His Majesty requests the Assembly to give him advice on the other great offices which remain on this State so that he may know to what extent their functions and power should be reduced . . .

(Source: Grillon, i. 581–91)

98. Louis XIII to the procurator-general of the *Parlement* of Paris, Molé. From the camp at La Rochelle, 15 November 1627

Monsieur Molé. I have had reported to me in my council the decrees issued in my *Parlement* concerning the allocation of salaries and other matters arising from the tax contracts which have been drawn up in my council to help pay for the affairs of my State. You will see what orders I have given. I cannot think that this matter has been properly discussed

---

[7] By edict of January 1627.

and considered, or that my court of *Parlement* took full account of the consequences for my affairs. I will leave on one side the attack on decrees of my council which were issued to carry out my edicts. This does not fall under the jurisdiction of my court of *Parlement*, since the edicts had been verified solely in my *Chambre des Comptes.* By trying to delay the enforcement of these edicts and to prohibit my judges from carrying out my commission, my court of *Parlement* makes itself arbiter of the obedience which should be rendered to my commands by my office-holders and subjects . . . I cannot be considered subordinate to a body which has power and existence only as a result of my own authority.

What astonishes me most is that all the works that I undertake, all the hazards in which I place myself, and all the labours that I carry for the peace of my subjects are of so little consideration that the course of my affairs is held up by the solicitation of three or four worthless people, and by the intrigues of interested parties who assemble troops, town vagabonds and former soldiers, to increase their number and boldness, as I have seen with my own eyes. Thus it is that those who have contracted to provide large sums of money to my Treasury for the assistance of my armies are banished by menaces and the orders of other bodies without any consideration of the importance of my plans for the glory of God, the peace of my State and of all my subjects. I am thus deprived of the assistance for which I wait in considerable necessity.

I am here in the middle of winter, in the continual rain, having just recovered from a great and perilous illness, acting personally in all matters, sparing neither my person nor my health, and all this to bring back into obedience my subjects of La Rochelle and to remove from my kingdom the root and the seed of the troubles and disturbances which have oppressed and afflicted it for sixty years. Instead of everyone contributing whatever is most secret and most precious of their means to advance such a praiseworthy plan and one that is so useful for the whole State, people are preventing me being assisted. Those who are able to assist me are being frightened off. My armies will thus perish for lack of payment. The courage and the forces of rebellion will be strengthened. The rebellion will thus not be subjugated by the armies presently available. If my enemies had done this, one would have no doubts about their intentions. When I receive such obstacles from my own office-holders, who ought to have the chief and keenest hopes for the success of my enterprises, and whom I have obliged by so many benefits, I would prefer to impute it to lack of consideration rather than other motives . . .

You should make my court of *Parlement* understand that I will not allow these altercations, nor any undertakings against my authority. I

95

will always consider remonstrances which they may wish to make to me, but no other procedures are acceptable. I know the conspiracies and intrigues of those who excite these dissensions and wish to importune my court. I will deliver such firm justice to them that others will heed the example. On this, I pray to God that He will always hold you in His protection. This day, 15th. November 1627, at the camp before La Rochelle.
LOUIS

(Source: Grillon, ii. 646–8)

99. Relation of what happened at the time of the registering of the ordinance of 1629 [i.e. the Code Michaud] [September 1629]

King Louis XIII issued in 1629 an ordinance on all the different aspects of his State . . . He went to hold his *lit de justice*[8] in his court of *Parlement* at Paris, on 15 January 1629, and took with him this ordinance, which he had read out and proclaimed. The King made it understood by the Keeper of the Seals that if the court found some articles in the ordinance which they felt required some limitation or interpretation, he would willingly consider their remonstrances. Since the presidents of the court asked the Keeper of the Seals for the King to suspend the enforcement of the ordinance until the *Parlement* had the chance to make its remonstrances, the King agreed that the sending of the edict to the tribunals in the jurisdiction of the court would be suspended for two months, during which time they could make remonstrances as they saw fit, the ordinance however retaining its force and authority . . .

The King, after completing his business in Languedoc, learnt on travelling back to Paris that the registration had still not been placed on the edict. He wrote to the procurator-general that he had to bring him the edict with the decree on it before he entered Paris, otherwise he would be seen at his court of *Parlement* . . . The court made further difficulties but finally satisfied the order, and placed the decree and the edict in the hands of the procurator-general, who carried them to His Majesty at Fontainebleau on 5 September. The King received him, and witnessed satisfaction at the obedience of his court, but said that it would have been better had it been sooner. He replaced the edict in the hands of the Keeper of the Seals to see if it was as it should be, then returned it to

[8] Literally 'bed of justice', a ceremonial session of the *Parlement* with the king present.

the procurator-general, instructing him to send it to the *bailliages* and *sénéchaussées*[9] without any delay, adding that if the court of *Parlement* wished to make remonstrances to him on any of the articles, he would always listen to them willingly. It has been noticed that this ordinance has been well received throughout the kingdom.

(Source: Grillon, iv. 619–20)

100. Marillac to Richelieu, 27 January 1630

The deputies of Burgundy have been heard by the King, with Monsieur de Bellegarde present, concerning the revocation of the *élections*[10] for which they offer 1.8 million *livres*; but the uniformity which the King wishes to establish in his kingdom has led him to refuse these offers and to persevere in the establishment of *élections*. There is one great advantage of them: no taxes can be levied in this province except by letters patent of the King, and the Estates will not be able to burden the people.

I have written to you concerning the *droit annuel*[11] in my previous letters. Yesterday, the King, considering the need to assist your army,[12] resolved to accord it to the financial office-holders and not to the judicial office-holders, whose offices will be abolished on their death. This shows that the failure to renew the *droit annuel* results from the wish to assist the people and for the good of justice. Financial office-holders are a charge on the King because of their great salaries, but judicial office-holders are a charge on the people because of their great number, and draw from the people in fees what they do not receive in salaries. I consider that, if this is carried out carefully, there will soon be a great diminution in the number of these offices and a great help to the people, besides which it will considerably reduce the price of offices, which may not be significant at the beginning but subsequently becomes the main wealth of the most notable families. This would also gain support for this measure and remove the opinion that it is just an expedient to gain vacant offices which can then be granted out by the crown . . .

(Source: Grillon, v. 51–4)

---

[9] Lesser judicial courts.

[10] These were lesser finance courts concerned with the levy of direct taxation. They existed throughout much of France (the so-called *pays d'élections*) but were not in the provinces with provincial estates (the so-called *pays d'états*).

[11] The so-called annual right (sometimes called the *paulette*) was an annual payment by an office-holder for the privilege of resigning his office to his heir.

[12] Richelieu was lieutenant-general in the army of Italy at this moment.

101. Marillac to Richelieu, 12 February 1630

. . . I do not write much about the *paulette*, since my last three letters informed you of what has happened. That two days ago the King accorded it to the lieutenants-general and office-holders in the *présidiaux*. My opinion had been to suspend for a while the granting of it generally to all the second order of justice, because the reasons for excluding the judicial office-holders were general ones, and there were no exceptions except for the *Parlements*. But the necessity for money led us to accept these suggestions. I have no means of resisting financial proposals, and hope that peace will give us the opportunity to undo the damage we are doing to various of the King's subjects . . .

(Source: Grillon, v. 76–7)

102. Brandon to Séguier, 10 December 1633

I have learnt from Madame de Ligny that you plan to send out Messieurs the masters of requests[13] into the provinces for the regulation[14] of the *taille*. [Brandon has received a commission but is unable to exercise it] . . . I beg you immediately to permit me to ask you humbly to gratify and honour my brother-in-law Monsieur de Bellejambe with the same commission . . .[15]

(Source: Mousnier, i. 216)

103. Commission as intendant for commissioners carrying out the regulation of the *taille*, 25 May 1634

We have by our letters patent of today, and for the considerations therein contained, commissioned you and deputed you to travel to our province of [   ] in order to carry out our letters of declaration in the form of an edict of January last, containing the order that we wish henceforth to be observed in the levy and imposition of the monies of our *taille* to the relief and discharge of our subjects . . . We commission you and order you by these letters signed in our hand to have during the exercise of your

---

[13] These were office-holders, from whose ranks councillors of state (and later, intendants) were traditionally chosen.

[14] *Règlement*; more usually termed *régalement*.

[15] Le Maistre de Bellejambe received a commission for Orléanais.

commission mentioned above the intendancy of justice in this province, and the *bailliages*, *sénéchaussées* and other justices in its extent. You are to ensure that justice is properly and sincerely administered, that our ordinances are kept and observed exactly, and that our subjects are preserved from burdens and oppressions. For these purposes, we order you . . . to enter, take your seat and preside whenever you see fit in the sessions and jurisdictions of the *bailliages*, *sénéchaussées* and other courts of the province . . . to ensure that our office-holders do their duty, hear the complaints and grievances of our subjects, and deal with these, giving them prompt and swift justice. You are to order and command the provosts marshals, their lieutenants, clerks, constables[16] and other judges and office-holders and all others as need be to do whatever you see required. We also give you power to pacify the debates and disagreements which may arise between our judicial office-holders because of the rights, emoluments, authority, prerogatives and privileges of their offices, such decisions to be provisional until otherwise ordered. In the assemblies of magistrates and town councillors which you will hold, you should inform yourself of the order and proper administration of the affairs of the communities . . . You are to investigate carefully the disposition and state of our affairs and service in the towns and province . . . We order very expressly all governors, lieutenants-generals, captains and governors of our towns and places that they should assist you and have your orders obeyed in all matters concerning the present commission, and to the members of the said *sièges* . . . that they obey you . . .

(Source: AG A[1] 21 no. 121)

104. Commission for the regulation of the *taille*, 25 May 1634

We have resolved to send out throughout our provinces persons of experience, quality and the required probity to proceed to reform the inequalities of the *taille* and other abuses and to inform them of our intention by full and ample instructions. For these reasons, having full confidence in your person by the proofs you have rendered to us on divers occasions, and of your probity, experience, affection and fidelity for the good of our service and that of the public, we have commissioned and deputed you . . . to transport yourselves to the *sièges* and *bureaux* of the *élections* of our *généralité* of [   ] within the jurisdiction of our *Cour des*

---

[16] *Archers.*

Aides of [   ] and in all the towns, villages, bourgs and parishes of the *élections* as you judge necessary even to the town of the *bureau des finances* of the *généralité* to proceed there to the regulating of our *taille, taillon* and additional levies[17] either by parishes or by *élections* following our letters of declaration of the month of January last . . . [Detailed powers follow.]

(Source: AG A^1 21 no. 120)

105. Instructions for the commissioners for the regulation of the *taille*, 25 May 1634

. . . The commissioners will visit as soon as is possible the principal town of the *généralité* to which they are sent. They will begin with a conference with the *trésoriers de France* to clarify the reasons for the arrears of the *taille* and the abuses and inequities in the assessments,[18] and the measures which they consider most suitable to remedy them. Nevertheless, the commissioners are not obliged to follow the proposals of the *trésoriers* unless they consider them sound and advantageous to the purpose of their commission.

At the towns where the *élections* are situated, the commissioners will summon the *élus*, controllers, receivers, the procurator of His Majesty and the clerk. They will have the rolls of the parishes presented to them, which ought to be in the registry of each *élection*, with the assessments for the present year and the preceding ones. They will then establish the sums which have been imposed on the people and will be able to observe the changes which have arisen, from the number of inhabitants, their status, whether there are manufactures, arrangements for the cultivation of the land, what relief the parishes received during the past wars, and other matters such as the relative fertility of one place as against another . . . . On all this they are to make diligent enquiries by consulting His Majesty's office-holders, ecclesiastics, gentlemen, and notable bourgeois in order to gain as much correct information as possible to carry out their commission.

Since the most important abuse arises from the assessments carried out by the *élus*, the commissioners are to investigate carefully the reasons which have led the *élus* to increase the levy on some parishes and to diminish it on others. They are to redraw the assessments on the basis of what each *élection* carries of the principal of the *taille* in accordance with the capacity of the parishes, as justly and equitably as possible . . . His

---

[17] *Crues.*
[18] Called the *département.*

Majesty reserves the right on the return of the commissioners, and having heard their report, to adjust the burden on entire *généralités* and on *élections* which are found to be over- or under-assessed for the relief of the poor and the common benefit of the people.

The commissioners will pay particular attention in the towns where the *élections* are established to see if they are imposed at the rate they should carry in relation to the rest of the *élection*. If they are imposed at less than they should be, they will have the separate assessments of the individual inhabitants shown to them, to see whether the office-holders and well-to-do pay sufficient *taille* in comparison with the poor. They are to correct any abuses they find, and to take to task the *élus* and assessors who have committed the fault . . .

Once the commissioners have the rolls of the *taille* to hand, they will have brought before them as many churchwardens and assessors of the parishes as they can deal with in a day, and learn from them about the wealth of the inhabitants in general, and especially that of the principal inhabitants of the parishes, and whether by abuse, force, favour, corruption or otherwise the best-off are not assessed at the rate they should and could be. They are to deal with this matter as they see fit in order to maintain equity and to ensure, in so far as is possible, that the strong relieve the weak . . .

To avoid omissions of individuals and abuses, if the commissioners find some doubt or obscurity in the claimed exemption and privilege of those who have not been included in the rolls of the *taille*, they will request them to bring their titles and letters of exemption, summoning them for this purpose at the request of the substitute of the procurator of the King. They will investigate such titles fully, in conformity with the declaration and will include them, if necessary, in the rolls of the tax-payers and instruct the assessors of the parishes to tax them and impose them in the future on the level of tax set by the commissioners, with the assessors keeping nevertheless the same rulings as for other taxes, namely to increase them if their wealth increases, and to diminish their tax if their wealth declines . . .

(Source: AG A^1 21 no. 122)

106. Decree of the council of finance, 28 September 1634

. . . The *trésoriers* in some *généralités* have created difficulty, and have even refused entry to their bureaux and denied the commissioners[19] the access which belongs to them, under pretext that their commissions have not been presented in their bureaux. His Majesty wishes to deal with this matter. The King in his council has ordered and orders the *trésoriers de France* of the *généralités* to register the commissions of the commissioners immediately they are presented, and to receive them in their bureaux whenever they wish to enter for the assessments of the *taille* and other matters concerning the regulation and other matters of the service of His Majesty. They are to accord them the first place at the high end of their bureaux. The *trésoriers* are prohibited from proceeding to the assessments of the *taille* without the commissioners being present, on penalty of annulment, provided that the commissioners arrive in the towns where the bureaux are established by the 20th of next month. After this date, His Majesty permits the *trésoriers* to carry out the assessments as they have been accustomed, enjoining them to establish such equity that his subjects in the *élections* have no occasion for complaint of being overburdened . . .

(Source: AN E 120a, fo. 478)

107. Verthamon, commissioner for the regulation of the *taille* at Bordeaux, to Séguier, 25 October 1634

[M. de Gourges, *trésorier de France* and myself] have ordered Messieurs the *élus* of the *généralité* to make their circuit-tours this year and mark down exactly for us the number and value of the hearths of their *élection* or the commoner lands[20] in areas of land tax, in order that by this means we could have more certain information of desirable changes in the assessments of this *généralité* in each of the *élections*. I think, my lord, that in a few days Messieurs the *trésoriers* will send out the assessments for next year, which they agreed upon in the presence of M. de Gourges and myself; we presided over them following the commission which it pleased you to give us. But I have already touched on the reason why they have not changed the assessments for this year, besides which they claim that this has been observed and consented to by the whole province for 60 years . . .

(Source: Mousnier, i. 241–4)

[19] For the regulation of the *taille*.
[20] Called *terres roturiers*.

108. Ruling of Verthamon, intendant and commissioner for the regulation of the *taille* at Bordeaux, 12 April 1635

. . . Having dealt with the complaints made by individuals throughout the *élection* of Bordeaux, terminated their differences, seen, examined and judged the titles presented to us by those who claim to be nobles or exempt from taxes . . . we have had regard not only to the nature and extent of the parishes, the fertility or sterility of the land, the number of hearths and inhabitants, considerations which in themselves are insufficient. In several towns and places within the *élection* which we have visited, and subsequently at this town of Bordeaux, we have had the principal inhabitants of the parishes brought before us. We have compared what each of them have said, listened to the office-holders of the localities, seen and examined all the rolls of the parishes from all the previous years and all the assessments of taxes since the year 1600, taken the advice of the officers of His Majesty in this *élection*, and conferred with several other principal officers of His Majesty in this province and with the best informed persons of this *sénéchaussée* . . .

(Source: AN E 123b, fo. 46)

109. Bertier de Montrave, first president of the *Parlement* of Toulouse, to Séguier, 6 June 1635

. . . I am obliged to inform you, my lord, that this province is vexed by several extraordinary commissions from which it is said that the King will gain very little benefit. Nevertheless, they enfeeble this province so much, that if they continue it will scarcely be possible to levy the King's taxes . . . The *Parlement* has received so many complaints that it has been forced, on the request presented by the King's attorneys[21] to order very humble remonstrances to His Majesty that it should please him for the good of his service to suspend the enforcement of these commissions and that in the meantime that they should be suspended under his good pleasure. The present state of affairs and the King's service seem to require this. However, my lord, if you judge otherwise, you have only to command, and I am certain that you will find complete obedience . . .

(Source: Mousnier, i. 255–6)

---

[21] Called the *gens du roi*.

110. Decree of the council of state, 16 June 1635

. . . The King in his council has declared, and declares, the decree of the court of *Parlement* of Toulouse of 21st May last given against his royal authority, against the peace and public tranquillity of his province of Languedoc, and against the good intentions His Majesty has always had to provide by the justice of his armies a universal peace and tranquillity throughout his state and the states of all Christian princes against the evil designs of those who have troubled them . . . These are just reasons and considerations for His Majesty to break, revoke and annul the decree, and order that it shall be torn from the registers of the court . . . His Majesty orders that the president who presided in the deliberation of the decree, the most senior of the other presidents and the four most senior councillors of the court of *Parlement* who participated and spoke, the senior advocate-general and the procurator-general be assigned to appear in person before the council of His Majesty within seven weeks and until then be suspended from their offices . . .

(Source: AN E 124a, fo. 81)

111. Laubardemont, intendant of Touraine, to Séguier, 15 May 1636

. . . As for the rest of my tasks, I will tell you, my lord, that the chief one is to prevent by all legitimate means the ill effects which the discontent of the populace and all the orders in general can produce, since the taxes which the necessity of the times requires are very onerous. But, my lord, the greatest evil comes from the abuses committed by those who receive the taxes and also from the troops whose violence can scarcely be described to you . . .

(Source: Mousnier, i. 289–90)

112. Villemontée, intendant of Poitou, to Séguier, 26 June 1637

. . . Having visited the greatest part of lower Poitou, I have observed that the villages which have not paid their taxes for five or six years are poorer than the others, either from not having dared carry on their ordinary commerce freely or from having consumed in debauchery the monies which they should have paid for the *taille* had the taxes been paid at the customary time. From experience I conclude that when payment dates for the *taille* are delayed, the money is lost. Those who are at present paying last year's taxes, which represents a quarter of the *généralité* of Poitiers and three-quarters of the *élections* of Saintes and Cognac, will have difficulty in making at the same time their payments for the present year. These payments, following the list which has been sent to me for the commissions, are heavier by one-third than the previous year, and include arrears. Since a large number of parishes will have to pay two years' taxes at the same time, there will be further great arrears. With the advice of some capable people with whom I have discussed the matter, I consider, my lord, that under your good pleasure one should reduce the levies in the *généralité* of Poitiers to 3.2 million *livres*, which will be 800 000 *livres* less than in the list sent to me ... and for Angoumois and Saintonge, a total of 1.42 million *livres* would be a reduction of 350 000 *livres* ...

> (Source: Mousnier, i. 390–2. A decree of the council of finance on 4 July 1637 implemented the intendant's suggested reductions: AN E 138a, fo. 27)

113. Bullion to Richelieu, 8 April 1639

The *Parlement*[22] vexes me considerably because of the consequence and example of its actions. It is certain that its stubbornness and disobedience gives great prejudice to the affairs of the King ... [We must recognise] the consequence for the other sovereign courts ... The *Parlement* is unreasonable in letting everyone else bleed themselves to death for the King's service while they enjoy their salaries and annuities[23] and do not wish to contribute anything for the public good ... We must draw on the *rentes* and *gages* as the late King resolved to do at the time of his death, and take half of them for the maintenance of the army. I know that this is not the intention of Your Eminence and that it should be avoided if there are ways of doing so, but at least we must put fear into them ...

> (Source: AAE France 833, fos. 93–4)

---

[22] Of Paris.
[23] *Rentes*.

114. Decree of the council of finance, 1 March 1640

The King wishes to deal with and remedy the disorders which are committed in the provinces by the *élus* in the *élections* of this Kingdom, who are the cause of the arrears in the levy of the *taille* and other impositions. He wishes to have the edicts and decrees of his council on this subject observed, particularly those by which the *trésoriers de France* of each *généralité* are ordered to participate in the assessments of each *élection* within their jurisdiction. The *élus* have . . . been left in liberty until now to carry out the assessments. Abusing the authority of their offices, they have retained the commissions of the *taille* and the attachments sent to them by the *trésoriers* for two or three months without working at the assessments. When they have finally been forced to carry out the assessments, they have created great inequities for their own interests, and have discharged the richest parishes which belong to them and where they have their houses, relatives and friends. The richest and most important inhabitants have thrown the main burden of the *taille* and other taxes on the weakest and poorest individuals, who lack influence . . .

Thus it is that the inhabitants are reduced to such extremity and necessity that most of the *taille* for 1637, 1638 and 1639 is in arrears, and only a third has been received for the present year, to the great prejudice of His Majesty's affairs . . . If it is found that because of their inequities there are arrears, His Majesty orders that the office-holders of the *élection* will be coerced jointly to pay the arrears in their private names . . .

(Source: AN E 154c, fo. 120)

115. Richelieu to Bouthillier, finance minister, 19 June 1641

I am very pleased that you have sent out commissioners for the sales tax. If they are wise and well instructed they will deal tactfully with the people instead of alienating them. I will not stop you sending one into Brittany for the same purpose,[24] but I ask you to choose the man you send carefully, ensuring that he is an agreeable and able person, and one who understands the mood of the province so that he can bring to a successful and smooth conclusion what it is you want . . .

(Source: Avenel, vi. 821–2)

[24] Richelieu was governor there.

116. Richelieu to Bouthillier and Séguier, 22 August 1641

The disorders which we have met in Champagne and in Picardy, not on the establishment of the sales tax as such, but on the demand that the tax contractors make of the tax which they claim due to them for the inventory of past business, obliges me to take up my pen to tell Messieurs of the council that if they do not moderate the excessive demands of their tax contractors, it will be impossible to avoid a revolt . . .

The size of the sums which you are trying to exact from the people for this tax throws them into despair and imperils the sales tax in those provinces which are willing to establish it voluntarily. I believe that the towns and populace can be brought to pay for the inventory of past business on the basis of four months' tax.

If Messieurs of the council demand more, I believe that they will be in the wrong. Not only should they accept promptly the offer that is made to them, but give orders to pacify the fears of the people that the vexations that they have suffered on this matter will continue . . .

(Source: Avenel, vi. 858)

117. Bouthillier to Richelieu, 13 September 1641

. . . I must tell Your Eminence, quite to the contrary of what the late Monsieur de Bullion used to say, that since we draw notable help in money from time to time from the sovereign courts and the other courts, we must assist them and favour them whenever we can within the just bounds of royal authority . . .

(Source: AAE France 839, fo. 246v., 13 Sept. 1641)

118. Bouthillier to Richelieu, 17 October 1641

. . . We are delaying the establishment of the sales tax at Limoges and at Les Sables d'Olonne, considering it appropriate that these places profit from their rebellion for a time. If it lasts, Your Eminence will judge what can be expected from this important affair, which ought to have produced (we thought) so much advantage for our affairs, and give us means to alleviate the people of the capitation taxes, that is to say, the *taille, taillon* and other poll taxes . . . [The establishment of the sales tax, however, has been suspended in Guyenne, Languedoc, Dauphiné, Burgundy, Brittany and Béarn]. Nor has it been established in most of

107

Poitou and in many other places in the *pays d'élections*. There are some provinces where it has been established effectively. But if the people in these places see the other provinces discharged, they will claim a similar exemption in time, there being nothing which so drives people to despair as the inequality of fiscal burden. Taxes seem lighter when they are well distributed . . .

(Source: Avenel, vi. 882–3)

119. Ruling on the *taille*, 9 November 1641

The King is well informed that the extraordinary delay in the levy of the *taille* in the present year proceeds less from the impoverishment of his people than poor organisation in the levy. Many of the clerks, sergeants and bailiffs used in the recovery of the taxes carry out such great exactions on the taxpayers under pretext of the costs of coercion that insufficient money remains to pay the original taxes. These officials take care only to levy their illicit profits . . . Moreover, most of the receivers-general and receivers of the *taille* keep no clear registers of their receipts, and misappropriate the money . . .

(Source: AN E 165b, fo. 191)

120. Decree of the council of finance, 4 January 1642

The King in his council has had brought before him the assessments for the *taille* in 1641 ordered in the *élections* of the *généralité* of Limoges by the sieur Fremin, councillor in his councils and intendant of justice, police and finance in the *généralité* presiding in consequence of his commission of 6 December 1640 for the regulation of the *taille*. His Majesty has considered the benefit and relief for his subjects, and that the levy of his *taille* has been rendered easier, the assessments having been carried out with more circumspection. His Majesty has ordered and orders that the sieur Fremin will preside again in the assessments of the *taille* in the *élections* in the present year 1642 and in the following years for however long he exercises the commission of intendant of justice, police and finance and while he considers his presence in the *élections* necessary for the good of His Majesty's service. This is not in any way to delay the assessments of the *taille* which the *élus* are to carry out with all diligence.

(Source: AN E 166, fo. 48. Similar decree for Barrin de Rézé, intendant at Bourges: E 167b, fo. 250, 13 Feb. 1642)

121. Richelieu to Bouthillier, 13 February 1642

... I am in agreement with the rest of you and not with Monsieur the prince and the sieur de Machault[25] who are only one voice. If one removes the sales tax from Languedoc and Burgundy, it must be removed from the rest of France. If it is left in the rest of France, it must necessarily be established in these provinces as in the others ...

(Source: Avenel, vi. 897–8)

122. Decree of the council of finance, 5 June 1642

The King, for the relief of his people, has ordered that the levy of taxes for the purpose of the payment of his troops during the next winter quarter will be made together with those of the *taille* for the year 1643. In order to assure this revenue, and to make certain the timing of the payments which are necessary for the expenses of the troops in winter quarter, for the expenses of the household and also for the very important expenses of the war, His Majesty has sought out various persons to whom he has assigned the revenues, on the assurance of which they have made loans payable at the necessary times and on the necessary conditions. Wishing that these sums be paid in entirety and without any arrears, His Majesty in his council has ordered and orders that the sieurs intendants of justice or the *trésoriers de France* of each *généralité* (whoever has carried out the levy of the *taille* and the subsistence) will carry out a verification of the arrears in taxes once the said year of 1643 has passed. They will draw up reports, which they will send to the council. Once these have been seen, the arrears will be levied on the *élections* and parishes which should carry them; failing this, those individuals who have received the assignment of the sums will obtain a replacement of funds as necessary.

(Source: AN E 171a, fo. 145)

123. Decree of the council of finance, 19 August 1642

It has been represented to the King in his council that some gentlemen delay, and others prevent, the levy of the revenues of the *taille* in their parishes and instigate rebellions against the bailiffs and sergeants employed to recover these taxes by the receivers of the *taille* so that they

---

[25] Respectively governor and intendant of Burgundy. Machault was Condé's client.

cannot carry out any distraint of goods. The officers of the *élections* have neglected to sent their orders into the parishes and the inhabitants, procurators, syndics,[26] churchwardens and assessors have not drawn up the tax rolls and assessments; nor have they appointed collectors who are solvent. The collectors, bailiffs and sergeants employed in recovering the taxes are in regular lawsuits with the receivers of the *taille* before the *élus*. These lawsuits and the accounts which they have to render the receivers of the *taille* occupy them and consume the time which they should spend on recovering the taxes, which is therefore delayed. Moreover, the bailiffs and sergeants commit exactions, abuses and malversations: instead of carrying out distraint of goods, they take money from individuals within the parishes, and afterwards draw up reports to the effect that they have not found any goods or possessions which can be distrained and thus declare these taxes in arrears. For these reasons, nothing has been paid to the Treasury for the *taille* this year, to the great prejudice of His Majesty and the good of his service and of his state.

Since it is necessary to deal with the matter promptly, the King in his council has ordered and orders that the matters mentioned above are to be investigated by the sieurs intendants of justice, police and finance, each in his *généralité*, who will carry out prosecutions where necessary without appeal . . . His Majesty enjoins the sieurs intendants to leave all other matters in order to organise the acceleration and levy of the taxes, advising His Majesty of any obstacles and impediments which arise in order for these to be dealt with immediately . . .

(Source: AN E 173a, fo. 175)

124. Ruling on the *taille*, 22 August 1642

. . . III. In order that there shall be no delay in the levying of the taxes, His Majesty orders the presidents and *trésoriers* general in each bureau to assemble together with the intendant of justice as soon as the commissions are received, and to nominate and delegate one of their number for each *élection* within their *généralité*. On the day allotted by the intendant they are to go to the town where the *élection* is situated and, together with those officers of the *élection* nominated and chosen by the intendant, carry out the assessments of the subsistence for next winter quarter and the *taille*, *taillon* and *crues* for next year 1643 with equity according to their conscience . . .

---

[26] Nominated parish representatives.

IV. The *trésoriers de France* may create difficulty in allowing the intendant presidency in their bureau, in expediting their attachments to the commissions, or in delegating their colleagues to go to the *élections* to work with the intendant and officers of the *élections* nominated by them on the assessments. At the first refusal or delay, the intendant will issue ordinances on his sole authority, have them signed by his clerks, and send them with commissions to the officers of the *élections* nominated and commissioned by him. In these ordinances he will stipulate a day on which he will arrive in the town where the *élection* is situated, so that he may proceed to hold the assessments without the *trésoriers de France*. Similarly if in the *élections* some of the officers do not appear on the appointed day, place or time that was notified them by the sieur intendant . . . he will nominate and choose in place of those defaulters such other officers or notables of the towns that he considers fit . . .

X. . . . In cases where the intendant and *trésorier de France* discover a receiver in arrears, or not carrying out his office in accordance with the ordinances, His Majesty orders them to establish a clerk who is solvent in each of the *élections* for the receipt and management of the taxes . . .

XVI. His Majesty also orders the intendant in each *généralité* to investigate cases of exactions, abuses and malversations committed against the taxpayers . . . by office-holders, receivers, clerks and others. His Majesty permits and gives power to the intendant to subdelegate officials in the places which he cannot visit. When the investigations have been made, they can be sent to the council. After they have been seen there, the necessary orders can be given . . .

(Source: AN AD + 271)

125. Extracts from the register of the *bureau des finances* of Paris, 17 October–23 November 1642

17 October 1642. It was ordered that when Monsieur de Montescot[27] comes to the bureau to carry out the ruling on the *taille* and the subsistence for next year, he will be given a seat below the presidents, or whoever in the company presides in their absence. No member of the company will co-operate with the sieur de Montescot in carrying out the ruling except by order of the company . . .

(Source: AN Z^{1f} 200, fo. 268)

[27] Intendant in the *généralité* of Paris.

5 November 1642. Orders under the King's private seal[28] were seen, addressed to us in the following terms:

. . . We have had our commissions for the levy of the taxes addressed to the sieur Montescot, councillor in our councils and intendant of justice, police and finance in our *généralité* of Paris and to you. He will present these to you, together with this letter by which we ask you to issue your attachments on the commissions and to send out one of your number into each *élection* to work jointly with the sieur de Montescot on the assessments of the sums contained therein. You are ordered to do this by our ruling and by our commissions. We are assured that you will satisfy us with the diligence which the necessity of our affairs requires. We will send another letter more expressly if this is not done. For this is our pleasure.

St. Germain-en-Laye 24 October 1642. Louis. De Lomenie

(Source: AN Z^{1f} 200, fo. 285)

23 November 1642: [Montescot's secretary asked the clerk of the bureau] to tell Messieurs the *trésoriers de France* that if they were prepared to receive the sieur intendant in accordance with the ruling of the council he would come on Saturday or Monday to bring the commissions of the *taille* and work with them on the attachments . . .

The company ordered that the clerk should return to the sieur de Montescot and tell him that it did not intend working with him in the terms of the ruling and that the sieur de Montescot had infringed this, having expedited ordinances and issued decrees of the council in which they are not named or included. He was to show him printed copies.

The clerk having reported to us that he said this, and wishing to show the printed copies, the sieur de Montescot refused to see them and replied that since Messieurs the *trésoriers de France* did not wish to co-operate, he would do it alone . . .

(Source: AN Z^{1f} 200, fo. 298)

126. Decree of the council of finance, 25 February 1643

. . . The sieur de la Potherie . . . intendant of justice, police and finance in the *généralité* of Caen . . . finds that in some of the *élections* of the *généralité* the receivers of the *taille* have not satisfied the ruling of 22 August 1642,

---

[28] *Lettres de cachet.*

and are still found to be in great arrears. It is essential for the security of the taxes, and their diligent recovery, to establish clerks for the receipt of the taxes in place of the receivers . . . [The council orders] that the sieur de la Potherie . . . shall establish clerks nominated and presented by Messire Gabriel Massienne[29] who carries the money order of the Treasury. They will be installed by the sieur de la Potherie, who will also deliver to them the necessary assessments and commissions. His Majesty expressly prohibits his officers or anyone else from troubling them or interfering with them on penalty of responding personally for the taxes and all expenses, damages and interests incurred.

(Source: AN E 177b, fo. 98)

127. Cazet de Vautorte, intendant of Provence, to Bouthillier, 7 April 1643

My lord,

I have received the letter with which you honoured me on 21 March, together with the decree of the council and commission of 25 February for the revocation of the sales tax, and the levy on this province of 82 500 *livres* for its part of the 150 000 *livres*. You are well aware, my lord, that we can do nothing without holding an Assembly of Communities[30] which accords this tax, the King having up to now conserved Provence in this privilege of not having any tax levied on it except in this way. We asked the procurators of the province[31] to do it, but they told us that they could not . . . In fact, they are powerless without a resolution of the Estates or the Assembly of Communities to levy or accord the tax. This has always been the practice. The commission of 25 February does not seem to apply either, because it is addressed to myself and the *trésoriers de France* jointly, with whom I am ordered to carry out the assessments of the *taille* and the subsistence for the present year. But you will be aware that they do not deal with this here, and that it is done by the Assembly of Communities . . .

(Source: Mousnier, i. 512)

[29] Nominee of the consortium of financiers which had lent the crown 1.8 million *livres* anticipating the receipts of taxation in the *généralité* of Caen.

[30] The Estates of Provence were not summoned after 1639. Instead, the Assembly of Communities was summoned, which represented the third estate together with one representative from each of the two privileged orders. These meetings were controlled more easily by the government, since there was no significant noble participation.

[31] An interim executive committee of the Assembly of Communities, called the *procureurs du pays*.

128. The *trésoriers de France* at Lyon to Séguier, July 1643

. . . By this ruling,[32] the intendants of justice are given the power which belongs to the *trésoriers de France*. It removes from us our principal function, including the assessment of the *taille*, which we have always exercised. We also ask you, my lord, to permit us to tell you that this also brings great costs and expenses to the King and his people. It is easy to see that the officers of the place have more knowledge of the relative capacity of the *élections* and parishes to pay than have extraordinary commissioners who often only pass through the province . . .

(Source: Mousnier, i. 525–8)

129. La Guette de Chazé, intendant at Grenoble, to Séguier, 12 July 1643

My lord,
I took the liberty in my last letter to inform you of the dispute which the bureau of the *trésoriers de France* sought to have with me on the subject of the clerk I established last December for the receipt of the *élection* of Vienne in accordance with the last ruling on the *taille*[33] . . . They have resolved, together with other courts, not to suffer any longer an intendant or any power and authority other than their own . . . [There is also a dispute between the intendant and the *Parlement* of Grenoble]. In those of my ordinances which they seek to annul, they cannot find one which I had not the right to issue because of my commissions as intendant, for the land tax or other particular commissions, or as the judge agreed to by the parties to a lawsuit either for their convenience or because of their poverty. I say no more than that justice in the *Parlement* is very expensive, while mine does not cost them a *sou* . . .

(Source: Mousnier, i. 530–2)

130. Decree of the council of finance, 22 July 1643

His Majesty has ordered the intendants of justice and finance of the

---

[32] The declaration of 16 April 1643, which extended the ruling of 22 April 1642 on the levy of the *taille*.
[33] That is, the ruling of 22 August 1642.

provinces to appoint only three *élus* in each *élection* to carry out the assessments of the *taille* and subsistence this year with equity and in full knowledge of the facts, following the ruling of the council of 16 April. Nevertheless most of the *élus* nominated and deputed for this task, in collusion with their colleagues, continue to overburden the weak parishes and favour the powerful parishes which have been protected and favoured for a long period of time. They do this in order to oblige the other officers of the *élections* to do the same for them when they find themselves in turn deputed to carry out the levy of the *taille* next year and the following year . . . [The council orders] the intendants of justice and finance sent into the provinces of this Kingdom to proceed to the assessment and levy of the *taille* and subsistence this year with the *trésoriers de France* deputed from their bureau and three *élus* chosen and nominated by the intendants in each *élection* in conformity with the ruling decided on in the council of 16 April. In cases where the officers of the *élections* fail to do their duty, or refuse to give the intendants all the information which they require concerning the strength or weakness of the parishes, His Majesty permits the sieurs intendants to dismiss them and to appoint in their place other *élus* or, if they refuse, such other office-holders as they see fit to work on the assessments with the same authority and function as that attributed to the *élus* chosen and nominated under the ruling . . .

(Source: AN E 181c, fo. 112)

131. Bosquet, intendant of Languedoc, to Séguier, 12 August 1643

My lord,
I thought that since I was in the neighbourhood of this city[34] I ought to come here and reside for a while. This will make the people realise that the intendancy is not proscribed, since I am able to exercise its functions in its capital town, and in full view of the *Parlement* which, it is rumoured, has annulled my commission, or at least suspended it from being carried out. I have found, my lord, great peace, and spirits which are repentant, claiming that their intentions were misunderstood . . .

(Source: Lublinskaya p. 38)

---

[34] Toulouse.

132. Decree of the council of finance, 12 November 1643

[Request of the sieur comte d'Arpajon, lieutenant-general for the King in Languedoc concerning his lands in Rouergue.]

. . . Some individuals told the sieur Foullé, master of requests then intendant of justice in Guyenne,[35] that the distribution in the land tax had not been carried out with equity and that some were taxed more than others. He issued an ordinance, by which he shifted part of the tax burden on to some of the places and parishes . . . belonging to the plaintiff, on the pretext that the inhabitants of the places had always paid the quarterly payments of the *taille* and were not in arrears even for the last quarter of the present year, notwithstanding this surcharge and the fact that taxes were much heavier than in previous years. It would be a bad example to overburden those parishes which attempt to pay their taxes. If there is an inequity in the distribution of taxes, a general investigation should be held, which has not been done . . .

(Source: AN E 184c, fo. 382)

133. Decree of the council of finance, 24 September 1644

The King's council has seen a copy of the decree issued by the *Cour des Comptes, Aides et Finances* of Montpellier on 27th August, at the request of its procurator-general, which is full of insults and invective against the sieur Baltazar[36] . . . and even against his function of intendant. In this decree, the court annuls an ordinance of the sieur Baltazar dated 22nd August, and prohibits the town councillors commissioned for the levy of the *taille* and all other persons from obeying it, his tax lists and procedures, and his authority regarding the assessments and levy of the *taille* on penalty of a 300 *livres'* fine . . . The King in his council has broken and annulled . . . the decree of the court . . . and orders that the ordinances of the sieur Baltazar of 16, 19 and 22 August shall be carried out according to their form and tenor. The court is prohibited from preventing them from being carried out on penalty of its councillors' being suspended from office . . .

(Source: AN E 194b, fo. 357)

---

[35] Intendant at Bordeaux in 1637 and again between 1639 and 1641.
[36] Intendant of Languedoc from 1643 to 1647.

134. Mesgringy, first president of the *Parlement* of Aix en Provence, to Séguier, 31 January 1645

My lord,

It is with great regret that the responsibilities of my office require me to write to you about the continual enterprises of Monsieur de Champigny[37] against the jurisdiction and authority of this *Parlement*. The old friendship that I have with him,[38] and the witness that I owe to truth, oblige me to tell you that everybody recognises in him a virtue and probity free from any sort of corruption. The complaint that we make against him is a result of a jealousy which has taken over his spirit, which seeks to subordinate the *Parlement* to a sort of tribunal that he calls an intendancy. This is composed of certain officers drawn from the *présidial* and unemployed advocates from the inferior courts, who have through this extraordinary means increased their wealth faster than if they had been employed in trade or seaborne commerce. In this intendancy he has established a procurator of the King and two clerks . . . These two clerks receive more presentations and expedite more judgements than the *Parlement, Chambre des Comptes, Cour des Aides,* and all the subordinate courts together. There is scarcely anyone in the province who does not hold a community debt. Under the pretext of verifying the debts of the communities, or a seizure order for a creditor, the clerk makes all sorts of people appear before him . . . and halts legitimate procedures before other courts . . .

(Source: Mousnier, ii. 715)

135. De Heere, intendant at Tours, to Séguier, 2 February 1645

My lord,

I am obliged to tell you that the *élus* of La Flèche have so taken leave of their senses that when I went to their bureau to work on the assessments of the *taille*, they told me frankly that they would not sign the assessments unless I followed their views, and other such insolent remarks . . . I carried out the assessments with the *trésorier de France* who had come here, and on the advice of the receiver, despite their opposition. Their plan is

---

[37] Bochart de Champigny, intendant of Provence between 1643 and 1647.
[38] They were both received as masters of requests in the same month (January 1634).

to carry out another assessment, and to send their commissions into the parishes, which I shall try to prevent. Nevertheless, in order to deal effectively with this it is necessary for the good of the King's affairs that you interpose your authority; otherwise, all the other *élus* will want to cause trouble in this way . . .

(Source: Mousnier, ii. 720–1. A decree of the council of finance was issued on 2 March 1645: AN E 200a, fo. 55)

136. Decree of the council of finance, 15 February 1645

It is represented to the King in his council that the sieur d'Argenson, councillor in the *Parlement* of Rouen, has been subdelegated following a decree of the council of state of His Majesty of 4 January last, by the sieur d'Argenson his father, councillor ordinary in the council of state, intendant of justice, police and finance in the provinces and islands between the rivers Loire and the Garonne[39] to carry out in his absence the function of intendant of justice, police and finance in the *élections* of Saintes and Cognac, in order to supervise the acceleration of the recovery of His Majesty's taxes in these *élections*. However, the sieur d'Argenson senior has not been able to give his son authority to commission other persons to investigate crimes of rebellion, disobedience and other disorders which are frequent occurrences there, or to give authority to judge criminal cases without appeal, assisted by the number of judges required by the ordinances, since such authority must come purely from His Majesty's power. Nevertheless, this is necessary to suppress the disorders there, and to facilitate the recovery of His Majesty's taxes, which will be greatly delayed unless there is a prompt remedy . . .

[D'Argenson junior is given powers to investigate cases of rebellion and to carry out prosecutions.]

(Source: AN E 199b, fo. 146)

137. Decree of the council of finance, 31 January 1646

The King is duly informed that the tax-payers in the *élection* of Les Sables d'Olonne[40] are in arrears for notable sums of money for the *taille* and

[39] René I Voyer, sieur d'Argenson, intendant of Poitou between 1644 and 1646.
[40] In the *généralité* of Poitiers.

subsistence from malice as much as from poverty. The intendants of justice in the province of Poitou have been obliged to send into the parishes fusiliers to take billets until they are paid what is owed. But since the resistance[41] of the tax-payers has reached such a point that they do not voluntarily take any taxes to the bureau of receipt, although they have received a very considerable diminution on the taxes of 1644–46, His Majesty is obliged to repeat the procedure of billeting fusiliers on them. Nevertheless, he does not wish this extraordinary vexation to be suffered by people who place themselves in obedience. For this purpose, it is necessary to commission an individual of the required ability and probity both to supervise the fusiliers and to have the tax rolls drawn up by the collectors of the *taille* and subsistence presented to him in order to ascertain from their quittances those who are in arrears . . . [Messire Philippe Richard, sieur Desbordes, is appointed by the council to follow the orders of Voyer d'Argenson, intendant, for the acceleration of the collection of taxes].

(Source: AN E 207b, fo. 539)

138. De Heere, intendant at Tours, to Séguier, 10 March 1646

Since my arrival, I have released more than 150 prisoners for the *taille*, gabelle and contraband of salt held in the prisons of Angers. There are still a large number held. They are in extreme misery because of the plague . . . [I released them] despite the objections of the financiers, particularly the farmers of the *gabelle*, who find it difficult to tolerate my releasing poor people who have languished for eight or nine months and sometimes even a year in prison. . . .

(Source: Mousnier, ii. 780)

139. Memoirs of Omer Talon, advocate-general in the *Parlement* of Paris, 1648

General reflexions on the present state of affairs according to my humble opinion. Monsieur the Cardinal de Richelieu entered the ministry, and surmounted all the obstacles placed before him. He elevated his fortune on the ruin of those who attacked him. He maintained himself

---

[41] *Endurcissement.*

principally by the profusion of the royal finances, with which he corrupted all the great nobles and those who were necessary to him both within the kingdom and abroad. In order to do this, he suffered that those who were in the administration of the King's finances did what they wanted at a time when the kingdom was rich and abundant in wealth. All sorts of means of obtaining money were permissible. The King went to the *Parlement* of Paris frequently to have fiscal edicts verified, and princes of the royal blood were sent to the *Chambre des Comptes* and *Cour des Aides*. As a result of these extraordinary measures, creations of offices and attributions of new rights, monstrous sums of money were raised, so that one might say that during the reign of Louis XIII more money was levied on the people than since the establishment of the monarchy.

All these new establishments, with which Messieurs the finance ministers easily obtained money to meet expenses, produced permanent charges on the State, that is to say, creations of offices produced great salaries for office-holders; there were many new rights on the *taille*; while all the revenues of the farms were alienated as annuities[42] or salaries for office-holders. Thus the riches of France were for the most part imaginary. Everyone who had an office, *rentes* or tax rights on the King thought that he was rich; for a time, the enjoyment of these rights was comfortable and easy.

[However, under the Regency] ordinary taxes would no longer suffice. The populace was exhausted, and could no longer suffer new taxes. Creations of offices were useless, because no-one wanted to levy them if they were unimportant, while no-one dared levy them if they were important because the great courts resisted them and mistreated those who had offices of recent creation. The King's revenues were thus reduced to the levy of the *taille* and income from the reductions in office-holders' salaries.

Monsieur d'Hémery had himself made finance minister in July 1647 although he had neither the birth nor dignity to undertake this office. To obtain this post, he had promised to provide all the necessary money to enable the State to subsist. In January 1648, he found himself unable to satisfy what he had promised, and had the King appear before the *Parlement* of Paris on 15 January bringing several fiscal edits . . . Monsieur d'Hémery took the view that provided the *Parlement* of Paris was dealt with and satisfied, the other courts of the kingdom would not pose a serious threat. To this end, he established the annual right[4]

[42] *Rentes.*
[43] *Droit annuel.*

advantageously for the *Parlement* of Paris, without any forced loan; with regard to all the other sovereign courts, he cut their salaries for four years. This royal declaration[44] offended all the honest people of the kingdom, either because they received a notable financial prejudice or because of jealousy at receiving different treatment from the *Parlement* of Paris.

The office-holders in the [sovereign courts at Paris] consented to a union . . . and agreed to nominate deputies to confer together.[45] In this conference[46] no-one spoke about the reasons why it had been called, that is to say, the annual right; but everyone spoke about the reform of the state, and the reasons for the chaos in the royal finances. This excited spirits, and gave the *Parlement* of Paris credence with the populace, which hoped from these assemblies for some sort of alleviation of its tax burden. The ministers wanted to stop the meetings, and having first of all tried mild measures, and these having failed, they decided that they would have recourse to rigorous methods and sovereign authority. But despite their menaces, they encountered great resistance. They did not want to risk a conflict, and thus demonstrated their weakness and lack of courage, which made them fall into contempt . . .

(Source: Michaud and Pojoulat, pp. 270–2; 299–300)

140. Lauzon, intendant of Guyenne, to Séguier, 10 June 1648

. . . Although I consider that I have continued to serve as best I can, there are rumours in the province that I have become odious to some and that the positions of Monsieur de La Marguerie[47] and myself are to be exchanged, and that the decision is taken to send me to Montauban and to bring him to Bordeaux . . .

I know the hostility of everyone in the provinces against intendants. However, it is certain that the *Parlement* of Bordeaux can make no accusation against me, since more than any other intendant I have refrained from issuing sentences, and have never sought jurisdiction over a matter without receiving special powers . . .

As for the alleviation of the populace, besides the fact that I have

---

[44] Issued on 29 April 1648.
[45] This was the decree of union (*arrêt d'union*) of 13 May 1648.
[46] Held at the *Chambre St. Louis* after 30 June 1648.
[47] Laisné de La Marguerie, intendant at Montauban between 1645 and 1648.

written on several occasions to my lords the finance ministers, I have often importuned you, my lord, on the same subject. If I have not succeeded, it is the necessity of the King's affairs which has been the cause, and not a lack of asking on my part. Those orders which I have received have been carried out as moderately as possible . . .

(Source: Mousnier, ii. 830–2)

141. Articles of proposals made by the deputies of the courts assembled in the *Chambre St Louis*, 30 June–29 July 1648

1. The [commissions of] intendants of justice, and all other extraordinary commissions which are not verified in the sovereign courts, will be immediately revoked.

2. The loan contracts of the *taille*, *taillon*, subsistence and other taxes are to be immediately revoked. The *taille* is to be levied in the ancient form as was the case before the loan contracts. The *taille* is to be reduced by a quarter, since this reduction is considerably less than the profit of the financiers. There is to be a remission of the arrears up to and including the year 1646. All prisoners for this reason are to be released . . .

3. The ordinary charges of the State are to be paid first, and then the revenues used for the payment of the royal household and the cost of the war. These revenues may not be diverted for any other purpose . . .

4. An extraordinary tribunal[48] will be established, composed of officers drawn from the four sovereign courts who will be nominated by them, to take cognisance, and judge cases, of abuses and malversation committed in the administration and management of the King's affairs, exactions on his subjects, including usurious and fictitious loans . . .

3 July 1648:

7. No new taxes are to be imposed except as a result of edicts and declarations properly verified in the sovereign courts which have cognisance, and the implementation of the edicts and declarations shall be reserved to the courts. All persons are prohibited from levying such taxes except those properly verified on penalty of death . . .

8. There may be no reduction in the salaries of office-holders, or reduction of annuities and other alienated rights of the crown, except as

---

[48] *Chambre de justice.*

result of edicts and declarations in the same form, properly verified by the courts on a free vote.

10 July 1648:

13. The use of secret expenses[49] has been recognised, by the Estates General and Assemblies of Notables, as a means of covering up all the abuses which arise in financial administration . . . However, in 1643 they rose to 48.2 million and in 1644 to 59.2 million. In common opinion they have risen still further in 1645, for which the accounts have not yet been finalised. These sums are so large that infinite disorders are easily committed. The administration of the King's finances will always be suspect to the public until the excessive level of such secret expenses has been remedied. His Majesty should either abolish them altogether, or at least use them only for expenses which must necessarily be kept very secret . . .

14 July 1648:

15. There should be no creations of offices, whether of justice or finance, except as a result of edicts verified in the sovereign court on a free vote. The establishment of the sovereign courts may not be changed or altered for any reason or circumstance, either by increasing the number of offices, establishing a second tribunal serving for half the year,[50] or by dismembering part of the area of jurisdiction of the court[51] in order to establish new ones . . .

19. . . . All matters within the ordinary jurisdiction[52] of the courts will be sent back to the *Parlement*, the *Grand Conseil*, the *Cour des Aides* and other ordinary courts to which cognisance belongs according to the ordinances, without this being withdrawn by separate commissions. All extraordinary commissions and commissions contrary to this . . . are to be revoked forthwith . . . No office-holder should be troubled in the exercise of his office by orders under the King's private seal.[53] There should also be a prohibition on entering the courts to arrest members, on exiling them to towns and castles of the kingdom, and on arresting and detaining them. Instead, there should simply be investigations against office-holders and prosecutions according to the ordinances.

---

[49] Called *comptants par certification*.
[50] Called a *semestre*.
[51] Called the *ressort*.
[52] Called the *juridiction contentieuse*.
[53] Called *lettres de cachet*.

17 July 1648:

20. Decrees issued by the sovereign courts may not be annulled, revoked or suspended except by the legal procedures permitted by the ordinances . . .

21. No subjects of the King, whatever their status, may be held prisoner for more than 24 hours without being interrogated, in accordance with the ordinances, and sent before their natural judges . . .

(Source: Michaud and Poujoulat, pp. 240–5, n.1)

142. Memoirs of Omer Talon, 6 July 1648

. . . The Queen, in the present state of affairs, wishes to revoke the function of the intendants, and to re-establish order in the administration of royal finance; but she fears that the proposed remedies, which she recognises to be legitimate, are not appropriate at the present time, and that they might have an effect contrary to that intended.

For this purpose, she desires that you should consider that the King's army, commanded by Monsieur the prince is situated on the frontier to oppose the enemy,[54] and that for it to subsist it must have bread for the soldiers, and that besides they must be paid one month's pay . . .

There is no cash in the Treasury to meet all these expenses but only promises and letters of financiers, who pay in monthly instalments the sums that they have promised. The war plans were drawn up on the assurance of their undertakings. Nevertheless, those who have promised to make these loans do not have cash at hand, but hope to find it in the possessions of their friends, or to recover it from the payment of the *taille,* for which they have contracted with the King.

As for any credit, it is a matter of public knowledge that the financiers have none. No-one will lend them money; what is worse, those who have lent them money withdraw it.

As for the payment of the *taille* by the populace, if the order established for the last eleven years[55] is changed, and the intendants are revoked, and the *trésoriers de France* and *élus* are all re-established in the functions of their offices, this great and dramatic change could not be brought about quickly. There is a great difference between employing 35[56] persons

---

[54] Condé won the battle of Lens in August 1648.
[55] *Sic*: actually six, that is, since 1642.
[56] *Sic*: there were 22 *généralités*, and the rule was one intendant for each *généralité*.

throughout the kingdom to give orders for the levying of the King's taxes (which is the function of the intendants) and employing 3000 persons, which is how many *trésoriers de France* and *élus* there are. If they are re-established in their functions and paid their salaries and rights for this year, then the people will be burdened with more than 9 million *livres*, which would have sufficed to complete the present campaign. It is also certain that the *trésoriers de France* and *élus* will feel obliged to change the orders observed at the moment to establish their own orders . . .

(Source: Michaud and Pojoulat, pp. 244–245)

143. Remonstrances of the *trésoriers de France*, 1648

The intendants of the provinces and the financiers of the *taille* have reduced the *trésoriers de France* of all the *généralités* of the Kingdom to a miserable state by removing them from their functions (which the intendants have usurped absolutely) and by the violent seizure of their salaries by the tax contractors.

These intendants and financiers have united not only for the ruination of the *trésoriers de France*, but all the other office-holders in the provinces, and have so unreasonably conducted themselves that they seem to have undertaken the general destruction of the provinces of the Kingdom to which they have been sent, and have committed so many misappropriations, peculations, fleecings and other violent actions that as a result of the great number of these abuses the state has fallen into the necessity in which it now finds itself . . .

Each intendant costs the King more than a whole *bureau*, and the financiers exact more in costs than the sums that are levied in the *taille* . . .

(Source: AN U 28, fos. 188v.–9)

[Additional remonstrances of the *trésoriers de France*, c. 1648]:
. . . The administration of provincial finance . . . has passed into the hands of the intendants of justice, who retain what is most honourable and important and leave to the *bureaux* only the burden of a large number of dispatches for the King . . .

The intendants in general are from a profession whose procedure and practice are very different from the order of finance. Several of them have been drawn from the council before they have gained great experience, and coming into the provinces as young men, and ill-informed, all the established office-holders being suspect to them, they have no other information on affairs than that given to them by interested persons who asked for their appointment.[57]

(Source: BL Harleian MSS 4472b, fo. 147)

144. Debates in the *Parlement* of Paris concerning the revocation of the intendants, July 1648

7 July 1648:

Decreed that very express prohibitions are made against intendants of justice in the provinces, their subdelegates and other persons carrying extraordinary commissions which have not been verified in the court. They are not to attempt to carry out these commissions or take any cognisance of the *taille*, the *aides*, the *gabelles*, the *traites foraines* and other taxes on penalty of misappropriation and falsity . . .

In doing so, it is ordered that the *trésoriers de France*, *élus*, officers of the salt bureaux, judges of the *traites* and other officials who have previously been troubled in the function of their offices will perform them in the customary manner in accordance with the ordinances, edicts, decrees and rulings of the court . . .

(Source: AN Z^{1a} 163, fo. 48)

9 July 1648:

[Objections of Chancellor Séguier to the revocation of the intendants]. It was a matter of finding money to undertake so many pressing necessities. In the provinces it was very difficult to obtain payment of taxes without the assistance of the intendants of justice, who ensured that the King's taxes were paid by the people . . . It was now only a question of implementing what they had begun, and it was to be feared that the *trésoriers de France* and the *élus* would not enforce their orders out of resentment at having seen the intendants carry out their functions. Since the intendants could no longer do any harm, and were nevertheless necessary in the provinces, it was preferable to leave them there until next year when matters could be returned to their former order . . .

[After accusations that the commissions of the intendants were expedited in blank, the names of the appointees being filled in at the wish of the financiers; and that the intendants were personally involved in loan contracts on their *généralités*, the Chancellor compromised:] Since there was an insistence on the revocation of the intendants . . . they

---

[57] An allusion to the financiers.

would be left in the provinces simply to judge ordinary matters with the officers of the *présidiaux* in their *bureaux*, and the disputes over the *taille* with the *élus* in their *bureaux*. [But the Chancellor's good will was not accepted. He said in a loud voice] that when a Chancellor of France said something on behalf of the King or the Queen [Mother] he ought to be believed, and his intention was not to avoid the issue.

[Councillor Nesmond wanted a royal declaration containing the words] 'the King being informed of the abuses which are committed in the provinces by the intendants of justice in the matter of the *taille*.' [The Chancellor intervened:] this would be tantamount to prosecuting 10 or 12 intendants. It could be the case that some of them had committed peculation. They should not all be condemned, however, but their honour spared. [Councillor Hodicq replied:] they were men without honour.

(Source: AN Z^{1a} 163, fo. 62)

145. Royal declaration, 10 July 1648

. . . The late King, and we following his example, commissioned in the *généralités* of the Kingdom certain of our office-holders as intendants of justice, police and finance with power to carry out the levy of our taxes. Certain abuses have inadvertently occurred in these arrangements, besides the notable interest which our ordinary officials suffer, since they find themselves by these measures deprived of the principal function of their offices. . . . [Revocation of the intendants within the jurisdiction of the *Parlement* of Paris. The intendants of Picardy, Lyonnais and Champagne may remain to assist the governors to carry out their functions].

(Source: AN K 117b, no. 37)

146. Royal declaration, 12 July 1648

. . . Complaints have been made to us from several provinces of the vexations and violences committed in the levy of our taxes . . .

[An extraordinary financial tribunal[58] is to be established] composed of a number of officers from our sovereign courts, with powers to proceed to investigate exactions, violences and extortions committed in the provinces of our kingdom, in the imposition and levy of our taxes,

---

[58] *Chambre de justice.*

whether the *taille, taillon,* subsistence and others, as also the abuses, malversations and dissipation of our finances. The tribunal is to order the penalties which such crimes merit in accordance with our ordinances . . .

(Source: AN K 117b, no. 38)

147. Favier du Boulay, intendant at Alençon, to Séguier, 18 July 1648

My lord,
The King's declaration for the revocation of intendants sent to the *Parlement* of Paris brings such a blow to these quarters that it is impossible to remain here any longer. I am assured that it is the resolution of the council to revoke all the intendants. Among these rumours there is one which is very prejudicial to us: it is claimed that you will send a similar declaration to the *Parlement* of Normandy. I consider myself obliged to ask you humbly on my own behalf that, if the revocation is determined, you should send a special order by a letter under the King's private seal,[59] as always has been practised, and not give malevolent people the advantage of sending a declaration to the *Parlement* of Normandy, which certainly would do harm both to us and to the King's affairs which are already in an extreme decadence and disorder. . . .

(Source: Mousnier, ii. 840)

148. Lauzon, intendant of Guyenne, to Séguier, 20 July 1648

My lord,
The rumours coming from Paris are so prejudicial to the King's service that I do not know if we will dare to demand from the people the *taille* for 1647 or 1648. A general discharge of taxes is expected as if new silver mines in Peru had suddenly been found in the Treasury . . .

(Source: Mousnier, ii. 841)

[59] *Lettre de cachet.*

149. Le Tonnelier de Breteuil, intendant of Languedoc, to Séguier, 27 July 1648

. . . I learn that all the intendants of justice in the provinces are to be revoked except for certain provinces, of which Languedoc is one. The functions of those intendants who remain will be limited to certain types of affairs only. I thought, my lord, that at a time of such changes I should take no other rule for my conduct than from you, and ask you what I should do in order not to undermine the new orders which may have been established in the Kingdom for the functions of an intendant of justice . . .

(Source: Mousnier, ii. 845)

150. Sève, intendant of Provence, to Séguier, 27 July 1648

My lord,

The exception made of Provence in the revocation of the intendants is like a renaissance of my task, which obliges me to renew to you the vows of my obedience. I will receive, when it pleases you, your orders for my conduct since there are to be new ones. I will not have to change my conduct with regard to ordinary jurisdiction because I have never interfered with this. But, my lord, since there are certain matters here outstanding with regard to the separate commission for the verification of community debts, and several other jurisdictions attributed to the intendant by decrees and royal commissions, please would you inform me which matters I should return. In the meantime I am resolved not to deal with them.

It is certain, my lord, that the King's service will not be less advantageously maintained by removing part of the intendants' jurisdiction. But unless they remain independent of the *Parlements* in order to enforce the King's authority, it is very difficult for them to serve effectively . . .

(Source: Mousnier, ii. 846–7)

151. De Heere, intendant at Grenoble, to Séguier, 2 August 1648

[Remonstrances of the *Parlement* of Grenoble on matters of its

129

jurisdiction, and particularly to demand] that no more intendants should be sent into this province,[60] whatever limited powers they may have and for whatever purpose. I believe that I am correct, my lord, in telling you that the deputies[61] have the task of observing what happens at Paris and in certain circumstances of requesting a union with the *Parlement* of Paris . . .

(Source: Mousnier, ii. 852–4)

152. Decision of the council of state, 4 October 1648

The article on security has been accorded in the form in which it was read out before the Queen, on condition that the *Parlement* of Paris demands nothing further, and that it will end all its debates including that on the tariff by the end of this week. It may not continue its assemblies . . . or recommence them under any pretext whatsoever . . .

[Gaston, Condé, Conty, Mazarin, Longueville, Séguier and La Meilleraye] have advised the Queen to bring matters to a head against the *Parlement* and have promised to use all their power to maintain the King's authority . . .

Decided in the King's council at St. Germain-en-Laye.

(Source: AAE France 860, fo. 173)

153. Remonstrances of the *Chambre des Comptes*, 14 October 1648. [Presented to the Queen Mother, 27 October 1648]

. . . It is just and reasonable that Your Majesties order that henceforth all wealth, of whatever type, acquired by financiers since they entered into financial business, given by them to their children as part of a marriage settlement, or otherwise held under false names, should be mortgaged to Your Majesties and their creditors . . .

The licence given to all persons to propose extraordinary taxes to the prejudice of Your Majesties' service, the good of the state and of your subjects, has for some years been so great that without considering the

---

[60] Dauphiné.
[61] Of the *Parlement*.

persons proposing such measures, the nature of their advice, or the consequences of it, they have all been accepted provided that an immediate loan was made. Thus the laws and ordinances of the Kingdom have been broken . . .

[The procedure of establishing loan contracts on the *taille* is compared to enemy troops levying 'contributions' from the populace]. By such extraordinarily rigorous methods, most of the tax-payers have been ruined and are powerless to continue to pay the *taille* in subsequent years . . . The loan contractors, in order to prevent an investigation of their rigorous treatment of the tax-payers, have had the receivers-general and receivers-particular of finance dismissed from their offices because they did not want to participate in their loan contracts. In their place they have appointed their servants, or persons who are unknown and not resident in the locality . . . [The court considers that the crown has] a very great interest in returning as soon as possible the levy of the *taille* to its former procedure, for the good of the people and the royal affairs.

(Source: AAE France 860, fo. 199f.)

154. Memoirs of Omer Talon, 6 January 1649

At four in the morning, the King left Paris. The Queen left at six in the morning . . . Monsieur the duc d'Orléans, Monsieur the prince and the chief members of the royal court left at the same time for Saint-Germain-en-Laye in about 20 carriages. There was consternation in Paris at this news. All the people, great and small, were excited. People ran after those who wanted to leave. Within three hours most of the gates were secured by the bourgeois militia, and some baggage trains that attempted to leave were pillaged. Many members of the *Parlement* went to the home of Monsieur the first president,[62] where they were told that the King had written to the mayor of Paris stating that his sudden departure was necessitated by the assault on his authority by some members of the *Parlement*, who were involved in intrigues with the enemies of the state. The town councillors came to the *Parlement* to bring this letter. On this matter, we presented three proposals to the court. Firstly, that the court should take care to prevent pillage within the town, and that the mayor, who commanded the armed forces of the town, should give the necessary orders for this purpose. Secondly, for the exterior of the town, the

[62] Molé.

131

lieutenant-civil should send out commissioners to obtain supplies. Thirdly, with regard to the letter written to the town council, that it should please the court to send a deputation to the Queen to inform her of the sincerity of the court's actions and to request her to bring the King back to Paris.

(Source: Michaud and Poujoulat, p. 318)

155. Letter of the *Parlement* of Paris to other provincial *Parlements*, 18 January 1649

. . . The design of the Cardinal Mazarin has no other purpose than to oppress and destroy the *Parlement* and the city of Paris, and to subject the other provinces to a common oppression. He seeks to establish his tyranny to such an extent that he would be absolute master of all that is most considerable in the State. This is completely unjust and contrary to the laws of this monarchy and royal authority . . . [Help from the other *Parlements* is requested. Paris has levied troops. Conty and other nobles command them]. Thus acting together, with a similar sentiment, we will secure the State by preventing a civil war which would have no other cause than the ambition of a foreigner . . .

(Source: Mousnier, ii. 901–2. BN MS. fr. 3854, fo. 35)

156. The *Parlement* of Provence to Séguier, 24 January 1649

My lord,

We dispatch this courier to His Majesty to advise him of what happened in this town four or five days ago, and to inform him particularly of a disorder which obliged us (in order to avoid the consequences of it) to take up our seats and use what credit we had among the people to maintain His Majesty's authority which would have received a great alteration without this remedy . . .

The news spread[63] that there were soldiers hidden in the town hall . . . The tocsin was sounded, and at this the whole town took to arms. Monsieur the Comte d'Alais[64] is besieged in the town hall without being able to leave. The same is true of the office-holders of the *semestre* of the *Parlement*. Monsieur the comte de Carcès[65] goes round the town with

[63] On 21 January.
[64] Governor of Provence.
[65] Lieutenant-general in Provence, who sided with the *Parlement*.

several of the sieurs of our court . . . attempting to stop the disorder . . .

The same day a decree was issued abolishing the *semestre*, and establishing a new town council at His Majesty's pleasure. It has also been necessary, in order to establish calm in the town, to prevent the levy of a tax on flour . . .

(Source: Mousnier, ii. 905–7)

157. Séguier to Le Tellier, war minister, 30 May 1649

. . . [Matters in Dauphiné] are of great consequence and a dangerous example for other provinces of the Kingdom, whose condition and state is undergoing change. They consider they have the same right of returning to their ancient privileges. If such violent procedures are useful and advantageous to Dauphiné, others will think that they can follow suit. Thus Languedoc, Provence, Guyenne and Normandy will demand freedom for their Estates, which it has rightly been thought necessary to weaken in order to establish royal authority. You will have been informed of the decree of the *Parlement* of Toulouse which changes the disposition of the edict of Béziers,[66] so that freedom is given to the estates to vote such taxes as they see fit to the King. These are dangerous steps which are difficult to halt. If such tendencies had appeared before our peace,[67] they would have been incapable of solution. This demonstrates how important it is to maintain peace at Paris. We have not considered it advisable to require any financial assistance from Paris. The proposal would not bring forth any fruit and would produce only a refusal which would give those who are disaffected the opportunity to make speeches and spread rumours which we would have great difficulty in stopping. It also seems inadvisable to give Parisians the idea that we are discontented with them: they would interpret this as our seeking a quarrel in order to besiege them again. There is some tendency for people to believe such things, which could have serious consequences. Means to assist the King can only be obtained with the authority of the *Parlement*, which would use the opportunity to hold assemblies and regain the good graces of the people by protecting them from new taxes. Such an alliance must be avoided. At present it is broken. This court has lost its reputation in the public esteem and has little power over the people. Financial assistance

---

[66] Issued in October 1632, after the Montmorency rebellion.
[67] The treaty of Rueil, 11 March 1649.

can be obtained only by authority or with the good will of the people. As to governmental authority, we should not be mistaken: there is none in Paris, where we must be content to conserve appearances and such power as remains. As for public good will, there is even less: if the people do not rebel, it is from fear of returning to past miseries and not from respect and love of the administration . . .

(Source: Mousnier, ii. 930–3)

158. Syndic of the *élus* to the *élections* of the kingdom, 1 June 1649

We are openly opposing the designs of Messieurs the *trésoriers généraux de France* who wish to remove your functions and authority and preside in the *bureaux* of the *élections* for the assessments of the *taille* . . . We have been strongly supported by our lords of the *Cour des Aides*. . . . [The *trésoriers*] have requested a conference in order to reach an entire reconciliation . . . Since the news of the division between the sieurs *trésoriers de France* and the officers of the *élections* has led to proposals in the council to send commissioners or rather intendants into the provinces, we have thought it necessary to accept the conference in order to arrive at a close union between the *trésoriers* and ourselves, which is the only means of preventing the sending out of extraordinary commissioners into the provinces . . .

(Source: AN Z^{1a} 206, p. 915)

159. Voyer d'Argenson, royal commissioner in Guyenne, to Séguier, 18 June 1649

. . . We are told today that the *Parlement* of Toulouse is enraged at the news that Monsieur de Tallemant, a relative of Monsieur de Montauron,[68] has been nominated as intendant in the *généralité* of Montauban. The name of his father-in-law could serve as their pretext. Though he himself is an honest person, they hate this title of intendant almost as much as his relative the financier . . .

[P.S.] It is necessary to send out masters of requests under a title other than intendant, on a pretext such as to investigate rebellions in this area.

[68] A great financier.

Monsieur de Tallemant could come under this pretext. Gradually they could regain their fiscal powers, in order to alleviate the people by a better administration of the recovery of the taxes . . .

(Source: Mousnier, ii. 939–41)

160. Syndics of the *élus* to the *élections* of the Kingdom, 23 July 1649

[At the meeting with the *trésoriers* the precedents for those who had carried out the assessments of the *taille* were discussed inconclusively. The *trésoriers* stated that] it was only the syndics of the *élections* who opposed them in the authority and jurisdiction of their offices. Without the opposition of the syndics, all the *élections*, or most of them, would have received them to preside over the assessments of the *taille* for the present year 1649. In certain *généralités* they had possessed this right for sixty years . . . [The *élus* replied] that if some *élection* or other had from weakness or timidity consented to their presidency in the assessments of the *taille*, this could not prejudice the general issue, it being certain that illegitimate possession gives no valid title. [As a result of these disputes, the negotiations broke down. The aim of the syndics was that the *élus* should ensure that] the royal taxes are paid more diligently, and with fewer complaints of the tax-payers than when there were intendants of justice in the provinces.

(Source: AN Z^{1a} 206, pp. 919–22)

161. Circular of the syndics of the *élus* to the *élections* of the Kingdom, 17 May 1650

We have received advice from some of the *élections* that in certain provinces where Messieurs the masters of requests have gone to make their circuit-tours and have remained with the function of intendants simply for military matters, they wish to take cognisance of the *taille*, to preside in the assessments, carry out the reductions accorded to certain *généralités* with regard to particular parishes and generally assume jurisdiction for themselves. We considered that we ought to advise our lords the sovereign courts of this enterprise. They are of the opinion that the officers of the *élections* must be maintained within the terms of the declaration of the King of October 1648, and ensure that nothing is altered in any manner whatever. If you have knowledge that Messieurs

135

the intendants attempt to act as judges and wish to revive their earlier commissions, in order conserve your jurisdiction you should write without delay, and send evidence, to my lord the procurator-general of the *Cour des Aides* of Paris.

(Source: AN Z^{1a} 206, p. 931)

162. Le Tellier to Mazarin, 6 September 1650

The letter written by the *Parlement* of Toulouse to the *Parlement* of Paris, following the decree of the former, proposing a union between the two courts, has been received and this morning deliberations commenced on it. Although this proposed alliance of the courts is judged very dangerous, since it will doubtless be received by all the other *Parlements* when Paris has accepted it, nevertheless it is not judged appropriate to oppose it, because far from preventing it, this would be sufficient to bring them to agree to it . . .

(Source: AAE France 872, fo. 33)

163. Anonymous memorandum to Mazarin, n.d. [late May or early June 1651]

. . . The financiers who are involved in the loan contracts may be divided into two groups, that is to say on the one hand the receivers-general, the chief treasurers, the revenue farmers and others who control the revenues; and the financiers who have no management of the revenues on the other hand. This second category are treated much worse than the others. Whereas those who are favourably treated receive more than a quarter[69] in interest payments or reimbursements, the others receive nothing at all . . . They have worked so hard and solicited so hard that they have been heard in the council of state in the presence of Monsieur the finance minister.[70] Monsieur Doublet spoke on their behalf. He alleged that actual revenues of the Crown, after the deduction of all charges, amounted to more than 40 million. Monsieur the finance minister would only admit to 33 million, with only 23 million net because the rest was consumed in interest payments. Monsieur Doublet exaggerated the maladministration of finance, and demonstrated with

[69] 25 per cent.
[70] Longueil des Maisons.

evidence that all the revenues could be paid in quarterly instalments and that there was no need of interest charges . . .

Monsieur the finance minister maintained on the contrary that he could obtain no money without making interest payments, which in truth were so excessive that the receivers-general and revenue farmers (who advanced nothing and paid nothing except out of the actual cash they raised in taxes) had more than a quarter[71] in interest payments and reimbursement, and this consumed 18 million as a result of loans anticipating other loans. In conclusion, the sieur Doublet claimed that if the administration of royal finance was in the hands of an intelligent and industrious man who kept order and kept his word, this proposal could easily be carried out. If one were appointed, he and his friends would pay 4.5 million in the months of May, June, July and August in order to complete the campaigning season. At this, those financiers and members of the public present demanded Monsieur de La Vieuville as the sole person capable of restoring the King's finances.

. . . The intrigue in the government is strong to retain Monsieur des Maisons, but his lack of intelligence and the necessity of affairs weaken his position . . . All the populace, including office-holders . . . cry out against Monsieur the finance minister and state loudly that he is kept on by Your Eminence because he gives you hope that the treasury bills for your loans will be honoured . . .

(Source: AAE France 875, fo. 115)

164. Decree of the council of state, 2 October 1651

[The council has seen a decree of the *Parlement* of Bordeaux of 30 September 1651] that very humble remonstrances should be made to His Majesty to reduce the *taille* and in the meantime that his subjects in the jurisdiction of the court should be discharged from paying half of the *taille*, including half the arrears due by them. [It also provides that] those who have made this half payment cannot be required to pay the other half . . . [The council orders that] the jurisdiction of the *Parlement* does not concern the matter of the *taille*. The discharge it has made of part of it is an enterprise against His Majesty's authority in order to divert his taxes and to use them to pay for the cost of troops levied in the province against his service and other expenses of the rebellion . . . [The council annuls the decree].

[71] 25 per cent.   (Source: AN E 249a, fo. 15. E 1697, fo. 221)

165. Extract from a diary of debates in the *Parlement* of Paris, 12 January 1652

Vedeau: in the present state to which affairs are reduced, we must act with circumspection and not fall into the mistake of 1649, when the perfidy of some betrayed and sacrificed the interests of this court for their particular advantage . . . For this purpose, he was of the opinion that Monsieur the duc d'Orléans should be asked to choose a number of good men from the court with whose counsel he would dispose of the military matters and to whom he would confide the administration of finance . . . It was a matter of war administration rather than judicial administration . . .

Pithou: . . . people were speaking as if open war were declared. We should carefully distinguish the King's authority from that of the Cardinal. In truth these two things seemed difficult to distinguish . . . With regard to Cardinal Mazarin and those who assisted him, we could not use too great a severity, including demolishing their residences in the environs of Paris.

[Gaston]: . . . he had had no personal interest in exiling Cardinal Mazarin from France and the King's council . . . But he would oppose his return by all means . . . and to do this the public taxes must be seized, otherwise these would fall into the hands of our enemies, without considering the funds from distant provinces for the payment of *rentes* since he was of the opinion that only the net revenues, after the *rentes* had been paid, should be seized. [Note: in all this speech and others on this day, he showed no criticism of the authority of the Queen].

President Le Coigneux: the evil was great, but did not yet require remedies of last resort . . . A distinction should be made between now and events at the time of the siege of Paris. Then, in truth, the *Parlement* took to arms and seized the public taxes. But at the time the city was besieged and people were talking of ruining us. But this is not presently the case . . . We should take care not to join a party, but to hold off from parties and act as mediators. If Monsieur the duc d'Orléans wants to seize the taxes and take to arms, we will suffer this and remain unaware of it; but there is a great deal of difference between suffering something and ordering it . . .

President de Mesmes: . . . It was necessary to consider that all the officers of the Kingdom, and particularly those of the sovereign courts, drew their subsistence from royal authority. The weakening of royal authority would bring about their own decline . . . At this time royal authority was damaged and could only be more seriously damaged by taking arms against the King. [At this point there was noise. But he continued on the risks of civil war . . .] This, gentlemen, is what it is to oppose force by force. It is impossible to make a distinction between the King's council and his person. I think we must take great care not to order the seizure of the King's revenues: this is to make ourselves sovereigns. The remedy will be worse than the evil, because it will bring about the cessation of the payment of *rentes* . . .

(Source: Courteault, pp. 226–36)

166. The articles of the recent deliberation of Messieurs the princes with the bourgeois of the city of Paris, carried out in the *Parlement* on 6 July and in the town council on 8 July 1652

. . .1. We will remain firm in, and will never depart from, the obedience and very humble submission that we owe as true and natural subjects to this crown of the King our prince and sovereign lord.

2. It is a notorious fact that a foreigner and his assistants have seized the person of the King and the entire administration and absolute government of the Kingdom, which they have taken over unjustly and exercise with an extreme tyranny and oppression . . .

3. . . . We will remove the public authority from the hands of its usurper, render to the King the dignity of his crown, guard it and maintain it in its entirety, remove his person from their hands, repair the offence they have committed, and have the instigator of this violence punished . . .

4. In order to return the state to its first form under the sovereign authority of the King, the legitimate council will be established with the princes of the blood and other princes and officers of the crown; with senior councillors of state who have held great offices; and those who are members of great and ancient families, who from natural affection and particular interest are concerned with the conservation of the State. They have as of right, during the minority of our Kings and during their indisposition, the administration, government, and direction of public

affairs in accordance with ancient and fundamental laws of the Kingdom, which exclude women and foreigners. If it happens (which God forbid) that the King should die, we declare that we intend to recognise as our King and sovereign lord my lord the duc d'Anjou, his true and natural heir and successor to the crown, and during his minority my lord the duc d'Orléans as Regent and legitimate guardian of the Kingdom, to whom this pre-eminence belongs, together with the above-mentioned council, for the joint direction and administration of the affairs of the Kingdom without suffering anyone else to have the Regency of the Kingdom, not even the Queen Mother, since this prejudices the laws of the state.

9. . . . We have no other aim than to conserve for the King the authority and dignity of the crown, to affirm the sceptre in his hands and his legitimate successors, under the common liberty of Frenchmen, to maintain our lives, property, honours and dignities against the disloyalty and perfidy of he who conspired for its ruin together with that of the royal family and the whole Kingdom.

(Source: BN L^b 37 2756 in 4°)

167. Moral testament [*sic*] of Omer Talon, advocate-general of the *Parlement* of Paris, 18 July 1652

. . . I have served 21 years in my office[72] without the loss of a single day, and without ever having failed, in my opinion, in what I owed the King, the public and my honour. I see that I am not in favour at court because I have never flattered the first minister. I am also suspect to those who are in the party of the princes, because I have never followed their views: they are offended because I have spoken too strongly in favour of royal authority, and I have said that no-one can dispense with it under any pretext.

I have seen the ill treatment which Messieurs of the *Parlement* received on the 25 June when leaving the hall of justice, and have reflected on what happened on 4 July at the town hall . . .[73] . . . I have perceived that one of the greatest evils which flatters men imperceptibly and precipitates them into misfortunes, from which there can be no return, is the habit of visiting, constant attendance on, and friendship with princes and great seigneurs of the Kingdom. I have seen this evil introduce itself

[72] As advocate-general of the *Parlement* of Paris.
[73] The so-called massacre at the *hôtel de ville*.

in the *Parlement* in the last five or six years, and in the other courts on a similar scale . . .

Princes and great nobles receive them with good countenance, and although they are sometimes importuned, they suffer this obligingly because they sell themselves dear and consider these men as their dogs and their slaves. When they want their vote in public or private affairs, they exact a sort of blind deference from them, which they believe due to them because of their status. These gentlemen do not dare refuse them, for fear of losing the good graces which they think they have acquired over a long period of constant attendance on them . . .

Many people consider that guile, artifice and duplicity are the necessary skills for succeeding in the world . . . Monsieur the president Jeannin,[74] who was one of the greatest personalities and the soundest minds of his age, despised all guile in ordinary affairs, and maintained that on occasions of consequence, it was necessary to speak sincerely, though not to the point of indiscretion, so that one secured the reputation of truthfulness and could not be accused of lying and duplicity . . .

Above all, faction, parties and undertakings must be avoided so that the King's authority, which cannot be in two places at the same time, may be defended. It is dishonest to flatter or to be absolutely committed to the thoughts of those in the government, who usually bring matters to extremities in order to advance the cause that they support. On the contrary, it is the duty of a good man to oppose strongly the insolence of ministers, who abuse the name and power of the King in order to do evil. However, this must never come to a schism. Nor should it break the union which ought to exist between the King and his office-holders. There should never be a league against the King under pretext of the common good and the desire for reform. Those who suggest these thoughts, and who are the instigators of these leagues, have no design other than personal aggrandisement. They wish to advance themselves at the expense of idiots whom they abuse. It is certain that after all civil wars, the people and the state are not alleviated, because the evils of the revolt itself cannot be cured. Reforms proposed for the future never bring alleviation. They are pious hopes and mere pieces of paper. Money is needed to allow the state to subsist and to satisfy the malcontents . . .

My late father, who was very wise, desired on his death-bed no more of his children than that they should not marry daughters of financiers and tax-contractors. I consider this counsel worthy of a man of good heart and virtue.

(Source: Mailfait, pp. 356–64)

[74] Formerly controller-general of finance, who died in 1622.

168. Royal declaration read out in the *lit de justice* held at the *Parlement* of Paris, 22 October 1652

. . . Henceforth the members of [the King's] court of *Parlement* at Paris are prohibited from taking any cognisance of general affairs of the state and the direction of his finances. They may not order anything, or undertake anything on such matters against those to whom His Majesty has confided the administration on penalty of disobedience. Everything which has been, or could hereafter be, resolved and decreed on such matters in the court in contravention to this declaration is as of now declared null and void.

(Source: AN U 30, fo. 356)

169. Decree of the council of finance, 17 September 1653

[The council has seen] a printed copy of the ordinance of the *trésoriers de France* of Paris dated [   ] August last . . . by which they cunningly allege that the masters of requests who are sent by His Majesty into the provinces are empowered to make new levies on His Majesty's subjects without letters patent. It is true that the masters of requests have been sent into the *généralités* of the kingdom to hold their circuit-tours[75] in accordance with the powers of their offices: to investigate the contravention of His Majesty's ordinances and rulings in the levy of the *taille* and his other revenues; to investigate the manner in which justice is administered to his subjects and the oppressions they suffer from the troops, their billeting and passage; to investigate the oppression of the weak and poor by powerful people who abuse their power; and finally to take a particular care that the money intended for the maintenance of troops in the frontier places where His Majesty has resolved to billet them during the next winter quarter is levied promptly and imposed equitably on all those who ought to contribute. The *trésoriers de France* have sent their ordinance into all the *élections* of the *généralité* of Paris, accompanied with letters to the *élus*, receivers of the *taille*, and officers of the salt tax bureaux, by which they prohibit them from recognising the masters of requests and other extraordinary commissioners whatever their status, and also prohibit them from obeying their orders and in the

---

[75] Called *chevauchées*.

142

case of the receivers from presenting their registers to them, on penalty of a 500 *livres'* fine. This is an outrage without example and worthy of punishment, since it displays contempt for His Majesty's authority with the design of depriving his subjects of the alleviation which they ought to expect . . . It also allows the disorders which have arisen in the levy of the *taille* to continue, which certain *trésoriers de France* in other parts of his kingdom foment and authorise instead of seeking to prevent. The *trésoriers de France* of Paris have been carried to this excess of audacity by their private interests . . . [The council annuls the 'reasons of the *trésoriers de France*' and prohibits them from issuing further ones on pain of deprivation of office]. His Majesty strictly forbids all persons, of whatever status, from troubling or interfering with the masters of requests, intendants of finance and other commissioners of His Majesty carrying out his orders on penalty of extraordinary procedures against them . . .
(Source: AN E 260b, fo. 158. The decree was inserted in the registers of the *bureau des finances* of Paris: AN Z1f 215, fo. 219)

170. Remonstrances of the *trésoriers de France* to the King, 17 September 1653

. . . Neither the masters of requests nor the intendants of finance can be informed of [local evidence for tax purposes] except from the reports of others . . . [The *trésoriers* claim that they proceed] with more equity than the masters of requests, who are simply commissioners and have no interest during their commission other than to take the fruit of the vine by tearing off the branches, whereas the *trésoriers* have an interest in conserving the plants since all their wealth and the subsistence of their family depends on their salaries.

The function of masters of requests in the provinces consists solely of making their circuit-tours each year according to the list given to them by Monsieur the Chancellor and to bring their reports to him of the complaints they have received and the contraventions of your ordinances which they have discovered . . . The masters of requests perform with a company of fusiliers and with force what the *trésoriers de France* have been accustomed to do without costs and without shocking your people. They consume part of the taxes which should arrive in your Treasury after the financiers have consumed the first part. The ravages which the troops cause your provinces render most of your subjects insolvent, or less willing to pay. This is the cause of the arrears which have become commonplace since their introduction violated the established procedures.

(Source: AN K 118b, no. 63)

171. Servien and Foucquet to Mazarin, 29 October 1653

[The *Parlement* of Toulouse has issued a decree] against the sieur de Machault, the royal commissioner deputed to the *généralité* of Montauban.[76] The terms of this decree are so seditious that we consider that the council cannot not issue too severe a decree to punish the court's insolence . . . It is a necessary remedy to stop the spread of the trouble throughout Guyenne and the neighbouring provinces . . .

(Source: AAE France 892, fo. 427)

172. Decree of the council of state, 31 October 1653

. . . This *Parlement*,[77] on the basis of reports it has received from certain office-holders, *trésoriers de France* at Montauban and other discontented persons, of the arrival of the sieur de Machault, master of requests deputed for this province, has assembled in extraordinary session without permission during the vacation. On the same pretext which formerly excited rebellion in the province, it has issued two decrees on 11 October, which require the sieur de Machault to place his commission in the registry of the court and in the meantime prohibits him from carrying it out on pain of falsity. It prohibits all office-holders, magistrates and others within its jurisdiction from recognising him as intendant and from deferring to his ordinances on penalty of punishment of their persons and suspension from their offices . . . It has also ordered very humble remonstrances to His Majesty, asking him to revoke the commission of the sieur de Machault . . . [The council has received a report of Machault on 'intrigues and cabals' in the province]. It is easy to see that these arise from those who are in the faction of the prince of Condé, in order to assist his evil plans in the province, and to excite new troubles and prevent His Majesty's orders from being carried out. [The council

---

[76] Louis de Machault, intendant at Montauban, 1653–6.
[77] Toulouse.

orders a decree of annulment against the decree of the *Parlement*] which was an outrage and enterprise against His Majesty's authority. It expressly prohibits the court in the future from issuing similar decrees on penalty of disobedience and suspension from office. [The decree of the *Parlement* is to be torn out of the registers and this decree is to be inserted in its place.]

(Source: AN E 1700, no. 212. E 261b, fo. 344)

173. Decree of the council of finance, 25 February 1654

[The council has received] the request of Thomas Bonneau, councillor and secretary of His Majesty,[78] containing his very humble remonstrances. For 40 years he has been involved in affairs. Those that he has undertaken have been with honour and the contentment both of Messieurs the finance ministers and the individuals with whom he has contracted. He acquired great credit with the late King, particularly after the year 1635 when war was declared, and His Majesty since his accession has received notable advantages . . . [But the loan contracts were revoked on 18 July 1648]. He remained a creditor of His Majesty for more than six million *livres*, even with interests reduced. Once the civil war began, he made considerable loans without interest charges. He has not received any interest payment for five years . . . He gave his assistance during the last movements[79] from no interest other than to contribute what he could by his zeal to the re-establishment of His Majesty's authority . . . His lack of re-imbursement has been a great prejudice to his creditors and his family . . . These assistances were given to His Majesty by borrowing on all sides. However, he is now scandalously and violently pursued by seizures of his property, even his furnishings, and a garrison has been established in his house at the request of Messire Pierre de Launay, who is charged with the recovery of taxes as a result of *rentes* that have been redeemed . . . He owes in tax no more than 120 000 *livres*, which he offers to compensate partly from the six million due to him, which the said de Launay has refused . . .

(Source: AN E 263b, fo. 620)

[78] A great financier.
[79] The Fronde.

174. Servien and Foucquet to Mazarin, 14 July 1654

[Dauphiné and Guyenne are] reduced to extreme suffering because of the disorders of the troops. Those who have made loan contracts on the *taille* of these two provinces cannot accomplish what they promised. We cannot find any other people to contract loans on these revenues next year, or for the winter quarter, except with great difficulty and excessive interest charges. When we complain to the intendants who are in those provinces, [those of Guyenne][80] reply that they are discharged of this task since the arrival of Monsieur Colbert de Terron.[81] We do not, however, believe that Your Eminence intended that they would not also deal with this matter while he was in Guyenne, since this is the principal reason they have been sent to their province. Perhaps also the sieur de Terron does not have enough authority to discipline the troops effectively . . .

(Source: AAE France 893/2, fo. 150)

175. Séguier to Mazarin, 9 August 1654

. . . The chamber of *Enquêtes* in the *Parlement* of Paris has demanded an assembly of chambers for general affairs and to deliberate on the new taxes which have been ordered. Monsieur the first president has promised an assembly next Tuesday, and is resolved to do all he can with his normal prudence to try to prevent this assembly, which will have a bad effect given people's disposition to bear new taxes only with considerable impatience. This matter merits being regulated, but it must come solely from the King's authority, and not from that of the *Parlement*, which seeks to find favour among the populace as its champion. This consideration is of great consequence, and it seems that this general assembly could be prevented if the King made it known that he wished to take cognisance of all the taxes being levied in order to regulate them for the alleviation of his subjects. It is difficult to bring about a reduction of these taxes, which provide also for repayment to those individuals who have advanced their capital. We wait on the decision of Your Eminence . . .

(Source: AAE France 893/2, fo. 222)

---

[80] Guyenne comprised two *généralités*, Bordeaux and Montauban.
[81] Intendant of the army in Foix, Bigorre and the frontier of Guyenne.

176. Séguier to Mazarin, 23 August 1656

[Concerning a decree issued by the *Parlement* of Paris on 18 August. It] has asserted its authority as if it were superior to the council, and as if it were in its power to correct the council's judgements . . . This is an affront to royal authority, an attempt to change the order established by Kings. It seeks to deprive the council of the cognisance which belongs to it, and to elevate the *Parlement* above it, making it the first company in the kingdom which can judge the faults of others . . . I see no establishment which would then not be subject to their will . . . In 1648 they claimed that edicts, taxes and tax-contracts which had not been verified in the *Parlement* could not be carried out. Thus all financial affairs were included within their definition of 'ordinary jurisdiction'[82] and could be prevented from being put into effect. The assistance which the King hopes to obtain from this sort of tax would thus become dependent on Messieurs of the *Parlement*, and all the King's affairs subject to their ambitions.

[MS B] . . . It is to be feared that all the other *Parlements* may undertake similar actions to that of Paris. It is indeed said that letters have been sent asking them to issue similar decrees . . . [The council is not infallible but] there is no court in the kingdom which serves the King better than the council or deals with matters with better rules. It may sometimes issue something ill-judged, but it is not the place of the *Parlement* to correct it . . .

(Source: [MS A:] AAE France 900, fo. 324. [MS B:] BL Harleian 4489, fo. 42. The decree of annulment was issued by the council of state on 19 October 1656: AN E 1704, fo. 52)

177. Le Tellier to Mazarin, 24 July 1657

. . . It is absolutely necessary that the assessments of the *taille* be carried out by Messieurs the intendants, on whose orders the troops are billeted. They take account of what the inhabitants of each parish have paid during the winter quarter and give due consideration of their burden, in accordance with His Majesty's intentions . . .

(Source: AAE France 904, fo. 49)

---

[82] *Juridiction contentieuse.*

178. Foucquet to Mazarin, 6 November 1658

[Negotiations over the money grant from the Estates of Burgundy.] Monsieur the Chancellor, who has suffered, it seems to me, a serious outrage against his person on this occasion, is of the opinion that the deputies should be required to attend, and give us proposals to increase the grant to the King.[83] We must initiate incidents such as this. They are opportunities to regain for the King the authority which he lacks in the *pays d'états*. Although in my office money must be my main concern, and the necessity for it is very great, nevertheless if money is needed to support an exemplary punishment, I offer my assistance. The *Cour des Comptes* of Montpellier did much less to Monsieur the Prince of Conty than this *Parlement*[84] has done to the King [in seeking a union with the Estates]. That court was suspended without its deputies being heard, in a province which is much more considerable and further away . . . [Foucquet recommends the exile or imprisonment of several of] those most guilty, and to suspend the *Parlement*, without entering into negotiations which could only be disadvantageous . . .

(Source: AAE France 905, fos. 481–2. The *Parlement* was suspended from January to July 1659)

179. Foucquet to Mazarin, 23 December 1658

[Discusses possible measures to be taken to punish the province of Burgundy for its disobedience]. . . . *Elections* cannot be established without abolishing the estates, which I am persuaded is not well-timed, because there would be too many matters on hand at the same time. Besides, the *Parlement*, the ecclesiastics who have entry into the Estates, the nobility, the people and the governor are all interested parties. This province would create difficulty for us, at a time when the King's armies are fully occupied, and the gentlemen of Burgundy, whom I am told are sought out by the conspirators of other provinces, will be the first to encourage them and join such a serious alliance . . .

(Source: AAE France 905, fo. 545)

180. Foucquet to Mazarin, 29 July 1659

I consider myself obliged to tell Your Eminence that all those who have

[83] Called the *don gratuit*.
[84] The *Parlement* of Dijon.

148

some knowledge of the affairs of Languedoc consider that it is very important to send orders immediately to the province to convoke the Estates on 8th or 10th September next, in the town of Toulouse. They will then fear that the King, who is not far away during his stay at Bordeaux, may come to hold them in person, and to impose a re-establishment of the edict of Béziers[85] on the Estates and the *Parlement*[86] if they do not give him prompt satisfaction. If they are delayed and they are slow in dealing with things, as is their custom, His Majesty must undertake another journey for them . . . It is important to draw greater assistance than has been the case in the past from Languedoc, and unless we do so now there is no doubt that their grant will be smaller after the peace . . .

(Source: France 907, fo. 255)

181. Le Tellier to Mazarin, 30 July 1659

I have arranged with Monsieur the procurator-general[87] the words the King must write to the towns of his kingdom to induce them to give money to His Majesty . . . Since then, having consulted the list of towns, it occurs to me that Messieurs the intendants may act in this with too much reserve, and doubtless may not propose sums as large as those for which we might reasonably hope. The reason for this is that they are happy to discharge the inhabitants because they have to live with them . . .

(Source: AAE France 907, fo. 264)

182. Colbert to Mazarin, 31 August 1659

[This paragraph has been deleted by Mazarin]. . . . Since I have gone so far in this discourse, I cannot prevent myself telling Your Eminence something which you know even better than me, that the royal finances have great need of a severe and vigorous extraordinary tribunal.[88] The officers composing it should have no link, either by marriage or by

---

[85] Imposed in 1632. Rescinded in 1649.
[86] Of Toulouse.
[87] Foucquet.
[88] *Chambre de justice.*

interest, with the financiers. (Thus they cannot be recruited at Paris).
The provinces have great need of ambulatory tribunals[89] to punish
undue vexations to the people.

(Source: Clément, i. 360–2)

183. Foucquet to Mazarin, 3 September 1659

[Levy on the towns.] I greatly fear that most of the towns which are
subject to the *taille*, and are consequently overburdened as is the rest of
the countryside, will be unable to make a great effort, and there are many
that will be unable to pay anything at all. But with the great ones which
have privileges, we must not abate our demands, because this is the most
legitimate assistance that we can hope for . . .

(Source: AAE France 908, fos. 23–31v.)

---

[89] *Chambres de grands jours.*

4 ARISTOCRATIC GRIEVANCES AND REBELLION

French society at the time of Richelieu and Mazarin was divided in many ways, but two categories appear particularly important. The first was the great gulf between privileged and unprivileged, basically between rich and poor, with the upper levels of the clergy, the old nobility of the sword and the new nobility of the robe (those ennobled through office) falling within the group of the privileged. The second was a less easily perceived, but still fundamental, subdivision within the privileged group. Thus, for example, the clergy stood apart from the rest of society, although the bishops might form a common interest with the nobility at a moment of crisis such as 1651 (cf. doc. 232), not least because most of the bishops were recruited from the sons of the nobility. It was observed in Chapter 3 that the office-holders were divided, some enjoying much greater privileges than others, some co-operating with the monarchy and its fiscal demands in time of war, while others tended to resist. The nobles, like the office-holders, lacked group cohesion. Magnates such as princes of the blood, provincial governors and other great nobles had little in common with lesser nobility or gentry. The experience of the Fronde demonstrated that the old nobility was too divided against itself to resist the encroachment of the new nobility of the robe. Nevertheless, the civil wars in Provence and Guyenne in 1649 were partly a conflict between robe and sword, with a significant part of the old nobility following the provincial governors in opposition to the local *Parlement* (doc. 214).

Among the old nobility, the magnates hoped that the lesser nobles and gentry could be mobilised to serve their interests. But they had their own concerns, which were very different from those of the magnates and reflected the limited extent of their landholdings. They enjoyed a much smaller income from land, offices and pensions. Magnates had access to the source of royal patronage, and exploited it ruthlessly. The gentry might hope for pensions or relatively unimportant military commands: but they could scarcely hope for provincial governorships, unless the rules were changed (doc. 226, clause 30). Most gentry were relatively poor (doc. 197). Indeed, some of the numerous Breton petty nobility (*hobereaux*) were indistinguishable from prosperous peasants except in terms of their pretension to noble status. The gentry had, to a large extent, been overtaken by economic progress in the sixteenth and early seventeenth centuries. They wanted to halt the process of assimilation of other social groups into the nobility, by restricting the purchase of noble lands by commoners, and preventing intermarriage between nobles and commoners (or at least preventing the transmission of noble status from such marriages). They tried to preserve the traditional noble lifestyle by, for example, making distinctions of dress (doc. 227).

Many provincial gentry seem to have lost sight of their fundamental purpose and did not even go to war. The feudal levy (*arrière-ban*) was summoned during the Thirty Years' War, but failed to produce an army. There was clearly some opposition to the idea of war against Catholic Spain, a crude view of foreign policy bequeathed posthumously by the Catholic League. Many of the gentry, however, excused themselves from military service on the grounds of poverty. They turned out in Poitou in 1627 and in Languedoc in 1637 to resist a sudden invasion, respectively by the English and the Spaniards; but elsewhere, the military service owed by the gentry was commuted into a small money payment.

The relative poverty of many gentry and their sense of being overtaken by economic change explains their attitude to those groups in society which had prospered in the period of their adversity. Above all, they were fiercely hostile to office-holders and financiers. The gentry denounced the 'common interests of the robe', which seemed to operate against them. They castigated the great rise in the price of offices which seemed to exclude any hope of placing their sons in the local lawcourts. They wanted a reduction in the number of offices and the abolition of the purchase of office, a drastic reversal of social and economic changes over the previous century (doc. 211). Denunciation of the financiers was to be expected, since this viewpoint was echoed by other social groups (doc. 226). The gentry also bitterly resented abuses committed by the army, whether in the levy of taxes or in taking billets on the population at large. They were prepared to form local leagues to make their views felt (doc. 235), and in 1652 and 1658 attempted to establish a general league in opposition to the excesses of the troops (docs. 232, 238).

The ministers clearly took this discontent seriously, fearing the prospect of widespread opposition to the war and the possibility of an alliance between rebellious gentry and rebellious peasants (docs. 236, 237). Although the gentry were exempt from the *taille*, their peasant farmers and tenants were subject to it. The gentry considered this policy to be unjust, since it amounted to an indirect tax on their own income (doc. 211, clause 18). They were realistic enough to perceive that they could not expect their tenants to pay simultaneous high rents and high taxes to the crown. A reduction in taxes would permit existing rents to be paid, and perhaps allow them to be increased. The gentry thus opposed high taxation and, although personally exempt, stood to benefit economically from the policies they advocated. If the peasant farmers were pressed too hard, all but the wealthiest would go under. Opposition to taxation could in turn lead to hostility to the war, and an overtly political stance of opposition to Mazarin as the personification of the French war effort (doc. 227, clauses 29, 34, 35). The gentry could have become politicised and a threat to the power of the ministers.

In retrospect, this threat seems more apparent than real, since the gentry lacked an organisational capacity due to the infrequency with which they met at national level. The meeting held in 1651 was exceptional, and the promise made by Gaston d'Orléans, Louis XIV's uncle, that they should be allowed to meet on a regular basis, was not kept. Fundamentally, the gentry wanted a meeting of the Estates General, the national representative institution in which they formed one of the three estates. They hoped that such a meeting would lead to an end of the war (docs. 220, 222, 238). The lack of political representation for most of the period of Richelieu and Mazarin was keenly felt in the provinces. There were demands for permanent gentry representatives called syndics (doc. 211, clause 3); in some provinces the gentry drew up their grievances though they were not legally entitled to do so because no meeting of the Estates General had been summoned (doc. 234).

The unpopular tasks of discouraging local leagues and policing the lesser nobility fell upon the provincial intendants (doc. 206). Machault in Languedoc and Laffemas in Champagne are famous early examples of intendants who were effective in dealing with this problem (docs. 192, 193, 194, 195). Later intendants were less successful (doc. 209), especially when dealing with the league of gentry in 1658. Colbert was particularly critical of the intendants of Normandy, and said that he would have recalled his own brother had he been so ineffective (doc. 241). On the other hand, Longueville, the governor of Normandy, sided with the gentry against the intendant (doc. 240). On an earlier occasion, in 1645, Longueville had also shown support for gentry privileges (doc. 207). In another context, Colbert recognised that an intendant might lack the power to deal with an alliance of magnates and gentry (doc. 242).

With magnate leadership such as that provided by d'Épernon in Guyenne and Pompadour in Limousin (doc. 205), it was scarcely surprising that the lesser nobility were reluctant to suppress tax rebellion and often actively encouraged it. The intendants' task was to investigate specific cases, backed by powers to confiscate noble estates, and to force the gentry to pay the taxes owed by the parishes they were protecting. In the last resort, they could declare noble status forfeited (docs. 201, 204). Sometimes, the intendants acted in a case where the facts were in dispute (doc. 208). Even after the Fronde, they continued to play an important policing role with regard to the gentry (doc. 239).

The provincial governors did little to discourage local leagues and associations of gentry. They were members of the upper aristocracy. Although appointed by the crown for political reasons, nevertheless they purchased the office. No limit was placed on the length of time served by governors at the beginning of Richelieu's ministry, although Richelieu may have tried to review appointments triennially and Louis XIV almost certainly did so. By 1632, members of the Montmorency family had held the governorship of Languedoc almost continuously since 1526; it was their name, their patronage and their influence, which counted in the province, not that of the King (doc. 191). From the point of view of the crown and the chief minister, control of the provincial governorships and the fortresses within the provinces was a key issue. Richelieu was governor of Brittany after 1631, Mazarin governor of Auvergne after 1650. The chief minister obviously could not hold all the provincial governorships in person, however. He had to find supporters and clients, which was no easy task. In Burgundy and Normandy there was no effective counterweight to the power of Condé and Longueville: this was an important factor in their arrest in 1650. They had intrigued to secure control of Le Havre, the most important fortress in France.

Instead, Mazarin had them arrested, retained control of the fortress, and indeed transferred the princes there later in 1650. The strategic implications of a transfer of governors were considerable: in 1651 the appointment of Condé to Guyenne gave him a new, and more dangerous, power base (doc. 224). He was able to turn this against Mazarin the following year in a general alliance, which for a time even the *Parlement* of Bordeaux was forced to support (doc. 230).

The ministers valued loyal governors because they could perform tasks which the intendants could not. The intendant could not act as the military leader of a vast patronage network. On the other hand, the intendant did not pose a political threat to the crown in the manner of a duc de Vendôme in Brittany in 1626 (doc. 186) or a duc de Montmorency in Languedoc in 1632 (docs. 189, 190). The intendant was usually a member of the nobility of the robe, appointed by the crown on merit to a position which could not be bought and sold, and from which he was usually recalled within three years of his appointment. There must inevitably have been a basis for tension, and sometimes conflict, between the two types of official. The intendants were probably not introduced as a means of deliberately weakening or destroying the authority of the governors. Several of the earliest intendants were chosen primarily as assistants of the governors. From the start, however, the 'assistance' given to the governor was double-edged. The intendant was commissioned to 'reside near' to the governor and to assist him with his advice and counsel. If that advice and counsel was ignored, the intendant wrote directly to Paris to inform the ministers. The real value of intendants was pre-emptive: to prevent the governor changing allegiance or declaring rebellion when his demands could still be met by the government. The governors appreciated the advantages of securing their own nominees as intendants, and the ministers often heeded their requests. They were certainly consulted about the choice of candidates and might well veto the nominee of the ministers. On the other hand, the ministers sought to appoint intendants who were of independent viewpoint and thus could not be easily integrated into the governor's patronage network (doc. 240).

In many cases, a loyal governor and a relatively compliant intendant were able to co-operate perfectly successfully. At other times, an intendant could advise, but it fell upon the ministers to

155

decide and act. Controlling the great nobility was a formidably difficult task, as becomes clear from the twenty or so conspiracies and revolts between 1602 and 1674. Richelieu dismissed many governors, but did not undertake a generalised attack upon the upper nobility as such. Nor did he attempt to undermine the importance of the governorships. He faced consistent difficulty with three of the most prominent of the great nobles: Gaston, Louis XIII's brother and heir presumptive until 1638, whose conspiracies culminated in an abortive rebellion in 1631 and an invasion of France the following year (docs. 184, 185, 188); the comte de Soissons, who led an invasion in 1641, won the battle of La Marfée – but accidently blew out his brains in the aftermath of victory (docs. 198, 199); and the duc de Bouillon, who participated in the rebellion in 1641 and lost his principality and fortress of Sedan the following year as a result of participation in the Cinq-Mars conspiracy, in which Gaston was also heavily implicated (docs. 200, 202, 203).

After 1643, the new Regency government could not afford to deal out its patronage in the high-handed manner of Richelieu. A number of the politically proscribed under Richelieu regained their positions during the first years of Mazarin's ministry. The policy of reconciliation was unsuccessful, however. Richelieu had dealt severely with so many nobles that there was a plethora of competing claims. By 1648, it was clear that Mazarin had undone some of Richelieu's achievements in quelling the unreliable magnates while failing to substitute any coherent alternative policy. The outbreak of civil war in January 1649 saw those whose claims Mazarin had been unable to satisfy on the side of the Fronde, though they were clearly divided (docs. 210, 212). Conty, governor of Champagne, and Longueville, governor of Normandy, turned against the government in the hope of extending their local power and their influence at the centre of political affairs. However, Gaston and the young Condé, who had only entered the council of state in 1647, sided with Mazarin. The chief minister was thus able to outmanœuvre his opponents, and elude demands for his exile and the signature of peace with Spain (doc. 213). Condé's own demands for rewards rapidly became exorbitant, however, and by the autumn of 1649 he was in effect seeking to impose himself as chief minister; a second round of demands in January 1650 precipitated his arrest, together with that of Conty and Longueville (docs. 217, 218). There is some evidence that Condé was opposed to the war against Spain by this date, which was the reason adduced for his arrest by his supporters (docs. 216, 219). The conditions on which Mazarin should have insisted for the release of the princes in February 1651, but mistakenly did not, make it clear that it was the princes' growing power in their provinces which the ministers most feared (doc. 221, clauses 4 and 6).

After the release of Condé, and Mazarin's self-imposed exile, there was no figure in France powerful enough to stop Condé using force to achieve his ambitions (docs. 225, 228, 229). The stage was set for Mazarin's invasion in December 1651, at the head of a force of German mercenaries. This led Gaston to throw in his lot with Condé, ostensibly for reasons of high principle, especially peace with Spain (doc. 231). But when Gaston made his peace, and Condé was forced into exile, and service to a foreign prince that lasted until the Peace of the Pyrenees, the government was able to reject the demand for peace with Spain (doc. 233). When Condé finally returned to France, it was after peace with Spain and on Mazarin's terms: he had to abandon his alliance with Spain as a prior condition of his restoration.

It was the misfortune of France during the Fronde to suffer from the rival ambitions of a Condé and a Mazarin. This was a recipe for civil war. If the Fronde was in part a personal rivalry, it was also an expression of aristocratic opposition to a form of government by a *parvenu* chief minister. To understand the Fronde of the nobles, the way in which the political process operated has to be seen in perspective – against the background and issues of previous aristocratic revolts, and through an appraisal of noble aspirations in which there was no convenient dividing-line between issues of principle and matters of self-interest. It should not be assumed that the nobles were motivated exclusively by self-interest during the Fronde. Many nobles seem to have wanted peace with Spain, yet they had no clear idea how to achieve this objective. Some of them wanted to replace the rule of a chief minister by a formal regency council, perhaps as a temporary measure until the King reached the age of sixteen (doc. 223). Above all, they seem to have assumed that if more great nobles participated in government, this would somehow solve the ills from which France was suffering. It is doubtful whether this was true: the nobles did not co-operate well during the Fronde. Marillac had seen that great nobles had to be educated into the tasks of government and the traditions of loyalty (doc. 187). The exclusion of the great nobility from government had been the work of Henri IV, not Louis XIII. Over two generations, this exclusion had become a self-fulfilling prophecy. It reinforced tendencies towards political naïvety, and above all, faction. The Fronde was important because it witnessed the last, desperate opposition of the French nobles to political change by means of armed rebellion. The nobles failed, and as a result, at the end of the civil war, the crown was left considerably stronger. In that sense, the 'absolutism' of Louis XIV was made possible by the achievements of Richelieu and Mazarin.

184. Writing signed by the King, the Queen Mother and Monsieur, Paris, 31 May 1626

Many false rumours have been spread of the discontent of Monsieur . . . He wishes to open his heart frankly to IIis Majesty so that the King may see the sincerity of his actions. He has full confidence in His Majesty's generosity, on which his fortune and happiness depends. He has promised to revere His Majesty not simply as brother but as father, King and sovereign lord. He is well aware of the division within the royal family, and would prefer death rather than to aggravate this dispute directly or indirectly, in any way whatsoever. He is resolved never to do other than support the King's interests and those of the State. He will have no dealings with persons, or enter any agreement, which could be prejudicial to the State or give offence to His Majesty. He wishes to subordinate his wishes and affections to those of His Majesty; he will always regard him as lawgiver and ruler of his actions. He undertakes that he will always advise His Majesty of any proposals or suggestions he receives from whatever quarter it may be. He will not conceal any words which might give offence to the King and his council . . .

(Source: Grillon, i. 344–6)

185. Considerations on the marriage of Monseigneur, the King's brother, 19 July 1626

To Monsieur the Cardinal de Richelieu.
Since the news of the proposed marriage of Monsieur to Mademoiselle de Montpensier has suddenly broken at court, the King's faithful

servants have all been astonished at the suddenness of the decision in an affair of such importance . . . His marriage could bring disorder to the kingdom without any likelihood of security or peace.

The day of Monsieur's marriage will see the court divided into cabals and the kingdom into factions. Everything is already disposed to such disunity. This tendency should be remedied, rather than encouraged . . . To marry him forthwith to Mademoiselle de Montpensier would be to make him too powerful too soon and at too young an age. In a word, it would run the risk of throwing France into the hands of the house of Lorraine. It would create a companion to the King, a master in the case of his having an heir before His Majesty . . . If Monsieur had children before him, it is certain that the King from then on would lose his authority and fall into the contempt of the great nobles and of all his people . . .

Another serious disadvantage in marrying Monsieur to Mademoiselle de Montpensier is that it will be very difficult to prevent the powerful house of Lorraine from controlling him, because of the large number of lords and ladies who are of this House, which will enlarge Monsieur's own entourage . . .

(Source: Grillon, i. 382–5. The espousal and marriage of Gaston to Mademoiselle de Montpensier took place on 5 August 1626)

186. Declaration of Monsieur de Vendôme, 16 January 1627

. . . Examining the faults which I know I committed in Brittany, I admit to Your Majesty that, with great care, I intrigued for, and sought out, the friendship of the *Parlement* of the province for no other reason than to prevail over my enemies and thus make myself a more considerable figure in the province.

I took the same care with regard to the nobility and the merchants. All of this was to put myself forward and increase my fortune. I do not doubt that such actions may legitimately have aroused some discontent on the part of Your Majesty. I further admit that when I visited the coast I demonstrated too much concern and affection for my province, although it must be said that I made this visit at the request of the Estates held at Ploermel that year . . .

(Source: Grillon, ii. 32–6)

187. Memorandum of Marillac to Richelieu, 24 July 1630

. . . It is necessary, in my opinion, to accustom the lords of the kingdom to the capacity and fidelity required for these tasks . . . If people are not employed in great offices, they will never be thought capable, and they will never become capable. The State will thus be deprived of great help and assistance.

Employment makes soldiers, captains and generals of armies; many will try to make themselves capable if they hope that they will be employed one day . . .

(Source: Gillon, v. 429–31)

188. Louis XIII to the provinces of his kingdom, 10 March 1631

. . . We were greatly shocked when we learnt that some of his[1] supporters had been negotiating on his behalf with ministers of several foreign powers, who hold our interests in little respect. He has sent representatives to foreign countries without informing us and without our permission. He has tried to make it appear to the towns and the people that we have tried to deprive him of his liberty. He has mobilised his guards with no official authority and quite unknown to us. His letters constitute a threat to our authority and suggest an evil intent on his part. He has incited other great nobles to leave the court, to follow him in rebellion, and to raise the provinces in which they hold governorships – but they have refused to listen to him.

He has assembled the nobility in his governorship,[2] although he has no authority to do this. Many people support him and are taking to arms. He has purchased arms and war materials. He has planned to seize bridges over the river Loire and has attempted to bring troops into Orléans, whose loyalty to us has been fully proven . . .

(Source: Mongrédien, pp. 212–14)

---

[1] Gaston's.
[2] Orléanais.

189. Marshal de Schomberg to Richelieu, 28 July 1632

I am in the greatest anxiety about the news of the rebellion of Monsieur de Montmorency. The courier from Marshal de la Force tells me that he has been greatly astonished and that, because his own army is small, he is unable to engage the enemy in Languedoc. I have sent him a courier immediately and told him that this is a great mistake. Monsieur de Montmorency may be lost, but we must still try to save the rest of the places which are not yet in his power. The people have need to be reassured by the presence of the army of the King: otherwise, fear and astonishment may lead them to do things which they would not otherwise allow to happen . . .

(Source: AAE France 802, fo. 286, 28 July 1632)

190. Marshal de Schomberg to Richelieu, 7 September 1632

My lord, this letter informs you that the good news continues . . . The army of the duke[3] lives in great necessity and many of his supporters in the province abandon him. The Spaniards still show no sign of invading, though I believe that they have been asked to do so. Since the news of the capture of Monsieur de Montmorency, Narbonne has reaffirmed its allegiance to the King, and I assure you that there is scarcely a small village which does not refuse entry to the army of Monsieur. The arrival of the King in Languedoc at this moment will promptly bring an end to this trouble . . .

(Source: *Histoire générale de Languedoc*, xiv. 1810. AAE France 803 fo. 23)

191. Bullion, finance minister, to Richelieu, 29 September 1632

. . . These people [of Languedoc] greatly need the King's presence. The character of the house of Montmorency has so impressed itself on them that they think the name of the King imaginary and entirely lack a sense of His Majesty's service. In my opinion, it is necessary to hold the Estates

---

[3] Of Orléans.

promptly in this place,[4] which adjoins several towns where the King's authority must be re-established . . .

(Source: AAE France 803, fo. 107)

192. Relation of what M. de Machault did in Languedoc after the arrival of the King until the end of February 1633

. . . His Majesty's authority and justice have been poorly recognised for a long time in the Vivarais, Velay, Cévennes and Gévaudan. Atrocious crimes have frequently been committed there for some years and have not been followed by due penalties and vigorous punishment according to the law. Those accused of such crimes use the natural advantages of the country to hold out against the King's authority and justice, withdrawing into fortresses, or leading revolts and rebellions. They finally demonstrated their pernicious designs on the recent occasion of rebellion . . .[5] His Majesty issued a commission on 28 September 1632 to the sieur Machault, councillor in his council, master of requests of his hôtel . . . to hold an ambulatory tribunal.[6] The [tribunal's] powers are to take cognisance of every crime, to transport themselves throughout the provinces in order to hear complaints made against persons of any status and condition. They are to investigate and prosecute those accused and to issue sentences without appeal. Their judgements are to be carried out notwithstanding opposition and appeals. They are to raze and demolish fortresses, walls, fortifications and houses of persons who participated in the recent rebellion or which have served as places of retreat for other crimes . . .

(Source: AAE France 807, fo. 30)

193. Commission of intendant in the province of Champagne to Isaac de Laffemas, 6 February 1633

. . . We commission you, order you and establish you by these present letters to carry out the function of intendant of justice, police and finance

---

[4] Béziers.
[5] The Montmorency rebellion.
[6] *Chambre de grands jours.*

in our armies and towns of the province of Champagne, Metz, Toul, Verdun and other places in our obedience and protection and wherever our armies are situated. You are to investigate the intrigues and conspiracies against us, the attempts to seize fortresses, and to levy troops without our permission, the amassing or transportation of arms, the holding of illicit assemblies and other similar matters within the province. You are to issue decrees against those accused, and to prosecute them without appeal . . .

(Source: AG A[1] 14 no. 44)

194. Laffemas, intendant of Champagne, to Séguier, Keeper of the Seals, 6 March 1633

. . . I will not bore you with affairs on this occasion except to tell you that I have issued decrees for the arrest of 34 gentlemen and others who have levied troops against the King, and I am ready to issue decrees against eight more, who cause much trouble in this province. Since most of them are absent, and have had to be sentenced in their absence, I would be very grateful if you would let me know what the King wishes to be done with their houses, particularly with regard to those which have served as places for assembly. The people expect to see them made an example to deter others from following suit. I have only just begun to disentangle this business . . .

(Source: Mousnier, i. 197–8)

195. Laffemas, intendant of Champagne, to Séguier, 20 March 1633

I am prosecuting many gentlemen of good birth, who are convicted of having levied troops, ransomed the King's subjects and carried arms against His Majesty in the defeat of Castelnaudary (where the duc de Montmorency was taken prisoner) . . . I have already issued more than 50 arrest warrants, which astonishes the whole province. I am hopeful that I have undertaken such strong investigations that the necessary evidence will not be lacking . . . You will learn from others in time what my presence has meant to those who could not defend themselves from the oppression of great nobles . . .

(Source: Mousnier, i. 198–200)

196. Humbert de Chaponay and Guérin, commissioners for the regulation of the *taille* at Lyon, to Séguier, 24 October 1634

... The power which the King has given us by his letters patent and separate instructions sent to us has obliged us to order the investigation of noble titles, to distinguish between the true nobles, exempted persons and privileged persons, and those who usurp these titles or have lost this status. We find plenty of people in this *généralité*, my lord, who usurp the title of noble, baron, viscount, count and marquis without any basis whatsoever, and who have no letters patent duly verified in the sovereign courts ... Such usurpers of nobility nearly all have ancestors who were in the third estate and they have never carried arms for the King's service. Others have farmed land, or continue to farm land directly or indirectly. The wealth of others is ignoble, arising from the sale of goods and mercantile activities at fairs and markets. They carry out ignoble acts which diminishes the dignity of nobility and oppresses the other subjects of the King who pay taxes. A good number of these usurpers have been found to have either changed their names or coats of arms, and claim to be members of families who are truly noble. Others call themselves chevaliers of the order of St. Michel, although many of them have been in trade or mechanic and unworthy activities, and have not carried arms for the King. Several of them present collated copies of their alleged titles, claiming that the originals were burnt or have been lost in the past disorders. On the basis of such collated copies or the testimony of gentlemen who are their friends, they have obtained sentences from the *élus* which declare them noble. We wish to deal with these abuses, from which the third estate is greatly oppressed ... The usurpation of the title of noble has been carried to such an extreme in this *généralité* that it is only little people in the towns that do not assume a noble title or that of *écuyer* with heraldic arms ...

(Source: Mousnier, i. 238–41)

197. Memorandum of Simon Estancheau, seigneurial judge in the chatellenie of Brossac, to Richelieu, n.d. [September 1636]

... With regard to the inequity at parish level, it seems that this cannot be remedied without the establishment of the land tax, because the office-holders, the richest men, and those who hold most of the inhabitants under their thumb because of debts, will shift their tax burdens on to the poor people.

What is worse, an even greater abuse is that for some years gentlemen participate in the parish assessments, preventing the freedom of the assessors and ensuring that their share-croppers and clients are not assessed at the tax rates which they should carry. By intimidation and menaces, these gentlemen prevent their share-croppers, and others who make gifts to them, from having to become parish collectors, which brings a great oppression to the rest of the people. This will only be removed by establishing the land tax . . .

The pinnacle of affliction and misfortune for the people is that some lesser provincial gentry of only 2000 or 3000 *livres* of revenue, who wish to make themselves seigneurs, have taken to crime and every sort of oppression and tyranny against the poor people and their tenants to satisfy their ambition to enlarge their plots and other small landholdings. They do this at the expense of the lands of poor people, knocking down houses, cutting trees, and changing the direction of roads at their whim . . .

(Source: Bercé, ii. 746–9)

198. Considerations [on a settlement with Monsieur the Comte de Soissons, 8 July 1637]

Two principal considerations could bring the King to accord to Monsieur the Count what he demands.

The first is that with vigilance no inconvenience will result to the state this summer from any graces accorded to the sieur Count.

The second is that by this means we could escape from present embarrassment and unfortunate consequences for the future. The name of the sieur Count joined to the enemy forces will give not a little encouragement to those who are disaffected within the Kingdom. The sieur Count, seeing his fortunes dashed forever in France, will give great support to the enemy to attempt all they can against the Kingdom.

At the very least, his alliance with the enemy could delay the peace unless we wish it on conditions which are shameful and altogether ruinous to France, and which would give him and the Queen Mother a power base. This would end the war only to restart it immediately afterwards . . .

(Source: AAE France 827, fo. 213)

199. Manifesto of rebellion of Messieurs the Comte de Soissons, the duc de Guise and the duc de Bouillon, July 1641

The Count of Soissons, the duc de Bouillon and other princes and officers of the crown are united to demand a general peace, and principally peace for France. They declare that the zeal which they have for the King's service and the good of his state forces them to take the only remedy which the violence and artifice of Cardinal de Richelieu leaves them, so that the King may hear what is happening in the conduct of his affairs . . . They wish to re-establish laws which have been overturned and to restore the immunities, rights and privileges of provinces, towns and individuals which have been violated. They wish to secure order in the King's councils and in the conduct of military and financial affairs. They seek to secure liberty for those who are held prisoner by an oppressive power, the return to France for those exiled abroad, and the restitution of lands and offices for those who have had them confiscated. They seek honour for those defamed; respect for ecclesiastics and nobles; dignity for the *Parlements*; wealth for those engaged in commerce; a discharge of taxes for the poor people; good relations with foreigners; and peace for all. To this end, they have taken the expedient which they judged appropriate of allying with those neighbouring powers which seek peace, a peace which cannot last if it is not with honour. They have received from the Emperor and the King of Spain all the assurances needed to satisfy the most scrupulous Frenchmen, as they will demonstrate in due course by treaties and above all by actions. Anyone who opposes their arms, counsels or otherwise opposes this great design, will be treated as an enemy of the King and of the Kingdom. Those who wish to live peaceably will be spared. All provinces, towns and individuals who join the cause will receive the promised assistance in this change hoped for from the justice of God and the King. They protest that they will never lay down their arms until everyone has received their fair entitlement.

(Source: BN Ms. fr. 17,331, fo. 46)

200. Louis XIII to Gaston d'Orléans, 3 August 1642

. . . I would have hoped with good heart that you would have had enough prudence and circumspection not to negotiate with my enemies against me and my state . . . and, moreover, against your birth and what you owe me.[7] If I did not have more natural goodness for you than you have affection for my person and the interests of France you would feel the consequences of your fifth fault. But I shall be very glad for everyone to see that there was no justification for you to enter cabals and treaties against my state, since I mean to use my goodness towards you after I have learnt fully about your cabals from your confession . . .

(Source: BN Ms. fr. 3843, fo. 62)

201. Ruling on the *taille*, 22 August 1642

VII. The intendant, *trésoriers de France* and officers will tax on their own authority office-holders and privileged persons whose exemptions have been revoked by the edict of November 1640. They will draw up a list which will be placed in the hands of the receiver, or the clerk receiving the revenues,[8] in order to make the levy. They are also to impose taxes on those powerful inhabitants of parishes who on their own authority, or by intimidating others, have gained exemption or who are taxed at very low rates in comparison with their capacity to pay. They will impose taxes on the farmers of gentlemen and seigneurs of the parishes, who up to now have paid little or no tax as a result of exemption gained on the authority of their masters. The farmers and powerful members of the parishes are to be taxed in regard not merely to their capacity to pay but also to what they should have paid in preceding years – this to be at the discharge of the poor, in order that they receive some alleviation, as His Majesty intends . . .

XV. His Majesty very expressly prohibits all gentlemen and seigneurs of parishes, ecclesiastics and others from hindering in any way in their parishes and elsewhere the levy of taxes, or preventing their farmers from paying their taxes. This is on penalty of being declared commoners and paying in their own names the *taille* and other taxes of the parishes, for which their wealth and possessions will be seized. His Majesty orders the sieur intendant . . . to prosecute those who are accused of hindering the levy . . .

(Source: AN AD + 271)

---

[7] Gaston signed the Cinq–Mars treaty with Philip IV on 3 March 1642.
[8] On behalf of a financier.

202. Amnesty for the duc de Bouillon, 17 September 1642

. . . My lord Cardinal de Richelieu not being fit enough to sign a promise for the liberty of Monsieur the duc de Bouillon, in accordance with the powers given to him by the King, I have been given charge to do it, and to sign it in the name of His Eminence. I promise to the sieur duc de Bouillon that as soon as the town and castle of Sedan have been placed in His Majesty's hands all the necessary orders will be given to release the sieur duc de Bouillon from the castle of Pierre en Cize so that he may go to Roussy, Turenne or one of his other residences as he so wishes.
At Lyon, 17 September 1642.   Cardinal Mazarin.

(Source: BN Ms. fr. 17,331, fo. 106v.)

203. Important declaration of my lord the duc de Bouillon on the violence done to him by Cardinal de Richelieu and on the innocence of his actions, 10 January 1643

. . . Far from having signed a treaty with the enemies of the King and of the State, I had on the contrary offered my life, my wealth, and my fortress to the Queen and to Monsieur. But I wished to prevent the subversion of the kingdom if Monsieur the Cardinal de Richelieu sought to seize the Regency . . .[9] All the fortresses in the kingdom and all the money of the kingdom were in his hands, and all the armies were commanded by his relatives and his clients . . .

Against my wishes and intention, I was constrained by force in order to save my life to write the letter to Cardinal de Richelieu by which I gave up Sedan to the King . . .

(Source: AN Musée AE II 835 [K 114b no. 42/12])

204. Decree of the council of finance, 18 November 1643

. . . The *taille* in most of the parishes in the *élections* of this kingdom and particularly in that of Falaise in the *généralité* of Alençon is in arrears because gentlemen protect these parishes, reclaiming cattle that is seized

---

[9] In the event of the King's death.

168

for non-payment of His Majesty's taxes, attacking and beating up the bailiffs and sergeants employed in recovering them, and preventing by their violence any distraint of goods being carried out against their parishes. [Article 18 of the ruling of 16 April 1643 is restated. His Majesty] expressly prohibits all gentlemen, seigneurs of parishes, ecclesiastics, troop commanders and all others persons from causing any difficulty in the assessment, levy and recovery of His Majesty's taxes, and from reclaiming cattle seized from their farmers or other persons in the parishes. They are not to prevent individuals from paying their taxes, whether directly or indirectly, on penalty of being declared commoners, and paying in their private names the *taille*, subsistence and other taxes of the parishes for which their wealth and possessions will be seized. His Majesty enjoins the intendants of the provinces to publicise this decree and enforce it, and to prosecute offenders without appeal.

(Source: AN E 184d, fo. 118)

205. Corberon, intendant at Limoges, to Séguier, 26 August 1644

. . . They[10] talk so much about their power and with such disdain for the authority of those who are in the province[11] that it is not difficult for the populace to believe that with the protection of the sieur and dame de Pompadour, no-one will dare take any action against them. As a result of this confidence, the inhabitants of these lands have paid their taxes badly since 1641 and have scarcely met a third of the sums that have been demanded . . . It is rumoured in the parishes that if the troops attempt to enter them, and their commanders are even told this, then there can be no guarantee for their safety and their lives will be in danger. The protection of Madame de Pompadour is even extended to lands which do not belong to her . . . The remedy, in my opinion, would be for the King to write a letter to the sieur and dame de Pompadour, ordering them to pay half the arrears of their parishes for 1642 and 1643 within a month or such other time-limit as is seen fit. They should be made to understand that if this is not done, His Majesty will expressly order the troops in the province to enter their lands and live on them at discretion until the taxes have been paid. This order should be so precise that neither the troops nor I myself could refuse to enforce it . . .

(Source: Mousnier, i. 640–3)

[10] Monsieur and Madame de Pompadour. Pompadour was lieutenant-general in Limousin and Séguier's brother-in-law.
[11] On the King's service.

206. Lauzon, intendant of Guyenne, to Séguier, 13 December 1644

My lord,

The affairs of the King have obliged me to return to Périgord, where the protection given by gentlemen to their share-croppers, their parishes and their friends causes a great delay in the levy of the King's taxes. They hold assemblies, try to frighten off tax-collectors and menace them. There are rebellions, but since I have not allowed the company of fusiliers to be divided they do not dare to attack a company marching as a body which provides a good guard. . . .

The small difficulties which I encounter here do not merit my importuning you nor writing to you about the murders which are committed daily. This is not a new development in Périgord. After the peace there should be an ambulatory tribunal[12] to purge this province of undesirables and gentlemen who give refuge to all sorts of criminals in their fortified residences and which need an army to remove them . . .

(Source: Mousnier, i. 666)

207. Favier du Boulay, intendant at Alençon, to Séguier, 1 February 1645

. . . On my travels[13] I learnt that there had been an assembly of 60 or 80 gentlemen at St. Pierre-sur-Dive in the *élection* of Falaise . . . concerning the distraint of their cattle, and to discuss the coercion of their farmers for the payment of taxes . . . and that we are trying to make the farmers pay the *taille* before they pay their rents. I thought I should advise you of this because it could become an important matter. It is true that there is no person of great status involved, but they have tried to draw such people in . . . Monsieur de Longueville has promised to support them in defending their privileges but has told them that he does not approve of assemblies. He has also said that they are demanding so many things that they cannot all be accorded. He considers that they should cease their complaints against those employed in levying the King's taxes . . .

(Source: Mousnier, ii. 718–20)

---

[12] *Grands Jours.*
[13] To see Longueville, governor of Normandy.

208. Decree of the council of finance, 29 April 1645

[Request of Léonard de Baillon, chevalier seigneur de Jons] . . . The baron de la Salle, his son, having been informed that the sieur de Lozières, councillor of the King in his council, intendant in Dauphiné, had sent on Easter Friday the company of fusiliers which he commands in the province to be billeted on the land of Jons. The sieur baron de La Salle travelled from Lyon to Jons when he heard from the commander that he intended to take billets there. At the same time, he offered to pay the amount of tax which the inhabitants owed. Moreover, he offered the lieutenant commanding the company that he could take his residence at the home of the plaintiff, and that the subsistence of the company would be paid. The lieutenant simply replied that he had orders only to take billets, which he intended to carry out. At the arrival of the fusiliers, the sieur de la Salle had the parish bells sounded to assemble the inhabitants, who are separated in several small hamlets, to ascertain from them whether they owed any taxes. The fusiliers thought that the tocsin was being sounded against them and withdrew without taking billets. [Legal procedures were begun by the intendant] . . . There was no reason to take procedures against the baron de la Salle, without any prior demand for payment being made, and despite all the offers to pay . . . [The council orders an investigation of the intendant's procedures].

(Source: AN E 201b, fo. 342)

209. Decree of the council of finance, 19 December 1647

. . . Although the method of taxing the well-to-do is the most just and legitimate measure that can be envisaged, nevertheless certain of the sieurs intendants of justice, and particularly those of the province of Normandy[14] find themselves persecuted by continual solicitations on the part of provincial gentlemen and office-holders who use all their favour, credit and authority to prevent the levy of taxes on the authority of the said intendants. As a result the intendants fail to carry out the rulings. The nobles and office-holders are thus left with the power and credit to tax their farmers as they see fit, having the tax rolls for the *taille*

---

[14] There were three intendants in Normandy, for the *généralités* of Alençon, Caen and Rouen.

drawn up in their residences, and intimidating the impoverished collectors of the *taille* . . .

(Source: AN E 227c, fo. 647)

210. Oath of union between the leaders of the Fronde of the nobles, 18 January 1649

We swear on the Holy Gospels to keep inviolably the word which we have given to one another, to do everything necessary to carry out the decree of the *Parlement* by which Cardinal Mazarin has been declared a disturber of the public peace,[15] to prevent the violent action which he has planned against the *Parlement* and the city of Paris, and generally do whatever is judged useful by the *Parlement* for the good of the King's service. Further to this, we promise that we will not listen to any proposal for a settlement until Cardinal Mazarin has been exiled permanently from the kingdom. We will render a true account of everything proposed by the royal court, and will not accept any conditions except on the authority and with the advice of the *Parlement* . . .

[Note from Molé's memoirs:] Copy of the union established between our generals, of which Monsieur the Coadjuteur[16] showed me the original. He wanted me to have it registered,[17] but I told him that I opposed this.

(Source: Feillet et al., iii. 636–7. BN Ms. fr. 3854, fo. 1. 500 Colbert 3, fo. 44)

211. *Cahier* of remonstrances of the nobility of the Angoumois to the projected meeting of the Estates General, 22–24 February 1649

2. In as much as the nobility has been frequently vexed by an infinite number of commissions and taxes which have no other basis than decrees of the council sought and obtained by financiers, His Majesty is very humbly requested that his declaration of October last should be carefully implemented with regard to the alleviations of his people. No edicts, declarations or commissions should be carried out before they

---

[15] A decree issued by the *Parlement* of Paris on 8 January 1649.
[16] Retz.
[17] In the *Parlement*.

have first been duly verified in his *Parlements* and other sovereign courts which have cognisance. And since it has pleased His Majesty to revoke the intendants of the provinces, he is requested not to re-establish them, but to abolish them permanently, since they are a great expense to the state and a burden on all the orders of the kingdom.

3. The nobility in provinces where there are no provincial estates are deprived of the means of presenting their complaints about matters prejudicial to their order . . . The King is very humbly requested to permit the nobility of provinces where there are no estates to nominate syndics[18] triennially in the presence of the governor of the province, who in the name of His Majesty will choose one of three names suggested by the nobility. These men will receive the complaints of individuals and act in the name of the whole nobility . . . [The governor will take] all necessary precautions so that nothing happens which is prejudicial to the King's service and public tranquillity . . .

4. The lack of a legitimate method of presenting grievances has resulted in the nobility of this province suffering many offences and injustices from the officers of the *présidiaux* to the prejudice of the prerogatives and advantages of being born a gentleman. These officials have wanted to take precedence in church festivals, which results in an insupportable shame and disgrace to the nobility, who can obtain no justice from the *Parlement* because of the common interests of the robe . . .

5. . . . His Majesty is very humbly requested that, in accordance with royal promises, the *taille* be reduced as much as possible. It should no longer be contracted to financiers, but levied by the traditional methods before the intendants and financiers were involved . . . The people are so ruined, and the nobility so discomforted because they are not paid their rents, that His Majesty's service is hindered: gentlemen lack the means to equip themselves for service. His Majesty is very humbly requested to commission as soon as possible a gentleman in each province, together with a judicial official, who should be men of recognised probity and ability, to investigate the levies of the intendants and financiers in excess of the taxes that have been ordered, and the peculation and malversation committed by them and fusiliers, clerks, bailiffs and other officials who have acted on their orders. They will obtain from restitution sufficient money not only to pay the cost of the commissioners but also to assist His Majesty's affairs and the necessities of the province.

---

[18] Agents or representatives of the nobility.

8. ... The immense wealth of an infinite number of financiers surpasses in revenues the greatest and most illustrious families of the kingdom and equals that of a prince. The King is humbly requested that a better order should be established in his financial administration in the future by the Estates which it has pleased His Majesty to assemble. The Estates should nominate and choose a sufficient number of persons of recognised probity and ability who are above suspicion of being partners of the tax-contractors and financiers in order to form an extraordinary financial tribunal[19] to which His Majesty is requested to give all the necessary powers to investigate the abuses and malversation of all the tax-contractors, sub-contractors, *partisans*, financiers and others ...

9. The Estates should be told, as earlier ones have been, that the nobility receives a notable prejudice from venality of offices, whether the offices are either in the king's household, or in the areas of war and justice. Entry to these offices has become practically impossible because of their excessive price. It is very damaging for nobles to be deprived of offices which formerly they exercised, and to see them in the hands of people of low birth, without merit and without ability. His Majesty is very humbly requested to bring about the reform to his state by abolishing venality ...

18. Although the nobility is exempt from the payment of *taille* and other subsidies, nevertheless contrary to their rights and privileges, they are indirectly forced to pay them in that their farmers are subject to taxation for alleged profits on their farms. This prevents the farmers from paying a just rent and diminishes the value of the lease, which falls upon the nobility. In order to prevent this, they humbly request His Majesty to order that in future farmers shall not be included in the *taille* and other subsidies for the profit of their farms ...

(Source: Mousnier, Durand, Labatut, pp. 78–91)

212. Second union of the *Frondeur* nobles, 25 March 1649

There are rumours circulating which seek to weaken us by promoting division. These encourage people to believe that we are more concerned with our private interest than the public interest and the King's service for which we originally united. Wishing to defend our honour which these calumnies attack, we declare that we neither wish nor intend in any

---

[19] *Chambre de justice.*

manner whatsoever to enter separate negotiations, and that on the contrary we are engaged to remain on all matters firmly allied under the authority of, and in union with, the *Parlement* of Paris. We protest that we intend to remain in this sentiment . . .

> (Source: Feillet et al., iii. 637–8. BN Ms. fr. 3854, fo. 77)

213. Memorandum of Conty, generalissimo of the *Frondeur* nobles, 25 March 1649

Messieurs the deputies[20] must insist with firmness[21] on the proposal for the exiling of Cardinal Mazarin . . . As for the point concerning a general peace,[22] which is our objective, Messieurs the deputies are to insist firmly on it, and that Monsieur de Longueville be appointed with deputies of the *Parlement* for this task. They will strongly request after this that the place and time of the negotiations be settled so that Monsieur de Longueville and Messieurs the deputies can go there.

> (Source: BN Ms. fr. 3854, fo. 73)

214. Sève, intendant of Provence, to Séguier, 17 April 1649

Monsieur,

I have already had the honour to give you an account of the state of this province and the seeds of division which I see developing every day. The party of the *Parlement* has a white and red livery. There is a more considerable sign in that Monsieur the Comte de Carcès[23] has always been clean shaven apart from wearing a moustache: everybody has followed suit and only Monsieur the president de la Roque and three or four councillors in the *Parlement* have not shaven off their beards. The party of Monsieur the comte d'Alais[24] wears blue ribbons, though unofficially . . .

You will have learnt, my lord, that the gentlemen supported the

---

[20] Of the nobles.
[21] At the Rueil negotiations.
[22] With Spain.
[23] Lieutenant-general in Provence and one of the few nobles of the sword to side with the *Parlement*. He sought a greater role for himself in the provincial government.
[24] The governor.

King's service during our detention.[25] Very few of the body of the nobility have detached themselves from it, and those that have are not in the first rank. These gentlemen have proposed a union and league for their common defence against the *Parlement* of Aix. The act of union is drawn up and signed by many of them. I have stopped their actions by encouraging their hopes of a general transfer of lawsuits away from Aix . . . There will not remain, my lord, any authority for the King in the province other than that which the *Parlement* is prepared to allow. It will thus retain the means of avenging itself on those who did not defend its interests unless these cases are transferred . . .

My lord, I see that everything now is a matter of dispute. I have no credit with Messieurs of the *Parlement*, and thus am useless as an instrument of mediation. It is necessary that a more effective hand than mine be employed; this cannot be too soon . . .

(Source: Mousnier, ii. 913–15)

215. Voyer d'Argenson, royal commissioner in Guyenne, to Séguier, 9 July 1649

. . . The rebels have asserted with great boldness that Monsieur the prince[26] will come to their assistance. Subsequently they have talked in the same way of Monsieur de Beaufort and Monsieur the Maréchal de Turenne.[27] At the moment they are convincing the people that Monsieur the Maréchal de La Motte will soon be theirs. The bourgeois of Bordeaux are at the moment greatly disillusioned and mock such rumours, but there are still partisans of the cabal who lend credence to them. It is necessary to remove the causes which produce these results. Above all, my lord, any talk of intendants or loan contracts on the *taille* must be stopped, because this would set everything aflame. There are other ways of ensuring that the people pay their taxes, which will alleviate them and give them justice. These methods must be adopted . . . I trust that you will not think that I argue in this way about intendants to prevent one from being sent to this province. I have no particular wish to remain here. I have already asked for my recall and hope to leave once the affairs of Bordeaux are settled . . .

(Source: Mousnier, ii. 947–9)

[25] The governor and the intendant were arrested by a rebellious mob, led by members of the *Parlement* of Aix, on 20 January 1649.

[26] Condé, who at this time had not broken with the government.

[27] Both of whom had sided with the Fronde in the rebellion of Paris between January and March 1649.

216. Letter of Guy Patin, a Parisian commentator, 24 September 1649

. . . It is said that Monsieur the prince demands three things:

1. Instead of Mazarin, a council of six great men of state should be established which will put the affairs of France into good order.

2. That an investigation be held of all those who have managed and stolen the King's finances since 1642.

3. That those who have prevented a general peace[28] in the last three years should be punished. Gaston still adheres to the party of Mazarin, which restrains and weakens the party of Monsieur the Prince. Monsieur de Longueville has arrived which could well strengthen it . . . It is said that Monsieur the first president of the *Parlement*[29] has spoken today strongly against Mazarin, and is apparently in Monsieur the prince's party although he has always been his enemy . . .

(Source: Thérive, pp. 155–7)

217. Letter written in the hand of Cardinal Mazarin to [. . .] announcing that he has counselled the Queen Regent to give the prince of Condé influence in the affairs of government, 2 October 1649

The Queen always considers matters which could contribute towards the King's service during her Regency, and for various reasons believes that nothing would be more appropriate than the establishment of a perfect understanding between Monsieur the prince and myself . . . Her Majesty has determined that I should promise (as I do at her wish and on her order) that no governorships, whether of provinces or fortresses, shall be filled, nor offices of the crown, principal offices in the King's household, in the army, and embassies, without first asking the opinion of Monsieur the prince; that no person should be exiled from court without similarly asking his opinion; and that no resolution on any important matter concerning the state should be taken without similarly asking his opinion. When Monsieur the prince proposes persons whom he considers capable of filling these offices, His Majesty will pay particular attention to them. In addition, I promise him my complete

---

[28] With Spain.
[29] Molé.

friendship, and that I shall serve him in matters of state and his own interests towards others and against others if necessary. In order to demonstrate this at the outset, I promise my sieur the prince not to marry my nephew or any of my nieces without having first settled the matter with him. I sign this document in all sincerity. Paris, 2 October 1649.

(Source: AN K 118a, no. 17 [AE II 843])

218. Document written by Cardinal Mazarin for Monsieur the prince two days before his arrest, 16 January 1650

I promise Monsieur the prince at the King's pleasure and at the command of the Queen Regent his mother, that I will never depart from his interests and that I will be attached to him and not other people and if need be against other people. I ask His Highness to regard me as his very humble servant and to favour me with his protection, which I shall seek to merit with the obedience he should be able to expect from me. I have signed this in the presence and at the command of the Queen.

(Source: BN Dupuy 775, fo. 122)

219. Union of the two Frondes, 30 January 1651

We, the undersigned, recognise from experience the prejudice which the King and the State receive from the detention of Messieurs the princes of Condé and of Conty and the duc de Longueville . . . We consider that we could do nothing more advantageous or useful for the public than to unite in order to halt, by all legitimate means possible, the oppression of these three princes, who have been arrested and held prisoner against the laws of the Kingdom . . . Cardinal Mazarin is notoriously the author of their detention, and the cause of the disorders which have preceded and followed it. He arrested them in order to delay a general peace, and by their arrest hoped further to secure the authority that he had usurped during the Regency. His conduct exposes France to the misfortunes which foreign and civil war can cause a State exhausted of men and money, and there can be no hope of seeing an end to war while he remains in government. We consider it necessary to obtain his exile from their Majesties in order to establish peace in the Kingdom and peace abroad . . .

(Source: Feillet et al., iii. 549–56

220. Le Tellier to Mazarin, 7 February 1651

... The assembly of the nobility which is held by permission of His Royal Highness[30] continues to grow every day. Today the *Parlement*[31] resolved to hold an assembly of the chambers to resolve on what should be done to halt this meeting of the nobility ...

(Source: AAE France 874, fo. 30)

221. Conditions for the release of the princes, 10 February 1651

Articles and conditions under which the King, with the advice of the Queen Regent his mother, and Monsieur the duc d'Orléans, wishes and understands that Messieurs the princes of Condé and Conty and the duc de Longueville are to be released from the citadel of Le Havre where they are presently held, without any delay once they have submitted to them and signed them.

1. Messieurs the princes and the duc de Longueville declare that they have not made any alliance, treaty or association, either within the Kingdom or abroad, against the service of their Majesties. If any of their relatives and friends have done so in their name, they declare that they disavow them and renounce such treaties ...

3. The princes may not return to the governorship of the fortresses they held at the time of their arrest until four years after the king's majority.[32]

4. The duc de Longueville will resign into the hands of His Majesty the governorship of Normandy, together with all the fortresses of the province of which he was captain and governor at the time of his arrest. His Majesty promises to give him the governorship of Guyenne if the comte d'Alais is prepared to resign it, or Provence, at the choice and option of His Majesty on the same conditions of expectancy which he had for the governorship of Normandy, immediately and without delay. He will also indemnify him for the costs for the château of Dieppe while he was governor of Normandy ...

---

[30] Gaston.
[31] Of Paris.
[32] I.e. September 1655.

6. The princes may not enter their governorships of Burgundy, Champagne and Berry until two years after the king's majority.[33] Nevertheless, they will enjoy all the honours, authority, rights, emoluments and salaries belonging to the governorships and will carry out the functions as they did before their detention. For the governorship of the fortresses, they will only enjoy the emoluments of captain and governor . . .

(Source: Feillet, p. 276 n.1. Eighteenth-century copy at BN n.a.f. 7806 fo. 184)

222. Le Tellier to Mazarin, 23 March 1651

The assembly of the nobility continues and strengthens as a result of the arrival of deputies sent from the provinces following requests from Paris . . . In order to halt this assembly it has been proposed . . . that the Estates General should be convened at Tours on 1st October . . .[34] Subsequently a command was sent to the assembly of the nobility to disperse . . . It refused to do so, on the grounds that it wanted the Estates General convened in the month of August . . .[35]

(Source: AAE France 874, fos. 175v–176r.)

223. Le Tellier to Mazarin, 21 April 1651

. . . Since the changes lately arrived at the Court,[36] the Queen is more powerful than she was and many people rally around her . . . Monsieur Colbert[37] tries to unravel Your Eminence's private interests and there is hardly a day when we do not confer together . . . It has been resolved to propose at the meeting of the Estates General that a council should be established for the first four years of the majority . . . It is certain that these Estates can be advantageous neither for His Royal Highness[38] nor for Monsieur the prince and that . . . they should not be refused, but rather eluded or deferred.

(Source: AAE France 874, fo. 286)

---

[33] I.e. September 1653.
[34] I.e. after the declaration of the king's majority.
[35] I.e. before the declaration of the king's majority.
[36] Molé was appointed Keeper of the Seals on 3 April, at Condé's insistence, but held office only until 13 April because Gaston required his dismissal.
[37] Mazarin's intendant of his household.
[38] Gaston.

224. Anonymous memorandum to Mazarin, 28 May 1651

. . . The *Parlement* of Paris is hostile to these changes of governors,[39] the great disadvantage of which is foreseen. The decision which has been made with regard to Guyenne has shocked everybody and not just the *Parlement*. This has renewed the hatred of Monsieur the prince, whose ambitions are greatly feared. It is thought that he wishes to distance himself from the King and to fortify himself against his power . . . and that he wants to gain the support of the Gascons by suppressing the *élus* and making Guyenne once more a *pays d'états*,[40] from which he would gain great advantages, not least 7 or 800 000 *livres* a year in gratifications from the estates of the province . . .

(Source: AAE France 875, fo. 106 ff.)

225. Anonymous memorandum to Mazarin, 8 July 1651

. . . Those who speak here on behalf of Monsieur the Prince wish to frighten us by saying that there can be no doubt that if he is not contented he will start a furious civil war, particularly if Monsieur d'Orléans is not on his side, in order to be the leader of the party. However, those who know his mind consider that he will always be restrained by consideration for his great wealth. The worst he may do is to withdraw to Guyenne with considerable forces, act as sovereign there, and not return to court. He spreads rumours that everything he does is to keep Monsieur the Cardinal out of the kingdom. But everybody says openly that it is rather to stir up trouble, in order to gain Provence and the fortresses that he wants in Guyenne, all his actions being for his private interest . . .

(Source: AAE France 876, fo. 66, 67v.)

---

[39] On 16 May, Condé secured appointment as governor of Guyenne, exchanging his governorship of Burgundy with the duc d'Epernon.
[40] Henri IV had established *élections* in Guyenne in 1603.

226. List of grievances of the nobility of Champagne, and particularly those of the *bailliage* of Troyes, and remonstrances to His Majesty at the Estates in 1651, 31 July 1651

23. . . . Your Majesty is asked to listen to a general complaint of the whole of France touching venality and the excessive price of judicial and financial offices, which is the cause of the great corruption found in those who exercise them . . . The cause of this immense price of offices is that enemy of the state, the annual right or *paulette*, which in the manner of a cancer, gnaws away at all the families of this kingdom. The nobility humbly requests His Majesty to revoke it immediately, and never to re-establish it under any pretext . . . Fifty or sixty years ago a gentleman of the robe could call to public offices three or four of his children. Now this is impossible for a gentleman following the career of arms. Even if his children are capable of exercising such offices of the robe, he cannot place them there because of their excessive price. It is a monstrosity to see such a great superfluity and excessive price of offices in the state . . .

29. The gentlemen humbly request that offices in the army, and in His Majesty's household should no longer be venal, and that no expectancies on such offices should be given . . .

30. [Request that governorships of provinces, towns and fortresses should be triennial] . . . The nobility will not attach itself to the interests of the governors, since they will only be temporary appointments. Instead, they will remain firmly in the service and loyalty they owe His Majesty. It will also give His Majesty means of recompensing a greater number of his servants . . .

45. The monstrous and unbridled multitude of new and useless offices of justice and finance is notoriously a cause of the ruin of the Kingdom because of the great salaries and emoluments of their incumbents . . . His Majesty is humbly requested by his nobility to reduce the number of office-holders, both of justice and finance, to the number prescribed by the ordinance of the estates of Blois of 1579, reimbursing the value of the offices or suppressing them when they fall vacant . . .

65. That the farmers of gentlemen should not be overburdened with the *taille* because of lands which they rent from those who are not subject to

taxation, but only taxed because of the wealth that they possess in their own right, otherwise it is the gentlemen who pay the *taille*, which is unreasonable . . .

73. His Majesty is asked to consider that at the Estates General held at Tours under Charles VIII in 1483, the King remitted three-fifths of the *taille* to his people . . . If a similar grace were made now to his people, and he contented himself with 10 million[41] instead of 50, they would give him eternal blessings and he would justly acquire the title of father of his people.

74. His Majesty is also requested to abolish the use of secret expenses,[42] or at least to limit them to a certain sum, since they are an invention which lead to the dissipation of your finances and great thefts and pillage . . .

77. [The King is also requested] to heed the pleas of the common people without whose labours none of us could subsist with honour. They have been overburdened for the last forty years with so many levies of taxes and other inventions of the financiers. We request His Majesty to have pity on their extreme misery and to alleviate them by remitting the *taille* and other taxes which have been increased . . . returning them to the state they were in between 1610 and 1619, revoking edicts levied since that time . . . and other inventions of financiers who have gorged themselves on the blood of the people as a vampire does on that of children . . .

(Source: Mousnier, Durand, Labatut, pp. 134–54)

227. List of grievances of the nobility of Périgord to the Estates General called to meet at Tours on 8 September 1651

1. His Majesty is humbly requested to restore the customary rights and privileges of the nobility as enjoyed under previous kings.

2. The demesnes, mills and tenants of gentlemen should be exempt from the *taille* and other taxes.

---

[41] *Sic*: should be 20 million.
[42] *Comptants*.

3. The King is asked to restore the Estates of this province, as it was before the reign of Louis XII[43] and the establishment of *élections*.

4. So much abuse and confusion has arisen in the summoning of the nobility that His Majesty is implored to order that the ancient registers be produced and the nobility summoned according to its rank – as was practised under Francis I in 1533 . . .

6. Those who hold fiefs through acquisition but who do not possess noble rank may not enter the Estates, and the status of their fief should remain in abeyance until held by a nobleman . . .

9. Many people have assumed noble status in order to gain exemption from the *taille*, to the great detriment of the common people. May it please His Majesty to enforce the ordinance of Blois[44] on this subject, and to determine a date after which those who have acquired noble status, either through purchase or gift of the King, shall be deemed members of the third estate . . .

10. In all *Parlements* and in the lesser judicial courts an equal number of nobles and clerics should be summoned so that the first two estates may enjoy the same privilege.

11. The number of judicial offices in the same courts should be reduced to that of Louis XII's reign, as was ordered by King Charles IX at the Estates General of Orléans.[45]

13. That all the *élections* and other financial offices be abolished and returned to the situation during Louis XII's reign.

20. Since great wealth has suddenly been acquired by the bourgeoisie so that it is now no longer possible to distinguish between nobility and commoners, His Majesty is implored to issue a ruling to make a distinction as to their manner of dress. This was ordered by Philip the Fair,[46] who prohibited commoners from travelling by coach, from wearing green and grey clothes, and from wearing ermine and jewels.

[43] I.e. 1498–1515.
[44] 1579.
[45] 1560.
[46] 1285–1314.

21. All nobles who marry below their rank should be stripped of their noble status, and their children – who are only semi-nobles[47] – debarred from claiming equality with those who have conserved the purity of their rank. This is the practice in Venice and other republics, which thus avoid contamination of the nobility.

26. . . . Those who hold offices because of their money and who are of low status should not claim the privileges of their offices, which ought to be the mark and recompense of virtuous people, and not conferred on bankers and merchants.

29. All foreigners should be excluded from the management of affairs of State in conformity with the decrees of the *Parlement* of Paris.[48]

32. That gentlemen alone be provided with offices in the King's household and the King's guard in conformity with the ordinance of the Estates of Blois of Henri III,[49] article 259.

34. That no foreigner should be provided with governorships of provinces and fortresses in the Kingdom, or benefices, in conformity with the ordinance of Charles VII.

35. All those who hold office and are not of the status stipulated by the ordinances must relinquish their positions. Such offices should be filled by the King with capable people of the required rank as specified by the ordinance of the Estates General at Blois, article 255, which it will please the King to enforce.

(Source: Bercé, ii. 815–19)

228. Decree of the council of state, 1 October 1651

The King has been advised that Monsieur the prince of Condé and his supporters have attempted to seize the taxes of the general and particular receipts, as also the tax farms of His Majesty, in the provinces of Guyenne, Poitou, Saintonge, Angoumois and Aunis. His Majesty

---

[47] *Sic*: this was not legally true.
[48] An allusion to the decree of 8 August 1617.
[49] 1579.

wishes to prevent these taxes being used for purposes against his service and to conserve them for the expenses of the royal households and the army which His Majesty is to send to Guyenne . . .

(Source: AN E 249a, fo. 1)

229. Second decree of the council of state, 1 October 1651

The King sees with extreme displeasure that he cannot provide for the conservation of his state and the maintenance of the peace of the provinces of the Kingdom unless he opposes the armaments and preparations for war and the intrigues to divert his subjects from their obedience which are occurring in several localities. In order to prevent these misfortunes, it is necessary not only to detach part of the armies which are presently in enemy lands, but also in order that these should not be weakened too much, to make new levies of troops whose costs will consume money which ought to be used for urgent necessities of the state . . .

(Source: AN E 249a, fo. 3)

230. Concordat of the Union between the *Parlement* and town of Bordeaux and our lords the Princes against the enemies of the State, 3 January 1652

. . . The court has seen the prosecution of Jules Mazarin, who had entered France in arms in contravention of decrees previously issued which prohibit his entry. His arrival is for the purpose of oppressing the *Parlement* and the town of Bordeaux, and to attack them and our governor, our lord the prince of Condé. With the advice of the said lord prince, the following treaty and contract of union was drawn up: . . .

1. The lord prince and those seigneurs in his following will take the *Parlement* and town of Bordeaux under their protection and defend them against the enemies of the King and those who seek to oppress them, even to the last drop of their blood.

2. Similarly, the *Parlement* and the town of Bordeaux, joined and united, will cordially and sincerely aid each other; the princes and *Parlement* and town councillors will in all their wishes, actions, passions

and interests generally follow the good of the State, and the conservation of the King and the kingdom.

3. The other *Parlements* of the kingdom, and other seigneurs, will be asked to conform to the objectives of this union.

8. My lord the Prince and those who follow him will not lay down their arms until they have exiled or exterminated Cardinal Mazarin.

36. It is notorious that these good intentions cannot be put into effect while Cardinal Mazarin is in charge of this state, due to the insolence and tyranny with which he comports himself . . . He has the audacity to attack the princes of the blood and to make war on them, and to attack members of the body of the *Parlement* and town of Bordeaux.

37. Because of this, with the advice of the princes, he has been declared a disturber of the public peace, an enemy of the King and his State. For this purpose, he will be pursued until he has been placed in the hands of justice to be publicly, and exemplarily executed, and his head placed on one of the gates of the town. The present union cannot be dissolved, with the grace of God, and its signatories agree not to separate from it, for whatever reason, until the present treaty is put into effect . . .

(Source: AD Gironde 4J 127)

31. Alliance between Gaston d'Orléans and Condé, 24 January 1652

The establishment of a general peace is one of the principal aims of this treaty . . . Cardinal Mazarin has always governed effectively although in appearance he was banished. He prevented the meeting of the Estates General which the King had promised for last 8th September, obliging the deputies who had arrived at Tours to depart in shame and confusion . . .

[Gaston and Condé] cannot regard as legitimate the council which has been established by Cardinal Mazarin, and refuse to recognise it. Those who form it have bought their positions with notable sums of money given to Cardinal Mazarin . . . There will be no settlement until the clients and open supporters of Cardinal Mazarin are excluded from the council of state. In future it will be composed of those who are not suspected of having any contact with him.

[They claim that] they have had no communication or correspondence with [foreigners] except with regard to the general peace, and that they will have none with foreign princes in the future except that

which is judged advantageous to the service of the King and the State by
the *Parlement* and the leading signatories of the present alliance . . .[50]
(Source: AAE France 881, fo. 136ff.)

232. Letter sent into the provinces to all the gentlemen of the kingdom: a union of nobility to prevent the disorders, excesses and ravages of the troops and to obtain a general peace. Drawn up on 16 May 1652 at Nogent-le-Roi

The necessity of the state and the oppression of the nobility obliged a
large number of gentlemen, princes, dukes and peers to assemble at the
Cordeliers in Paris in February 1651 with the consent of His Royal
Highness,[51] lieutenant-general of the State. Having obtained an alliance
with the clergy, they concluded that the sole remedy for so many evils
could only be found in the Estates General. His Majesty agreed to
summon the Estates General in such solemn words that everybody
thought that our alleviation was near to hand, since such a salutary
means of obtaining it was assured . . . Public miseries have since
increased because of new causes, and these have provided ample matter
for new requests. These principally concern the licence of the troops
whose outrageous conduct has reached such a point that it seems that
agreements have had to be reached with them at the expense of our
property and lives, and the honour of our wives and daughters.

These numerous oppressions have brought the nobility, which is
divided by the diversity of its private interests and lack of
communication, to unite as a body. As a result of several proposals, it
was resolved that it was necessary to sign an act of union between
individuals within *bailliages* and between the different *bailliages*. This was
carried out at Magny on 27 February last . . .

The deputies of the united *bailliages* met at Maintenon on 16 April last
and judged it suitable to communicate our plan to the neighbouring
bailliages, to which deputies were sent, since we all have the same interest
and we are all working by the same means towards our conservation . . .
(Source: Feillet, pp. 365–6

---

[50] However, Condé had signed a treaty with Philip IV of Spain on 6 November 1651
[51] Gaston d'Orléans.

233. Proposals which the marquis de Joyeuse must make to the King on the part of Monsieur the duc d'Orléans, 3 October 1652

. . . The King is very humbly requested by Monsieur the duc d'Orléans to consider seriously and immediately a general peace abroad, and to consider employing Monsieur the duc and Monsieur the prince for the advancement of this great benefit. All of this would be at the good pleasure of His Majesty and the Queen his mother to whom the glory of this great task would be reserved. Monsieur the duc de Lorraine may be able to assist, is well-intentioned and offers his services. Their Majesties might consider whether he would be a suitable intermediary.

These articles were signed at Paris on 3 October and taken by the marquis de Joyeuse on 4 October. They were presented and rejected on 5 October.

(Source: B. N. Dupuy 775, fo. 197)

234. De Heere, intendant at Tours, to Séguier, 25 May 1656

He reports difficulties] with the nobility of Upper Touraine on the question of the taxes imposed by royal authority[52] on their farmers and share-croppers. They have since met as secretly as they could, which has alarmed the receivers of the *taille* . . . [He is informed] that several gentlemen were resolved to petition the council in the name of two or three of them only and that all the others would contribute towards the costs as an affair common to all of them. They would complain of the exactions and thefts of the receivers. [The intendant was shown] a written memorandum which was unsigned and was a list of grievances as for an Estates General . . .

(Source: BL Harleian 4489, fo. 59)

235. Méliand, intendant at Montauban, to Séguier, 24 March 1657

Monsieur Le Tellier has sent me the King's orders to bring from

---

[52] Called *taxes d'office.*

Languedoc into Gascony a company of cavalry of the regiment of Piloy in order to punish certain rebellious communities which are not paying the King's taxes . . . This remedy is absolutely necessary, since for the last two years there has been a league among the nobles of the mountain areas, formed originally to exercise control over the troops living there. The league has since been extended to resist orders coming from the King, whether on the matter of the *taille*, the troops, or anything else . . .

(Source: BL Harleian 4490, fo. 204)

236. Foucquet to Mazarin, 5 June 1658

[Revolt of the Sabotiers of the Sologne]. The trouble at Orléans increases. The town is in rebellion. Everyone talks in a seditious way. There is no governor there or mayor. The officers are ill-disposed, the countryside ruined and the peasants summon all the parishes to join them in revolt and menace them with burning their property if they refuse . . . It is thought that there are agents of Monsieur the prince there. Gentlemen wearing rich clothes under linen cloaks have been spotted . . .

(Source: AAE France 905, fo. 139)

237. Servien to Mazarin, 3 July 1658

. . . It is absolutely necessary to root out by some great example the errors which have slipped into the spirit of the nobility, so that the whole state is not imperilled when military reasons oblige one to fight a battle against the enemy . . . The kingdom was menaced with a general uprising if the battle of Dunkirk[53] had been lost . . .

(Source: AAE France 905, fo. 228v.

238. Result of the assembly of the forest of Conches in Perche, 20 July 1658

. . . It was agreed that, in conformity with the union of the nobility at Paris on 4 July 1651 at the King's permission and under the protection of My lord the duc d'Orléans that, if any of the gentlemen were taken, or their persons and property attacked, all the others were obliged on oath

---

[53] An allusion to the Battle of the Dunes, and the subsequent capture of Dunkirk.

and by their signatures, on their honour and on pain of being declared cowards and infamous, to mount on horseback and ride as quickly as possible to the assistance of whoever was attacked. If by misfortune (which is scarcely believable) one of them failed in this duty, he would be declared to have forfeited forever his rank of nobility. Similarly those who refuse to sign the present union . . .

His Royal Highness[54] would also be very humbly requested to continue his intercession with the King for the convocation and holding without any delay of the Estates General, as the sole remedy for all the injuries to our rights, franchises and immunities . . .

Messieurs the governors of the provinces will be asked to act on their own authority under the King's orders for the billeting of troops in their provinces, without suffering the interference of intendants. All this was decided together with an inviolable protestation never to depart from the true service of the King for any reason and to die in his obedience . . .

(Source: Legrelle, pp. 323–8)

239. Colbert, intendant of the Cardinal's household, to Mazarin, 8 August 1658

. . . [The nobles] claim that they have a union signed by 14 provinces and even flatter themselves that a governor[55] is not against them . . . In order that this union does not gain ground in all the provinces of the Kingdom and provoke a real crisis, I think it essential to have good intendants in all the suspect *généralités* who will reside there permanently . . .

(Source: AAE France 905, fo. 357)

240. Foucquet to Mazarin, 10 December 1658

. . . It is important for the King's authority to support Monsieur Morant[56] and make it known to Monsieur de Longueville[57] that His Majesty does not approve such conduct, and that it would be a serious matter to tamper with the ruling.[58] There would be serious

[54] Gaston d'Orléans.
[55] Longueville, governor of Normandy.
[56] Intendant at Rouen.
[57] Governor of Normandy. He was in dispute with the intendant over the billeting of troops.
[58] On the winter quarter for the troops.

consequences if intendants, who are normally chosen from among those most opposed to the interests of the governors, became their valets and dependants . . .

(Source: AAE France 905, fo. 519/2)

241. Colbert to Mazarin, 20 August 1659

. . . Monsieur the procurator-general[59] approves my initiative in sending back the intendants of the three *généralités*[60] to Normandy, making it perfectly clear to them that the King is not satisfied with their conduct. They take great salaries yet there is a considerable conspiracy against His Majesty's service in their province. There are even decrees ordering the arrest of a large number of nobles, without any of them actually having been arrested. The complaints which Your Eminence has made for a long time on this subject are so just and reasonable that it is not surprising to see the King so badly served. For my part, I cannot avoid saying to Your Eminence that if I had a brother who was intendant in one of these *généralités*, and who had been so lacking in zeal as not to have unravelled a matter of this importance, I could not prevent myself from asking for his recall . . .

(Source: Clément, i. 357–8)

242. Colbert to Mazarin, 31 August 1659

. . . I must remind Your Eminence that their arrears[61] are great, and that these do not come from the poverty of the people but the vexation of the officers of the *Parlements* of Bordeaux and Toulouse, the great seigneurs and gentlemen of highest status, and even the King's lieutenants in the province . . . The lands of Monsieur [the duc] d'Epernon in the *élection* of Bordeaux are not only in arrears, but have paid nothing and not drawn up the tax rolls for more than seven or eight years. All persons of status in Guyenne follow this example . . . Intendants have insufficient authority to deal with this. Your Eminence should consider that in peacetime the King must not come away from this province without having restored his authority, which is greatly damaged, particularly in financial affairs. If he does not, instead of it being persons of quality who act in this manner,

---

[59] Foucquet.
[60] Rouen, Caen and Alençon.
[61] Those of the *généralités* of Bordeaux and Montauban.

all the gentry will act in this way. Since their interests will be similar, and they will fear punishment, there will be a close alliance between them. Your Eminence should not have to be involved in such details, but you must encourage either the council or the provincial administration to take the matter up and to proceed vigorously against the chief culprits. Whoever undertakes this task must receive the King's powerful protection, otherwise he can do nothing.

(Source: Clément, i. 360–2)

5 POPULAR REBELLION

Popular rebellion was not a new phenomenon at the time of Richelieu and Mazarin: there had been a significant number of large rural disturbances in sixteenth-century France. The more important of these were the risings of the Pitauds in south-west France (1548), the *Ligue des Vilains* in Dauphiné (1579–80), the Gautiers in Normandy (1589), the risings in Brittany (1589–91), the Bonnets Rouges in Burgundy (1594), and the Tard-Avisés in the Limousin, Périgord and Saintonge (1594–5). The rebellions during the later stages of the French wars of religion show some signs of social antagonism, a consequence of the breakdown of civil order and the resulting oppressive behaviour of local gentry and office-holders. A second period of large-scale disturbances followed French intervention in the Thirty Years' War. The most famous risings are those in the Angoumois and Saintonge (1636), the Croquants of Périgord (1637), the Va-Nu-Pieds in Lower Normandy (1639), and the Croquants of the Rouergue (1643). There were no large-scale risings during the Fronde, though small-scale tax rebellion was particularly serious. After the Fronde, there were further large rebellions in Guyenne in 1655–6, followed by the risings of the Sabotiers in Sologne (1658), and the Lustucru in the Boulonnais (1662) (Map 3).

Thus the ministries of Richelieu and Mazarin were marked by a wave of popular rebellions that had serious implications for the conduct of the long war against Spain. These rebellions defy any simple explanation. In 1948 the Russian Marxist historian Boris Porchnev asserted that they were not directed against the monarchy itself, but against the dominant social classes. The rebellions, in his view, demonstrated an early form of class conflict, and were initiated by the lower classes in the towns and countryside. They were destined to failure because class consciousness had not developed sufficiently. The alliance of the crown with the dominant social groups – clergy, nobility and office-holders – also proved too powerful.

Ten years later, this interpretation received a systematic riposte from the French historian Roland Mousnier. He contested the view that the rebellions were spontaneously initiated by the lower

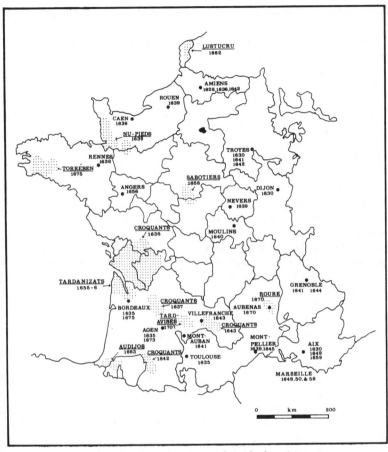

Map 3 *Certain peasant revolts and urban riots*

classes, and stressed that in many instances landlord and peasant had a common interest in opposing royal taxation. They were not directed against the monarchy as such, but confronted monarchical policy through opposition to its fiscal agents. Mousnier denied the relevance of class consciousness, arguing that society was organised differently, by social orders, with ties of fidelity linking the powerful and the weak. The crown, in this interpretation, did not form an alliance with the dominant social

195

groups but undermined the autonomy of other social groups while developing its own power.

Most commentators would agree with Mousnier that the popular rebellions do not, for the most part, reveal any profound social antagonisms within the rural communities. The peasants did not criticise their seigneurs, but sought protection – and, sometimes, leadership – from them. The most famous example was La Motte La Forêt, a nobleman who led the Croquants in 1637 because he recognised the justice of their cause (docs. 256, 257). The absence of any real threat to the social position of the gentry is revealed by the fact that they rarely turned out to suppress rebellion, a profound contrast with the German peasants' war. On the contrary, considerable evidence was supplied to the government by the intendants that the gentry encouraged their tenants and farmers to resist an increasing burden of taxation which would make it very difficult for them to pay their rents (docs. 211, clause 18; 280). Such support might take the form of physical protection for the peasants' goods when the crown's fiscal agents sought distraint for non-payment. It was usually royal troops, sent by the government from outside the province, who suppressed armed revolts, and at times, suffered heavy casualties (doc. 297). On occasion, the gentry might even form leagues and take to arms to support their tenants (doc. 235). Only the Breton rising of 1675 shows a significant degree of social antagonism between peasants and their lords.

The Porchnev–Mousnier controversy, now some thirty years old, has had the virtue of stimulating historical enquiry into the subject of popular rebellion at the time of Richelieu and Mazarin. A number of important studies have resulted, most notably by Madeleine Foisil on the Normandy revolts in 1639, by Yves-Marie Bercé on the south-west and by René Pillorget on Provence. Much work remains to be done. Important provinces still await their historian. There needs to be a careful collation of fiscal sources with the surviving evidence on revolts to establish whether, as the intendants claimed (docs. 269, 274, 282), it was often the rich parishes which refused to pay their taxes and led the violent resistance. If this is found to be generally true, then the fundamental cause of popular rebellion has to be seen as the defence of fiscal privilege rather than resistance to an increased burden of taxes. On the other hand, opposition to any increase in taxes as a novelty was sufficiently widespread as to arouse comment from Richelieu himself (doc. 258) and to have led to wild rumours of the intolerable nature of particular new taxes (docs. 248, 249, 288). Sometimes, the peasants demanded a return to the level of taxes at the time of Louis XIII's accession in 1610 (docs. 245, 250). This evidence suggests that taxes customarily paid were acceptable but that any increase, whether or not it could be paid, was rapidly viewed as intolerable. In some cases, it was the method of collection, rather than the actual amount levied, which caused the protest (doc. 244). Some taxes aroused more opposition than others (doc. 271).

The obvious sources for the historian wishing to understand the attitudes of a rebellious peasantry are manifestos, but relatively few of these survive. Those that do, for example from the 1636–7 risings, demonstrate the peasants' loyalty to their king, but their acceptance of the myth that he was deceived by evil ministers who failed to inform him of the true state of his kingdom. The evil ministers, who mocked the sufferings of the peasants and levied increased taxes under the pretext of necessity of state, were not, however, the main focus of hostility. It was the central and local agents of the fiscal system who were seen as the oppressive force (doc. 253). The ideology of the peasants was simple and is best expressed in slogans of rebellion such as 'long live the king without the *gabelle*', and 'long live the king, death to the *gabeleurs*' (doc. 246). The main focus for hatred was the financier, called the *gabeleur* or *maltotier*, terms which could vary considerably in their precise application according to local conditions (docs. 250, 254).

The danger of a rebellion spreading outside a single *pays* or province was slight. Each revolt had its own particular causes, each province its distinctive fiscal régime and social structure. The relevance of the slogans of rebellion is explained by the existence of privileged regions of France which paid much less than others in salt tax (*gabelle*). The rumour that the king sought to undermine these privileges, which Francis I had attempted in 1542, was sufficient to threaten a general insurrection in the south-west in 1635 (doc. 252). The removal in 1639 of the salt-tax privileges of a region in Normandy known as the *pays du quart bouillon* provoked one of the greatest rebellions, the revolt of the Va-Nu-Pieds (docs. 260, 261).

Few rural protests were entirely without townsmens' participation; similarly, agricultural labourers were involved in urban discontent (doc. 243), sometimes seeking to dominate the town to find support for their own cause (doc. 306). On occasion, leaders of urban faction used outsiders for their own ends (doc. 303). But there were also revolts that were predominantly urban in character. Because of the great political importance of cities as centres of wealth and administration, such revolts tended to assume a political significance not often achieved by rural rebellion. Urban insurrections seem to fall into five general categories: food riots, riots against outsiders, riots resulting from faction rivalry, tax riots and large-scale political rebellions. As with rural protest, there was some overlapping: a food riot might develop into a tax riot, and so on. Despite the bad harvests of 1628–31 and 1649–52, the period of Richelieu and Mazarin witnessed relatively few bread riots.

There were several different types of outsider against whom urban rioting was directed. The outsider might simply be the suburb-dweller; he might hold jurisdictional privileges which were resented (for example, a bishop or seigneur); he might be a representative of the judicial, fiscal or military power of the crown; finally, he might simply be a foreigner: at Marseille in March 1620, 45 Algerians and six local inhabitants were killed in a xenophobic riot. Faction-fighting in the town council, or within a provincial sovereign court, might lead directly to rioting. The struggle between factions within the oligarchy at Marseille was a primary cause of the frequent rioting in the seventeenth century. The faction within the *Parlement* of Aix-en-Provence that was opposed to the policies of the crown was largely responsible for the urban revolts of 1630, 1649 and 1659. In seventeenth-century France, charges of financial mismanagement played an important part in the development of factions. Election disputes and the suspension of elections might intensify the problem of urban rioting. Sometimes the conflict might take the form of a struggle between the lower orders and the rich (doc. 273). During the Fronde there were popular revolutions of this type at Bordeaux and Angers in 1652, known respectively as the *Ormée* and the *Loricards*, but they proved to be isolated phenomena of short duration. Conflicts resulting from one faction seeking support from the lower orders against a rival faction (doc. 295) were more common.

Tax riots were more frequent even than these, since the privileges of towns were partly fiscal in character. Any attempt by the government to increase the tax burden on new urban wealth was resisted as an encroachment on privilege. Most of the smaller French urban disturbances started in this way and most were single-grievance movements of short duration. Overwhelmingly, the aim was the defence of the *status quo.* This required little either in the way of manifesto to justify the rebellion, or of leadership to provide a focus. The immediate cause of rioting was usually self-evident: a forced loan, a tax on the well-to-do, a sales tax, the appropriation by the central government of municipal revenues and so on. Once the grievance was removed, the rioting ceased (docs. 255, 289, 290). On occasion, the fiscal threat was more generalised, involving no longer merely a single town, but a number of them in a movement against the central government's encroachment on provincial privilege. The riots in Provence in 1630, 1634, 1649 and 1659 fall into this category. So too do the riots at Dijon in 1630, in the Guyenne towns in 1635, the towns of Normandy in 1639, and those of Orléanais (doc. 307). Doubtless there would have been riots in the Languedoc towns in 1632 had Montmorency's rebellion not been defeated promptly. Not surprisingly, the fiscal imposition which had given rise to the trouble was rescinded in all these cases (doc. 284).

Extremes of violence in urban rebellion were rare. Between 1596 and 1660 it is estimated that there were 264 'insurrectional movements' in the Provençal (mostly small) towns, but only 69 deaths before 1648. The towns became more law-abiding with the passing of time: only three deaths in riots occurred in Provence between 1660 and 1715. Moreover, rioting affected only sixty out of the total of 600 communities in Provence. A riot such as at Agen in 1635, where there were 24 victims of the mob, including twelve financial office-holders, several of whom were vilely mutilated, was exceptional (docs. 246, 251). The intendant might point on occasion to the difference between an urban riot which was orchestrated by the local notables for reasons of self-interest, and which was restrained in its outcome, and one which was leaderless, popular in its participation and violent in its outcome (doc. 298).

If much remains to be known, our documents tell us a good deal about the reasons for popular rebellion and the development of small- and large-scale movements of resistance. Rumours of tax remissions were an important factor in spreading disaffection at the time of the illness and death of Louis XIII in 1643 (docs. 267,

268), at the outbreak of the Fronde in 1648 (docs. 292, 293) and on the signing of the Peace of the Pyrenees in 1659 (doc. 309). It is very difficult to establish how such rumours started, although there was evidently much wishful thinking that tax increases were purely temporary and would be removed once the immediate crisis had passed. Sometimes there is clear evidence of falsified decrees of the council in circulation to substantiate these rumours (doc. 283); on occasion a pedlar who was selling them is actually named (docs. 300, 305). At other times the evidence suggests that a local notable might start the rumour, for his own purposes (doc. 279). In the towns, the role of women as the instigators of the troubles, and perhaps those more susceptible to rumours of crushing tax increases because they were responsible for the family budget, is also attested (docs. 286, 287). Sometimes the women appeared with their children (doc. 308). When the riot developed in a town, then clearly the topography played a crucial part – the relationship of town and suburb, the existence of town gates, drawbridges and so on could be of great importance (doc. 247). The tax-collector might escape from his house over the rooftops (doc. 301). He might barricade himself in the house and hope that the bourgeois militia would come to his rescue (doc. 259), though fire might be used against him before they did. However, the bourgeois militia did not always act in the interests of the government (doc. 264). An unpopular intendant, heavily implicated in the collection of a particular tax, might need to take refuge in the citadel for a few days (doc. 285). Posters were sometimes used to stir up urban riots, and the intendants sent examples to the Chancellor (doc. 302).

Both social structure and regional topography played a crucial part in the development of rural movements. Gentry lawlessness and gentry-led resistance was a common feature (doc. 206). The intendant found himself in great difficulties when protection was given to tenants by the provincial governor (docs. 299, 242) or by magnates who were relatives of the ministers themselves (doc. 205). In such cases, the government had to intervene, for fear that the gentry might follow this example. The gentry might orchestrate an attack on the intendant in person (doc. 304). The council sought to reinforce the intendant's powers by all possible means, such as making the crime of tax rebellion equivalent to a crime of treason (doc. 272), and refusing payment of pensions to gentry whose parishes had not paid their tax demands (doc. 275).

If the situation became serious, the intendant was empowered to raise a brigade of special troops to enforce the levy, though this was an unpopular step and a further source of discontent (docs. 270, 276).

Resistance to taxation took different forms according to the nature of the regional economy and the possibilities provided by the terrain. The principal wealth of Limousin consisted in cattle-breeding so that distraint of goods had to be in cattle (doc. 277). Subsequently, the peasants might have recourse to the mountainous terrain (doc. 278), or make use of local administrative boundaries to escape distraint orders; they might block a river crossing to prevent the billeting of troops (doc. 281). Elsewhere, in Picardy, villages might be fortified to prevent the distraint of goods, or the movable wealth of the community might be transferred to the protection of the home of the local gentleman for safekeeping (doc. 263). In some cases, weapons were stockpiled for use in a prolonged insurrection (doc. 296).

The intendant made careful distinctions between parishes which were unable to pay their taxes because of poverty and those which were 'hardened and experienced in revolt' (doc. 274). The persistent, nagging, problem of deliberate tax rebellion by a relatively small number of parishes within a province was a more serious difficulty for the government than the great peasant uprisings, which were sporadic in nature. Tax rebellion could never be eliminated by force alone. The intendant could not police an entire province so that rebellion never occurred – to be really effective, more intendants would have been needed (doc. 291). The methods used to suppress tax rebellion – summary prosecutions by the intendant and the enforced levy of taxation by troops – were likely to intensify the problem. However, the alternative was worse, as was demonstrated clearly in the last years of the Fronde. Such a negative policy would have led to rapidly diminishing tax returns and a creeping paralysis of government. This had been clearly perceived by the finance minister in 1642, shortly before the transfer of fiscal powers to the intendants by the ruling of August 1642 (doc. 265). The intendants were given the task of reforming the fiscal system; it was inevitable that they would also be given the decidedly unenviable task of suppressing revolt. Their activity in coercing payment of taxes was one of the chief reasons for their unpopularity during the ministries of Richelieu and Mazarin.

243. Marillac to Richelieu, 26 April 1630

... The King arrives tomorrow to issue his judgement on the sedition which has occurred in this town.[1] In my opinion, the example will be a considerable one, but I will let you know the details after the decision is taken. His Majesty did not consider that the vineyard workers who started the sedition should be present in the town when he entered ...

(Source: Grillon, v. 232–4)

244. Marillac to Richelieu, 13 July 1630

... The method of collecting four types of taxes by four different agents of the financiers, in different ways in different places, causes great vexation and thus provokes sedition, quite apart from the sum to be paid. We are trying to commute all these taxes into a single levy to be paid once only and in one place, which will thus be less likely to provoke the people. We will then obtain the same amount of revenue with greater ease, a significant benefit if we are successful ...

(Source: Grillon, v. 392)

245. Verthamon, intendant of Bordeaux, to Séguier, 4 June 1635

Since I had the honour to write to you on the 28th of last month nothing has arisen in this town[2] which merits my report to you. Things are still quiet. The people nevertheless continue to threaten rebellion when one seeks to make some punishment which ought not, or cannot, be omitted in order to repair the damaged authority of the King. This same evil humour is very apparent in the rest of the province, and it is reported that some have spoken of not paying the *taille* or other taxes above the rate they paid on the accession of the King.[3] They are still in the malevolent spirit of finishing off those who are employed in tax collecting, including anybody who simply comes from Paris ... We also have plenty of information, my lord, concerning the ill disposition of several gentlemen and the menaces of the populace towards others that they will burn their houses if they come here when we punish this town for what has happened ...

(Source: Mousnier, i. 253–5)

[1] Dijon. The incident referred to is the Lanturelu rising.
[2] Bordeaux.
[3] 1610.

246. Description, by the town councillors of Agen, of the sedition which arrived in the town on 17 June 1635

On Sunday 17th of the month at 9 o'clock in the morning the riot and popular sedition on the rumour of the *gabelle* began . . . Plenty of people assembled and began to troop together, shouting that 'we must kill the *gabeleurs*' and 'long live the King without the *gabelle*' . . .

This riot and popular sedition was so great and arose so suddenly among the plebs and common people of Agen that when the sieur Meja met the sieur d'Espalais, a town councillor and captain of St. Caprazy at the St. Gilles road, he ordered him to go to his quarter and prevent the evil plans of this mob. The said sieur d'Espalais placed himself in front of his house in a state to rally the good inhabitants among his neighbours to resist the mob on the road, but was killed and butchered on the spot and his house sacked, pillaged and put on fire; his eldest son killed, together with the La Tour sieur de Sauvebère, a councillor of the *Cour des Aides* who had taken refuge there; he was killed and butchered, as well as a man named Guérineau, a student, who was thrown from the window and burnt alive. The adjoining house of the sieur de Barbier, a councillor in the *Cours des Aides*, was also pillaged and burnt. The sieurs de Maures, the father a town councillor, the son an *élu*, were murdered, killed and butchered in the convent of the Carmelites where they had taken refuge. The house of the sieur Codoing, an *élu*, was pillaged and he was killed, butchered and dragged to the river. Thomas, the jailkeeper was killed and butchered in front of the jail. Messieurs president Dubernet and other Messieurs of the chamber,[4] of the Catholic or Protestant faith, went with Monsieur Delpech, the *lieutenant criminel* and the sieurs Meja, Grousses and Cancer, town councillors, to protect the town hall with certain town councillors and bourgeois of the rue de Garonne, and established barricades and fortified the doors of the town hall. At this moment, certain gentlemen, seigneurs and litigants at the chamber offered themselves to assist us and serve the King and the town by defeating the incendiaries and seditious persons . . .

The town hall was menaced with arson. We got out the cannon and other pieces and falconets, established barricades at the four corners and approaches to the town hall, installed a good guard throughout, even at the five gates and at the St. Caprazy church. The people barricaded themselves throughout the streets and alleys.

[4] Of the edict (*chambre de l'édit*). This was one of several special tribunals set up under the terms of the edict of Nantes to hear cases involving Protestants.

Behind the barricades, the mob discussed who they intended to kill if the rumoured *gabelle* was not abolished. They demanded a decree of amnesty for their murders and incendiarism and forced Messieurs of the Chamber to draw up this declaration and have it printed. If they had not agreed, everything would have been put to fire and blood. As long as the *gabelle* was abolished they said that they would return to obedience. The decree was announced by trumpet call throughout the town . . .

(Source: Bercé, ii. 718–20)

247. Verthamon, intendant of Guyenne, to Séguier, 18 June 1635

. . . The news of what happened on Friday at Bordeaux has arrived here.[5] The populace began to rise when the cannons which had been used for celebrations remained outside the Taillefer gate. They imagined that we wanted to use them against the town to establish some new taxes . . . [I informed them that] they had no reason to be alarmed, and that they would be in danger if they embarked on something which displeased the King. I succeeded in separating them, and they seemed to calm down. However, my lord, while I was on a visit outside the city for half an hour the people returned to their melancholy, and came back to the town to look for those they consider *gabeleurs*. Throughout the night the alarm was sounded both inside the town and outside in the suburb towards Bergerac. Within the town the seditious mob continued their insolences and kept a guard close to the town hall . . . It happened, my lord, that the mob captured the two gates which were the only ones we had left open, the others being closed and the drawbridges raised. I also found the suburbs in arms . . . worse still, we have had information that peasants summoned by the night alarm call wish to join them . . .

This, my lord, is our situation in this town . . . The people around here are less long suffering than elsewhere. After the necessary punishment of certain offenders, it would be in the King's service to issue a public declaration that by his grace and goodness he will not overburden them with taxes. They will be relieved of this fear which otherwise could degenerate into a complete frenzy of pillage, upheaval and mindless killing, which has not yet happened . . .

(Source: Mousnier, i. 259–64)

---

[5] Périgueux.

248. Decree of the *Parlement* of Toulouse, 19 June 1635

. . . Request made orally by the King's procurator-general, that he is informed that certain unknown persons, disguised as pilgrims and beggars, travel from town to town spreading rumours against the King's service and the administration of the State. These people give very pernicious and false impressions to the people of the establishment of certain *gabelles* and other taxes and impositions on every sort of item, even on children to be born and the bodies of people who have just died. These damnable ideas have excited popular uprisings in several towns and several parts of the jurisdiction of the court, to such an extent that the roads are blocked by armed peasants, and passers-by run the risk of their lives. These abominable ideas can only arise from the malice of enemies of the state. His Majesty's paternal goodness wishes only for the relief of his subjects in so far as the necessity of his affairs permits it . . . He has no wish to establish new *gabelles* or other taxes, but merely to obtain the help that is absolutely necessary to sustain the expense of several armies beyond the frontiers . . .

(Source: Bercé, ii. 722–3)

249. Bertier de Montrave, first president of the *Parlement* of Toulouse, to Séguier, 19 June 1635

. . . Following the example of Bordeaux, all Guyenne is full of sedition. We have observed that unknown people dressed as pilgrims or beggars travel from one town to another, spreading rumours that the *gabelle* is to be established, that taxes are to be placed on the birth of children and on dead people, and that it is intended to establish everywhere monopoly ovens and special taverns beyond which it will not be permitted to sell wine.

. . . A new fury has since changed everything. The *Parlement* has judged it necessary to issue the only thing which these rioters believe in, that is, a decree. This makes it clear from the narration of the request of the King's attorneys that His Majesty does not wish to overburden them with his taxes, and that these are merely rumours spread by enemies of the State to bring about their ruin. After this action, I know of none other than punishment, and we will not spare this . . .

(Source: Mousnier, i. 270–2)

250. Decree of the council of finance, 30 June 1635

The King is informed that there has arrived at the town of Lectoure a rumour and popular sedition on pretext of the *gabelle*, against both the officers of the *élection* established in the said town and against other persons whom the people suspected of being *gabeleurs*, and that it lasted from Monday to Wednesday last. The rioters sounded the tocsin several times in order to excite the people to massacre, burning and pillage. They even broke down the doors of the house of one of the office-holders, and searched there, as well as that of the president of the *élection*. They gravely wounded and emprisoned one of the town councillors of the town, an official of the *élection*, a sergeant and an outsider pursuing some lawsuit in the town . . . Without the prudence, assistance and help of the sieur Marquis de Rocquelaure, governor of the town, many murders would have been committed, principally against the officers of the *élection*. He gave them refuge in the citadel and assisted others to escape from the town and to withdraw in safety to avoid the fury of the populace, which was ill-disposed to His Majesty's service. They called out continually against the *gabeleurs* and *élus*, whom they menaced with death if they imposed more taxes than those levied in 1616 [sic] . . .

(Source: AN E 124b, fo. 172)

251. Second decree of the council of finance, 30 June 1635

Complaint is made to the King in his council by the officers of the *élection* of Agen that on 17th. June last there was a massacre and sedition in the town of Agen and other horrible, cruel, and inhuman actions by many of the lower classes and peasants living there which lasted three days. This was caused by their offices of *élu*[6] and on the pretext of great taxes, levies and other rumours of the *gabelle* which the people imagined would lead to their utter ruin. The mob killed and mutilated three *élus*. They dragged to the river these bodies, and those of other persons, including a sergeant of the *élection*; they attacked and pursued the other officers of the *élection*; they also demolished, pillaged and burnt six of their houses in the town and three in the countryside. His Majesty's

---

[6] The officials in the *élection*, the local court of finance with responsibility for direct taxation.

commissions for the levy of the *taille* and *crues* were in one of these houses: these were also burnt with unheard-of insolence. Moreover, several persons of condition, including officers of the *Cour des Aides*, were killed during the massacre and arson: their houses were burnt and their possessions pillaged. None of the said officers of the said *Cour des Aides* and *élection* was spared. With the help of the town councillors, they fled to the town hall, where guard was kept for its protection and that of the said officers. Since the whole province of Guyenne was in similar rebellion, the officers did not know where to go without risking a miserable death . . .

(Source: AN E 124b, fo. 204)

252. Letters of amnesty accorded to the inhabitants of Bordeaux after the riot of 1635, September 1635

. . . We have been notified that several outsiders, disguised and unknown persons, instigated by enemies who are envious of the grandeur of this State, have slipped among the people of our province of Guyenne, including its capital and principal cities and by a pernicious design have persuaded people that we wish to establish the *gabelle* on salt and other new taxes such as are levied elsewhere in our kingdom. Previous kings had revoked these taxes in our province of Guyenne on the very humble remonstrances of their people and for certain specific reasons . . . We do not wish further investigation to be carried out, but prefer our clemency and mercy to the rigour of justice. They have assured us that most of the people recognize their faults and have for some days obeyed our letters patent and levied the taxes of our *taille*, *taillon*, *crues* and other levies contained in our commissions . . . We wish it, and it pleases us, that the memory of such acts and seditions should remain suppressed and the whole matter be treated as something which never happened . . .

(Source: Bercé, ii. 731–3)

253. Anonymous account of the revolt of the peasants of Saintonge and Angoumois, n.d. [1636]

. . They protest[7] that they are good Frenchmen who would rather die

[7] The peasants of Saintonge.

than continue under the tyranny of the Parisians and the financiers, who have reduced them to the despair and extreme poverty under which their province labours presently as a result of new and heavy taxes invented during the course of this reign. These burdens have forced many to abandon their landholdings in order to beg for bread, leaving the land uncultivated, the draught animals unable to live off the saffron crop, abandoning clothes and farm implements to be seized by the bailiffs. These seizures do not reduce their debts to the receiver, but merely cover the costs of collection. The peasants have made their complaints known on numerous occasions, but the gentlemen of Paris and the Council have ridiculed their sufferings, levying new taxes every year under the fine pretext of necessity of state. The aim of these gentlemen is to increase the personal wealth of a few individuals and the clients of the ruler of the state by extracting all the money from the province – thus they will achieve the ruin of the kingdom. The peasants have been forced to go to these extremes in order to gain redress of their grievances and to ensure that their complaints may be heard by the king and not just by his ministers who counsel him so badly . . . The people have paid more taxes in two years of this reign than in the whole of the reign of the king his father, and all the reigns of his predecessors since the beginning of the monarchy . . . All new taxes apart from the *taille* should be abolished as being for the ruin of the people. Properly spent, the *taille*, *taillon* and traditional levies are sufficient for the upkeep of any army necessary for the protection of the realm against enemies. If these taxes should prove insufficient, the peasants are willing to contribute wholeheartedly provided that they are not taxed by the present ministers, who must no longer be allowed the power to impose arbitrarily new taxes and exactions upon the people. Such taxes should be levied only in times of national crisis, after a vote of the Estates General as has been the custom since time immemorial . . .

(Source: Mousnier, ii, 1103–5. Bercé, ii. 736–7)

254. Ordinance of the peasants of Poitou [Angoumois], n.d. [1636]

. . . We enjoin each parish to have all the gentlemen march with them, and give them arms, on pain of their houses being burnt down and not being paid their rents and dues.

We enjoin the parishes to give out copies of this decree on pain of being ruined by the commune:

Messieurs, we advise you that the true *gabeleurs* are the *élus*, one, two, three, four, five and six of the richest men in each parish who pay practically no taxes. It is verified at Paris that the *élus* of Saintes and Fontenay levied 60 000 *livres* above the limit in the letters patent of His Majesty. Having considered all this, we have ordered without appeal that the *élus* will be brought to justice by the commune and to suffer restitution of their notorious thefts together with interest charges to the present.

As regards the rich in each parish who have achieved the ruin of the people, in future they will not be permitted to interfere in the assessment of the *taille* in favour of the share-croppers of Monsieur of this place and Monsieur of that place who hold most of the wealth of their parish.

The late-arrivals (*Tard avisés*) . . .

(Source: Bercé, ii. 738–9. Mousnier, ii. 1105–7)

255. Bertier de Montrave, first president of the *Parlement* of Toulouse, to Séguier, 3 June 1637

The noise of those people who have risen in Périgord on pretext of the *gabelle* attracts the attention of people in these parts . . . In order to prevent this evil from spreading, the *Parlement* has been forced to suspend certain extraordinary commissions which are being carried out in this province, which are not of great consequence. It requests you very humbly, my lord, to agree to this, since both towns and private individuals complain very justly about the commission of the *francs-fiefs*.[8] It seems that it is being carried out at an inopportune moment when it would be more appropriate to allieviate those who can only pay their *taille* and other taxes with great difficulty. From all these small commissions only a small revenue is raised for His Majesty . . .

(Source: Mousnier, ii. 378–9)

[8] A payment owed by commoners who bought noble lands.

256. Anonymous account of the rising of the *Croquants* of Périgord between 1st May and 6th June 1637, 7 June 1637

Advice of the assemblies of communes of inhabitants making known their assemblies and the election of La Motte La Forêt as their general.

... We have elected a general with absolute power to command and order whatever is necessary for the said assemblies. Nothing will be permitted to be undertaken or carried out except by his ordinances. There will be a specific prohibition on the use of violence against the goods and persons of individuals without such measures having first been ordered by the sieur general and his council.

And if one of the communities is fully informed that certain enemies of the people's liberty approve the overburdening, extraordinary and illegitimate imposition of taxation, they will be asked to inform their leaders and captains, and the sieurs captains to inform the sieur general, for him to decide on the matter in his council. None of the said communities, leaders or captains are to use violence against property and individuals without a declaration or ordinance of the sieur general in his council, on pain of being punished as criminal disturbers of the public peace ... The leader is called Monsieur de la Motte de La Forêt, a man of some years and spirit experienced in the career of arms.

This resolution having been taken, the communities assembled in the fields adjoining the city of Périgueux, because their leader had not yet arrived. First of all they demolished a house in the country belonging to sieur Saleton, a receiver of the *taille*, and some other houses of Vincenot. This assembly could have been of 4000 or 5000 men ...

[Rendez-vous of deputies on 7 or 8 May]. In this assembly there were 20 000 to 25 000 men, from whom the general chose the 8000 or 9000 best men that he could find, and gave them the best weapons from among those that they had all brought. This general is the sieur de la Motte La Forêt, who married a daughter of La Douze.

The other captains are disbanded soldiers from the Périgord, the best that he could find, because ... he takes only 20 men from each parish who are fed and maintained by the parish itself at 5 *sous* a day ...

The principal subject of these rebellions arises from the fact that according to the rebels themselves, extraordinary taxes are levied over and above the *taille* and *taillon*. 150 000 *écus*[9] have been imposed for th

---

[9] 450 000 *livres*.

pay of the army of Bayonne, grain has been levied to feed the said army, and finally there has been a third levy called Rations. For none of these three taxes has there been a King's commission . . .

(Source: Bercé, ii. 751–2, 764–9)

257. Mesgringy, intendant of Auvergne, to Séguier, 19 June 1637

. . . Every day there are new rumours of a great number of *Croquants* in Guyenne who have for general a gentleman named La Motte La Forêt. It is said that the marquis d'Aubeterre joined them a few days ago, and that M. the duc de La Valette retook Bergerac and Ste. Foy only on condition that he would confirm the request of these rebels, a copy of which has fallen into my hands and which I send you. There is no more to fear from Upper Auvergne: none of the 6000 or 7000 men who took to arms against the regiment of d'Effiat, and to prevent the levy of the King's taxes, is now in arms. The worst aspect of this is that they are still in the woods and hills and have abandoned their houses to prevent the punishments which I am having carried out. They hope to obtain an amnesty from you, my lord. If this made an exception of the leaders, it would be extremely useful for the King's affairs, because while the land remains uncultivated, the *tailles* and other taxes cannot be paid. It is also to be feared that the discontented will ally with the rebels of neighbouring provinces . . .

(Source: Mousnier, ii. 388–9)

258. Richelieu to Messieurs of the council, 27 August 1639

. . . It would be prudent for you to scrutinise closely any new taxes which you wish to make, so that inconveniences similar to those in Normandy do not arise.

The word '*gabelle*' is so odious, and the benefit of the establishment of it of so little consequence, that I can scarcely express my astonishment that you wished to extend the revenue farm of the *gabelle* when it could bring so much trouble and so little profit.

It seems to me that we should be circumspect in such matters when the distance of the King gives evil-doers the chance to hatch their evil designs. Whenever any new tax is levied, the people remember everything which they suffer, and because the most recent novelty is the true cause of their rising and makes their cause more plausible, they place the blame for everything with which they are burdened on it.

I request Messieurs of the council to consider the future by reflecting on the past, and not to embark on affairs where the consequences are so disastrous that the rebellion can only be pacified by shamefully revoking what has been ordered.

The King fears that the tax-contract that is proposed for the feudal levy[10] will produce a still worse effect, and had made up his own mind that he does not wish it to be established, judging as I do that it will lead part of the nobility to rebel.

His Majesty also fears that the new tax on the small towns called the tax on the well-to-do[11] will also produce a bad effect. I can only comment that if it is extended to the frontier towns, an inconvenience might arise that would be very difficult subsequently to remedy.

I well understand that Messieurs the finance ministers will say that nothing can be done with nothing, and that necessity obliges you to do many things which you would condemn in happier times; but I ask you to consider that measures which will not merely give support to our enemies but also deliver places up to them stand condemned in all times.

(Source: Avenel, vi. 494–6)

259. Memorandum of two seditions in the town of Rouen in the year 1639 [August 1639]

. . . After midnight on Sunday night[12] the house of the general clerk of the *gabelle* was threatened. On Monday morning he was besieged. He sent to Monsieur the first president of the *Parlement*, and to the town council . . . asking for help since the King's papers and public money were in his house. He was told that the matter would be dealt with.

On Monday morning he brought 50 men into his house to defend it, barricaded it, and provided weapons and everything necessary for the protection of the money and his house. That day there were several attacks on it by seditious people without weapons, which were repulsed.

The bourgeoisie was in arms in the town, especially in the square and at the guard-house; but they did not wish to leave it. Nor did the captains

---

[10] *Arrière-ban.*
[11] *Taxe des aisés.*
[12] 21 August.

of the militia, who were commanded to go to the rescue of the said house . . .

The bourgeois stated boldly that they were armed only for their own conservation and not for the conservation of tax-contractors and that they would not get themselves killed for them . . .

(Source: Floquet, pp. 344–53)

260. Relation of the revolt of Lower Normandy, 1639

The *gabelle*, which it was intended to establish in Lower Normandy, was what began this revolt; private hatreds and rumours fomented it; and the misery of the populace would have continued it if the arms of the King had not restored his authority and suppressed the insolence of the rebels who had already begun to make themselves masters of public liberty . . .

The people . . . saw themselves already overburdened with the *taille*, and a second burden ready to overwhelm them, one moreover from which they had previously been exempt. They became possessed by a furious despair and assaulted the sieur Poupinel[13] in the open street, hitting him cruelly with stones, sticks and other weapons. There were no more than 40 or 50 rogues at the beginning, most of them salt-makers and wood-carriers; but in less than a quarter of an hour the people gathered together so that at the end there were more than 400 . . .

The name of Jean Barefoot (*Nu-Pieds*) was chosen the same day for the name of the leader of the rebellion . . . the name . . . was taken from a poor unfortunate salt-maker who was called this fine title because he walked barefoot on the sand at the edge of the sea. It was given to the leader of the revolt, who did not dare declare himself openly for it, but contented himself to give orders secretly to those who were bolder than him. The true name of the general of this 'army of suffrance', as they called those in revolt, is not known . . .

A manifesto was drawn up under the name of Jean Barefoot, which was printed at Avranches. Copies were sent into all the parishes . . .

Manifesto of the high and indomitable captain Jean Barefoot, general of the army of suffrance.

---

[13] The sieur de la Besnardière Poupinel, *lieutenant particulier* in the *bailliage* of Coutances.

The rich people with their taxes,
Oppress the public by their conspiracies,
They sell off the province with their intrigues,
They are so vainglorious they mock us,
Wearing satin and velvet at our expense.
This would not be without their treason,
Complete Barefoot as I am, I shall lower their ambition.

They seek the help of all tax-contractors,
They run to Paris to seek the *gabelle*,
I know, with my peasants, how to discover
Their secret treasons; and with zeal,
I shall halt the spread of so many thefts,
Which every day oppress the people,
Who succumb to the burden, and require the help of friends;
All Barefeet oppose the rape of their possessions . . .

(Source: Floquet, pp. 397–421)

261. Further relation of the seditions which arrived in Lower Normandy, 1639

The disorders of the province of Normandy arose in the month of June last, when a rumour spread in Lower Normandy that in the lease of the *gabelles* which was to commence in 1641, there was a clause which read that the *gabelle* was to be established in the *élections* of Avranches, Valognes, Carentan, Coutances, Mortagne and Domfront, and that the salt-works of white salt were to be destroyed. Those who spread these rumours said boldly that this change should not be tolerated since it would cause the ruin and desolation of these *élections*, and subsequently of the rest of Normandy, since there were 10 000 or 12 000 souls who had no other, and knew no other, means of gaining their livelihood, and that if there was no wood burnt in the salt-works, then there would be no profits on sales and the ecclesiastics, nobility and populace would be reduced to necessity and poverty without any remedy . . .

(Source: Floquet, pp. 421, 425)

262. Summary of things which happened in Lower Normandy during the rebellion, 1639

All Lower Normandy generally was in the revolt, some having committed the crime of rebellion, others having tolerated it. The nobility in the countryside allowed the tocsin to be sounded every day in their parishes for the rebels (including their tenants) to assemble, without taking any remedial action. The office-holders in the towns tolerated the revolt of the people and allowed houses to be destroyed. Persons loyal to the King's service, such as receivers of the *taille* and other taxes of His Majesty, were assassinated without any individual or joint action being taken to stop the spread of a disorder of such perilous consequence . . .

(Source: Floquet, pp. 440–1)

263. Decree of the council of finance, 28 April 1640

Instead of satisfying [tax arrears in the *généralité* of Amiens] . . . [certain individuals] spread rumours that His Majesty has remitted and entirely acquitted payment of the *taille* while the war lasts. They attack and assault the collectors, and refuse to allow them to carry out the duty of their offices. To prevent distraint of their goods, they gather together all their grain, cattle and other possessions into forts constructed in their villages and in the houses and castles of gentlemen and seigneurs of the parishes of the *généralité*. Protected by some of them, they rebel against the bailiffs[14] carrying the orders of the receivers of the *taille*, and by this means remain obstinately in their disobedience and rebellion. . . .

(Source: AN E 155a, fo. 264)

264. Humbert de Chaponay, intendant at Moulins, to Séguier, 23 January 1641

[Sedition at Moulins in June 1640] . . . I had good reason to ask you to permit me to judge cases concerning the sedition outside this town, which you found reasonable by letters patent of December last year sent by the last courier. You recognised that protection was being given to these murderers and thieves by the principal officers and magistrates of

---

[14] *Sergents et archers.*

the town who openly supported their crimes against the wishes of the King . . . I have required from the *lieutenant-général* in his capacity as mayor the names and surnames of the officers and captains of the bourgeois *quartiers* and the inhabitants of the town and suburbs who did not wish to take up arms and refused to follow him to oppose the violence of the murderers and thieves . . .

(Source: Mousnier, i. 479–82)

265. Bouthillier to Richelieu, 17 February 1642

The affair of the sales tax goes very badly in Guyenne, and no-one dares talk of it in the town of Bordeaux, where Messieurs the Marshal de Schomberg[15] and de Lauzon[16] have not dared go to the *Cour des Aides* to take the special orders which were sent to them more than two months ago. They tell us that the people are extremely angered and that unless they have some good troops, there is no hope of establishing the tax . . . The Bonneau brothers who are farmers of the revenue farm of the *convoy et comptablie* of Bordeaux tell us that their clerks have run into trouble and have been obliged to give way a little to the popular fury without nevertheless abandoning the levy. The people of Bordeaux menace them with having their throats cut and being thrown into the river Garonne. If this continues, not only will we not establish the sales tax in this province, which is judged the most innocent tax which can be envisaged, but even those taxes which have been established for a long time will be threatened . . .

I remark on these difficulties in the levy of the *taille* only to make known to you the need to establish the necessary order because otherwise our revenues from taxes in the provinces will be progressively reduced. We will no longer be able to expect loans from financiers and others, which can only be assigned on these revenues; nor will we be able to expect anything from the 18.6 million *livres* in subsistence for the troops levied on the people in the same manner as the *taille*. I recognise that these words will not be at all agreeable to you, but it is necessary to bring about remedies so that the evil does not spread . . .

(Source: AAE France 842, fo. 43)

[15] Lieutenant-general in Guyenne.
[16] Intendant in Guyenne.

266. Lauzon, intendant of Guyenne, to Séguier, 2 March 1643

My lord,

It is not my place to penetrate the conduct taken for the peace of this town.[17] But the populace takes pleasure in rioting and nobody does anything about it.

The last few days, not from lack of grain but poor administration, there was no cheap bread at the bakers' and the populace gathered together in a mob and shouted seditious words.

. . . Last Saturday instead of calming spirits down, the printed request (which I join to this letter) was shouted out in the streets, informing the populace of the reasons why they should prevent the establishment of the sales tax.[18] It would be an unfortunate diversion at the beginning of a new campaigning season to have a sedition in Bordeaux. There is no governor in the province. There are no troops. You know the people of this area and what they can do . . .

(Source: Mousnier, i. 506–7)

267. Decree of the council of finance, 2 May 1643

The King is advised that persons who are ill-disposed to his service spread rumours in the parishes of the *généralité* of Tours which prevent His Majesty being assisted from the taxes imposed for the *taille* and subsistence of the troops. They suggest to the populace that the arrears of the previous years have been remitted; they also suggest that the sales tax, the subsistence for last winter quarter and the *taille* of the present year have been remitted. As a result of this, very little is being paid to the receivers of the *taille* and subsistence . . .

(Source: AN E 179b, fo. 93)

268. Decree of the council of finance, 20 May 1643

. . . Several individuals who are ill-disposed towards the good of the State and its service are taking advantage of the death of the late King

---

[17] Bordeaux.

[18] The intendant presumably had not received news of its revocation on 25 February 1643.

217

. . . and spreading rumours in the provinces that His Majesty before his death remitted and quitted his people of the taxes ordered in previous years and part of those in the present year. This has delayed the levy of the taxes and given rise to rebellions, riots and uprisings of taxpayers against clerks, receivers and others employed in the recovery and receipt of the taxes. It is very important that the taxes be levied. His Majesty can make no remission or moderation of them on any pretext whatsoever, since they are the sole funds on which the expenses of the army are assigned. The army must of necessity be maintained during the present campaign so as to arrive at a peace after which the tax-payers may be discharged of the greater part of the taxes . . .

(Source: AN E 179b, fo. 502)

269. Le Roy de la Potherie, intendant at Caen, to Séguier, 8 June 1643

. . . The poor taxpayers everywhere have paid their taxes. It is only the rich and the office-holders who make difficulties. Some well-meaning persons consider that I have been too mild and think this likely to cause trouble. It is easy to repair this fault. If I do not do so quickly, the lower classes say that they will demand back the taxes they have paid and will go to the house of the receiver to obtain payment. The riot at Caen[19] began in similar circumstances, for a tax of only 35 *livres* . . .

(Source: Mousnier, i. 516)

270. Decree of the council of state, 13 June 1643

The King wishes to deal with the disorders in the *généralité* of Orléans, particularly in the *élections* of Chartres, Orléans, Châteaudun, Vendôme and Montargis, in which the parishes refuse to pay what they owe His Majesty in *taille*, subsistence and other taxes for several years including the present year 1643, and commit continual rebellions against the bailiffs carrying the orders for distraint from the receivers . . . A garrison of infantry and cavalry will be established in the parishes of the *élections* as judged suitable and necessary by the sieur de Bragelongne, councillor of the King in his councils of state and privy council and intendant of justice, police and finance . . . He will send the troops into those parishes which do not obey our orders and do not pay their taxes. The troops will

[19] In 1639.

live there at the expense of the parishes in a good order and conduct established by the sieur de Bragelongne. This will also be carried out in all the other parishes of the *généralité* which are in similar rebellion as the sieur intendant sees fit . . .

(Source: AN E 1687, fo. 13 and E 180a, fo. 278)

271. Favier du Boulay, intendant at Alençon, to Séguier, 23 June 1643

My lord,

. . . Rumours of the remission of the *taille* have spread since the death of the King . . . The difficulty is increased by the support given underhand by the nobility to this rebellion . . . The *élection* of Domfront is one of the most malevolent in this *généralité*. It is also in great misery, partly because of the high price of grain, partly because of the great arrears owed by the inhabitants, of whom many are forced to eat oatcakes . . .

One of the principal causes of these disorders this year is the linking of the subsistence with the *taille*. If this had not been done, the subsistence would be paid by now. It is clear that the more rebellious parishes which have not paid the *taille* for four or five years have always paid the subsistence . . .

(Source: Mousnier, i. 519–21)

272. Decree of the council of state, 11 July 1643

. . . The populace are encouraged in the frequent rebellions which occur in the levy of the *taille* and subsistence by the protection and support of the judges and the magistrates. Either from private interest or because of ill-will towards the service of His Majesty, they cover up crimes and excuse them, alleging lack of proof and lack of witnesses. They refuse to accept depositions of the bailiffs carrying the orders for coercion, or depositions from the troops established for the maintenance of the affairs and authority of His Majesty, because they allege that these come from interested parties. They do so to avoid taking action on such depositions. It is unusual for other types of depositions to be obtained in cases of sedition and public rebellion . . . [The king in his council] has declared and declares all those accused and convicted of sedition and public rebellion guilty of treason.[20] He orders the intendants to prosecute them.

[20] *Lèse-majesté.*

Judges and magistrates who are called by the intendants to judge the cases according to the rigour of the ordinances are to do so, on penalty of being declared accomplices and instigators of the rebellions . . .

(Source: AN E 1687, fo. 35 and E 181b, fo. 128)

273. Decree of the council of finance, 22 July 1643

[The inhabitants of the town of Châteaurenaud in the *élection* of Montargis have not drawn up any tax rolls]. Each time they have been summoned to obey His Majesty's orders, and to satisfy the payment of their taxes, they have assembled in numbers of 500 or 600 people at the sound of the tocsin. The example of their impunity has brought the rest of the parishes to the same disobedience. All this has been fomented by the most powerful and well-to-do citizens of the town of Châteaurenaud, who wish to exempt themselves from taxes at the expense of the poor citizens. In order to remedy this, the sieur de Bragelongne, intendant of justice at Orléans, went to the town and was obliged to arrest and have removed to the prisons of Montargis the lieutenant of the said town, his brother, and one of his nephews who are noted as among the most seditious citizens and the authors of the rebellion and disobedience . . .

(Source: AN E 181c, fo. 94)

274. Favier du Boulay, intendant at Alençon, to Séguier, 5 August 1643

My lord,
Since I had the honour to write to you, I have done all that is possible in the *élection* of Conches, which truly is greatly in arrears because of the frequent rebellions over the last six years. There are thirty parishes which have not paid any *taille* at this time. I have prosecuted some of the rebels and condemned them, and by this means I have reduced some of the parishes to render the obedience which they owe the King. I have visited the principal small towns which are in rebellion. I have drawn up the tax rolls myself and have forced them back into their duty with great difficulty. Le Neufbourg is one of these, and is of such importance that it has ruled all the rebellious countryside for a long time: its inhabitants have made no assessment nor paid any taxes for three years. There is an extreme misery in this *élection*. But there are also inhabitants who are

220

hardened and experienced in revolt, and who can only be reduced to obedience by force. I am now in the *élection* of Bernay. The misery is no less, but the rebellions are less frequent. It is true that I find that there are parishes which have not carried out assessments for three or four years; some of these are poor rather than wicked . . .

(Source: Mousnier, i. 537–9)

275. Decree of the council of finance, 6 August 1643

. . . His Majesty prohibits governors of places, seigneurs, gentlemen and other persons of status[21] from preventing the levy of His Majesty's taxes and protecting those liable to the *taille* and subsistence. They are not to allow such persons refuge in their residences or châteaux, nor to hoard their grain, cattle or other possessions on penalty of being forced to pay His Majesty's taxes in their own name. Moreover His Majesty orders the seigneurs of the parishes, whether ecclesiastics, gentlemen or officers who receive emoluments from His Majesty that hereafter they may not be paid until the tax rolls have been drawn up, the levy carried out, and the inhabitants of their parishes are entirely in obedience . . .

(Source: AN E 182a, fo. 341)

276. Decree of the council of state, 14 August 1643

The King has received advice that some persons who are disaffected delay his affairs and maintain the inhabitants of several parishes in the *élections* of the *généralité* of Poitiers in rebellion and in a refusal to assess and levy the *taille* and other taxes, by sowing and spreading rumours that the said taxes must not be paid and that those who require them are thieves. They even assert that the riflemen and fusiliers established in the province to reduce the parishes to obedience and assist the bailiffs and sergeants carrying the orders of coercion for these taxes commit great violence and peculation against the taxpayers and that there is to be an investigation against them. All of this is to render them odious to the people and to create further riots of the people against them, which could place all the said province in rebellion . . . [The council orders] the sieur

---

[21] In the *généralité* of Tours.

de Villemontée intendant at Poitiers to investigate such rumours of a remission of taxes and rumours against the riflemen employed on his orders and to prosecute the instigators of such rumours . . . [The intendant is] to continue to use the riflemen and to use greater force if need be to punish the rebellious parishes and the instigators and participants in rebellion.

(Source: AN E 182b, fo. 61)

277. Cazet de Vautorte, intendant at Limoges, to De Bailleul, finance minister, 10 September 1643

My lord,

I have already told you that this province is in disorder on the matter of the *taille* . . . The people here are neither pliant nor prompt in paying their taxes, and the gentlemen maintain their vassals [*sic*] in this attitude and profit from it . . . The burden of taxes is greater, and certainly the capacity to pay is less not only because the burden in previous years has exhausted them, but because last year's harvest was poor, the present one is no better, and the last hope is the chestnut harvest, the outcome of which is uncertain: without the chestnuts, this province will be desolated. To this lack of capacity to pay I add . . . the association of the subsistence with the *taille*, which although in practice it assists them, nevertheless alienates them considerably because of the fear that it will not end with the war but will be confused with the *taille* and thus continue after the peace, as does the *taillon* . . . As to enforcing payment, we must use rigour because mildness will not bring any results . . . The province produces no grain or wine except for the subsistence of the people, who have no other means of making money than through the sale of cattle. This is the principal wealth which must be seized by the receivers if they are to be paid; without doing so they will certainly remain unpaid . . . However, this procedure of seizing cattle is rendered difficult by fraudulent lease contracts which the share-croppers have drawn up for their own cattle. It would be a long process and often impossible to ascertain this fraud, and to seize – as it is permitted – only the calves . . . The receivers strongly request the right to seize all cattle with the exception only of those serving to till the land. Such seizures would be for individual non-payment and not for claims against the entire parish. This demand would be excessive and unnecessary in any other province where the principal wealth and the easiest way of making money did not consist in cattle-breeding. There is a fear that this proposal will ruin the commerce of this province, making men withdraw their cattle. People will not want to lease their cattle, and thus by attacking the fraudulent contracts we may harm the legitimate ones. You must decide on a course of action that you consider to be just and necessary. For my part, I am not yet sufficiently well informed to be able to give you my opinion . . .

(Source: Mousnier, i. 543–6)

278. De Sève, intendant at Riom, to Séguier, 18 January 1644

. . . I am taking action all the time to combat the disobedience of parishes in the payment of their *taille*, and I am fairly strong in the countryside. But there is so much ill-will in the mountains and the lie of the land gives so much confidence to the tax-payers to oppose the distraint of goods, that it is very difficult with the few bailiffs that I have to bring them back to their duty. To use troops is a worse remedy than the evil, which usually adds impoverishment to the ill-will of the parishes where they are lodged. If those involved in the loan contract wish to advance the cost of fifty arquebusiers instead of the companies of riflemen which they pay for in other provinces, within two months I would hope to draw from the people everything that it is possible to obtain. Moreover, this cost would not be very considerable and less than a week's service of the company of a provost marshal . . .

(Source: Mousnier, i. 618–19)

279. Decree of the council of finance, 9 November 1644

. . . Messire Léonard Bezanne, president of the court,[22] who resides ordinarily in the parish of Ouroux-en-Morvan within the *élection*, stated that the *taille* of the past years and this year had been remitted and that if Gerard [a receiver] tried to levy the *taille* in the parish through the use of collectors he would have him assaulted with clubs. He said that the bailiffs and sergeants who came to the parish to demand payment of the *taille* should all be killed. He has prevented the seizure of possessions

[22] The *élection* of Châteauchinon.

for non-payment and spreads rumours among the populace so that rebellions arise frequently . . . He has threatened Messire Guillaume de St. Mesmin, clerk for the receipt of the *taille*, that he would wait for him with guns if he should return to the parish . . .

[The council orders Bezanne to appear before it and until then suspends him from office].

(Source: AN E 196a, fo. 156)

280. Favier du Boulay, intendant at Alençon, to Séguier, 10 January 1645

My lord,

I am obliged to give you an account of this *généralité*. Although it has received some diminution, it is certainly overburdened. Both malice and poverty are powerful factors in preventing payment. It is true that whole *élections* could pay the sums which are imposed on them, if they were not placed in a manifest rebellion by the protection of gentlemen, who ensure that if their farmers increase their rents, they pay little or no tax. The *élection* of Domfront is in a deep-seated malice. Although there has been some exemplary punishment, the taxpayers' rebellion has continued for the last seven years . . . The judges and the gentlemen ruin everything; the whole province is deeply infected with rebellion. I am nearly beside myself, having used both mild and rigorous methods. If it was just the *taille* to be paid in the *généralité*, then with some diminution I think it could be obtained. But since there are also many extraordinary levies, the people are extremely hard-pressed and lose courage to pay up . . .

(Source: Mousnier, ii. 706–7)

281. Corberon, intendant at Limoges, to Séguier, 15 January 1645

My lord,

I have great displeasure in telling you that the parishes of the *élection* of Tulle, which last September rebelled and attacked the fusiliers, continue their crimes and rebellion. Despite all my diligence and care, I have not been able to surprise the rebels, because of the mountainous terrain and also the proximity of *élections* in another *généralité*, where they find refuge for themselves and their cattle. No alternative remains for me but to ruin and burn their villages. I have not dared do so, fearing to punish the innocent as well as the guilty. Instead, I chose a second billeting of troops. This was prevented by 400 or 500 men, gathered from several parishes, who blocked the crossing of a small river at the entry of the bourg of Le Cugeat, where the fusiliers had received orders to take quarters . . . [The fusiliers were forced to withdraw after shots were fired and there was hand-to-hand fighting]. These parishes have been in rebellion for five or six years. It is necessary to have more considerable forces to reduce them to obedience . . .

(Source: Mousnier, ii. 708–9)

282. Corberon, intendant at Limoges, to Séguier, 10 March 1645

. . . Having marched the troops with the best order possible . . . the peasants of the guilty parishes disappeared at their approach. A few days earlier they had appeared in arms and had beaten the drum before the gates of Treignac. The fear of justice made them abandon their houses . . . The abundance of goods found in their houses demonstrates their crime and proves that there has been much more ill-will than impoverishment . . .

(Source: Mousnier, ii. 723)

283. Decree of the council of finance, 1 April 1645

The King has received information that in several *généralités* of this kingdom a false decree of the council discharging parishes from having to pay the arrears of the *taille* from the years 1638 to 1643 has been published. It also alleges that the intendants of justice are to carry out investigations against the receivers and clerks receiving the *taille* and subsistence and other taxes of His Majesty . . . Although this decree is false, it nevertheless hinders the levy of the *taille* . . . [The council] orders the intendants of justice and finance in the *généralités* of this kingdom to carry out investigations where pedlars are found in possession of this false decree . . .

(Source: AN E 201a, fo. 1)

284. Bosquet, intendant of Languedoc, to Séguier, 3 July 1645

My lord,

For the last four days Monsieur the Maréchal de Schomberg[23] has combated with his brains and his force the most desperate and stubborn riot that I have ever seen.[24] Having sought to exploit the respect which is owed to his person and the fear in which his troops are held, he seeks to bring the populace, infuriated with tax contracts and tax contractors, back to obedience. The orders which he gave today have been so effective that they have given a different appearance to the city. The officers of all the courts have taken to arms, together with the principal bourgeois of both religions, and have made themselves masters of the town [in order to resist the rebellion]. In order to bring matters to a public peace, Monsieur the Maréchal has been obliged to issue a fulminating ordinance against tax contracts and tax contractors . . .

(Source: Mousnier, ii. 737)

285. Bosquet, intendant of Languedoc, to Séguier, 4 July 1645

. . . Monsieur Baltazar[25] is still at the citadel, where it is said he draws up lengthy reports. I visited him there yesterday, where he welcomed me less civilly than my charity merited. Because he seeks to avenge himself of the hatred of the whole province for him, he is trying to counsel Monsieur the Maréchal[26] to violent retaliation, which would result in the loss of the town and perhaps the province. Had his counsels prevailed, and the regiment of Normandy entered the town, the sedition would have become more serious than before. The inhabitants of high and low condition were resolved to arm themselves against it . . .

(Source: Mousnier, ii. 738)

---

[23] Lieutenant-general of Languedoc.
[24] At Montpellier.
[25] The other intendant of Languedoc.
[26] Schomberg, lieutenant-general of Languedoc.

286. The *Cour des Comptes, Aides et Finances* of Montpellier to Séguier, 4 July 1645

My lord,
We have been greatly surprised by the riot which arrived in this town on the last day of last month and continued on the 1st, 2nd and 3rd of this month but which was at last quietened down on the same day of the 3rd by the great care and diligence of Monsieur the Maréchal de Schomberg and monsieur the intendant Bosquet, assisted by all the officers of our company and most of the other officers and town councillors. Together we have halted the disorders begun by women complaining of taxes on artisans because of the happy accession of His Majesty to the throne and coercion by ordinances of Monsieur de Baltazar, so-called sole commissioner for the levy of the taxes . . .

(Source: Porchnev, pp. 643–4)

287. Schomberg, lieutenant-general of Languedoc, to Séguier, 4 July 1645

. . . For the last two days the town has been quiet as a result of the ordinances which I have issued to prevent the levy of the taxes for the king's happy accession to the throne which were the cause of the sedition. In truth, Monsieur, the taxes are excessive, and since they were levied on all the masters of the trades as well as the wives of all the artisans, the women began the disorder which their husbands then took over. No bourgeois or rich merchant is involved in this matter, but the tax contractors are held in such horror in this town that no-one takes any great trouble to prevent the riot . . .

(Source: Porchnev, p. 644)

288. Report of Bosquet [on the riot at Montpellier], 4 July 1645

Monsieur Baltazar issued an ordinance to carry out the levy of taxes on the guilds. Romanet, the tax contractor, had it printed and placarded throughout the town of Montpellier at the end of June and at the same time attempted to make the artisans of the said town pay their taxes. This attempt was followed by a vehement desire on the part of the artisans to gain discharge from payment: they thought they could do this only by chasing out or otherwise intimidating the tax contractors. They stirred up their wives and spread rumours that women were to be taxed according to the number of their children, that servants and valets would pay a proportion of their wage each year in tax, and made other similar allegations. The artisans and the poor made public complaint at the long list of taxes and crafts subject to them contained in the ordinance. This excited everybody's compassion.

Monsieur Baltazar, having heard the shouts of the people against tax contractors and intendants, withdrew to the citadel . . .

(Source: AAE France 1634, fo. 139)

289. Baltazar, intendant of Languedoc, to Séguier, 5 July 1645

My lord,

. . . without the presence of M. the Maréchal de Schomberg,[27] who placed himself in continual danger [the riot at Montpellier] would not have been pacified so easily. He did all he could to bring people round; no-one could have done more. I can assure you, my lord, that the ordinance which he had publicised discharging the inhabitants of Montpellier from all taxes and getting tax contractors and their clerks out of the town was a most prompt and effective remedy for stopping the rioters. Sufficient force was lacking to deal with the mutinous populace. It was an absolute necessity to take this step in order to humour them and stop their fury . . .

(Source: Porchnev, pp. 645–6)

290. Bertier de Montrave, first president of the *Parlement* of Toulouse, to Séguier, 13 August 1645

. . . The town councillors who remain in this town[28] during the last few days have had announced at the sound of trumpet the ordinance of Monsieur the Maréchal de Schomberg which suspended all levies of taxes and tax contracts in the province. He should not have issued this ordinance without informing the *Parlement*. This announcement has put

[27] Lieutenant-general of Languedoc.
[28] Toulouse.

228

the lower classes in such a mood that they are shouting that the king no longer wants payment of the *taille* or any other taxes; all the tax-contractors and their clerks have fled the towns within the jurisdiction of this court and disappeared . . .[29]

(Source: Lublinskaya, p. 153)

291. Remonstrances of the *trésoriers de France*, 1648 [?]

. . . Since the intendants have only entered into jurisdiction over finance at a time of new fiscal measures which had to be established by extraordinary authority, it has entered the minds of people that all their ministry is violent, and that they are employed simply to exact from them what is required beyond the traditional levies. As a result, without seeking further information, they hate all orders emanating from the intendants; they regard such orders as suspect, and cannot be persuaded that judges other than the ordinary ones are necessary if what they do is just.

This viewpoint is greatly strengthened by the terror in which the troops levied by the intendants to exact payment of the *taille* are held.

. . . Fear follows the intendant everywhere, but he cannot be in more than one place at a time. Thus to hold a province in firm order by this method, if it were not excessively severe, it would be necessary to have as many intendants as there are *élections* . . .

(Source: BL Harleian MSS 4472b, fo. 147)

292. Lauzon, intendant of Guyenne, to Séguier, 20 July 1648

My lord,

The rumours coming from Paris are so prejudicial to the King's service that I do not know how we will dare demand from the people the *taille* for 1647 or 1648. A general discharge of taxes is expected as if the silver mines of Peru had suddenly been found in the Treasury. This is at a time when the assemblies of the sovereign courts of Paris have demonstrated their zeal for reducing the tax burden on the people . . .

(Source: Mousnier, ii. 841)

---

[29] This ordinance was not revoked by a decree of the council until 2 January 1647: AN E 219a, fo. 26.

293. Decree of the council of finance, 8 July 1649

[Remissions of taxes accorded in 1648]. This has given tax-payers the impression that if they do not pay their taxes they will obtain a similar discharge in the future. Whether this rebellion has been fomented by certain gentlemen or caused by the ill will of the people, several parishes, particularly in the *généralités* of Orléans and Moulins, have become so disobedient to the wishes of His Majesty and the payment of the *taille* that they have not drawn up tax rolls for several years or nominated collectors. Others refuse to allow distraint orders of the receivers to be carried out by bailiffs and others, and add assault to the disobedience to His Majesty's wishes and ordinances of his office-holders. They attack, kill and murder those who are sent out to make the recovery of taxes . . .

(Source: AN E 235a, fo. 197)

294. Decree of the council of finance, 29 July 1649

[In the *généralité* of Châlons] most of the parishes have not drawn up their tax rolls, nor paid any of the taxes imposed in the present year 1649. Certain individuals who are ill disposed to the King's service claim that the payment of the *taille*, the *étapes* and other taxes . . . is prohibited. They are supported by certain gentlemen and seigneurs of the parishes of the said *généralité*, who allow forts to be built in the villages or else allow the property and cattle of tax-payers to be hidden in their houses and châteaux. Thus the bailiffs holding the distraint orders of the receivers find no possessions to seize . . . [The council orders the demolition of forts. The *élus* are ordered to investigate those who spread rumours of tax remissions. Gentlemen may not delay the king's tax returns on penalty of being held personally responsible for this.]

(Source: AN E 235b, fo. 304)

295. Decree of the council of finance, 28 June 1650

[Report of the sieur Foullé, councillor of the King in his councils, master of requests ordinary of his *hôtel*, intendant of finance, commissioner sent to the *généralité* of Limoges on] the popular riots stirred up at the town of Limoges as a result of rumours of the establishment of the *gabelle* and the sales tax, and the attacks and murders which followed against the person of the sieur Guillaume, *trésorier de France* and others on 16th and 24th May last, and against the receivers-general of finance, their clerks and others employed in recovering His Majesty's taxes by those called Boyel the prince, Baluffre and other accomplices at the instigation of du Peyrat, Chenaille, Alesme, Maledent the younger and Hardy, *trésoriers de France* of the *généralité* suspended from the function of their offices by decrees of September 1649, 3 February 1650 and 6 May 1650. [The sieur Guillaume and the grand provost-marshal] were forced to abandon their houses in the town, as were all the *trésoriers* who had not been suspended from office, and the receivers-general, in order to escape the violence . . .

(Source: AN E 242c, fo. 414)

296. Tallemant, intendant at Bordeaux, to Séguier, 1 May 1656

I have been at Coutras with Monsieur de Saint-Luc, although the Tardanizats[30] had boasted that they would prevent the crossing of the river. No-one was there to dispute it. We have found no-one in Coutras or in the surrounding villages of its jurisdiction. Both innocent and guilty have fled and have left nothing behind in their houses. We have not been able to capture any of the rebels. I therefore carry out their prosecutions *in absentia*. However, I have had the bells taken down from the churches of five parishes because they sounded them to get people to assemble. I have also had 10 or 12 houses demolished which belong to their leaders against whom I have evidence that they have committed all sorts of crimes during the last three years and that they have stolen from peasants and killed them. I have found in one of these houses nearly half a barrel of shot, ready primed. You will well appreciate, My lord, that people who make this sort of provision do not have plans to use it for good purposes. I hope shortly that we will be able to seize one of these leaders to make a good example of him, which I consider absolutely necessary. If this evil is not promptly remedied in its commencement, it will quickly spread . . .

(Source: BL Harleian MSS 4489, fo. 61)

---

[30] The rebels.

297. Decree of the council of finance, 17 May 1656

For several years frequent rebellions and uprisings have arisen in several towns and parishes of the *élection* of Bordeaux, notably in the places within the county of Benauges, the jurisdiction of Cadillac, Rions, Lesparre, Castelnau, Tête de Buch and others . . . The inhabitants of most of the places have not imposed the taxes for the winter quarter for 1655 nor the taxes ordered for the present year 1656 . . . They have attacked and assaulted the bailiffs and fusiliers sent to coerce payment from them, and have killed several of them. There has been no punishment or justice meted out to those who have committed such offences and acts of violence because of consideration for the seigneurs to whom these lands belong. This impunity gives audacity to the inhabitants of the bourg of Coutras and the parishes within the jurisdiction of the place not only to refuse to levy their taxes, but also to form armed mobs to chase off or assault the bailiffs and fusiliers . . . and to attack the commissioners of the *Cour des Aides* of Guyenne. [Thus Tallement, the royal commissioner at Bordeaux, issued an ordinance on 28 March 1656 ordering the billeting of a company of troops at Coutras]. The inhabitants, far from obeying . . . armed the whole area against them, tore the brigade to pieces . . . and killed La Roche [its commander] and 18 of his cavaliers. [Tallement is ordered by the council to carry out prosecutions. St. Luc, lieutenant-general of Guyenne, is to move to the area with the number of troops he considers necessary to deal with the rebellion.]

(Source: AN E 289b, fo. 122)

298. Fortia, intendant at Poitiers, to Séguier, 8 June 1656

I am obliged to give you an account of the implementation of the decrees of the council ordering me to investigate what happened at La Rochelle and at Marenne, and to let you know the difference between the two incidents. That of La Rochelle was planned in the town council between the great merchants who thought that the tax which the King had ordered on dried and salt fish would cause great prejudice to their commerce. This plan was shown in the event. The individual who was charged with recovering this tax was taken in his bed and dragged through the streets to show him to the people. Once he had been taken for this walk, he was left alone without otherwise being ill-treated. I find so much caution in this misdeed that someone had to have planned it: it is unusual for a rioting mob to show such restraint and for some poor devil not to be sacrificed to the fury of the people.

The incident at Marenne was much more cruel. The people, with one accord, elected a leader and marched in order to a distance of three leagues from the town, gathering their supporters as they marched, and besieged a captain and two guards in their houses, which they set alight. These poor individuals were obliged to give themselves up on the word of the commander of the mob, who handed them over to the people. They were conducted to three separate places and murdered with unheard of cruelty . . .

(Source: BL Harleian MSS 4489, fos. 99–100)

299. Tallemant, intendant at Bordeaux, to Séguier, c. 27 June 1656

It is now a month since I received the command of the King to go with Monsieur de Saint-Luc and his troops into the pays de Benauge[31] and the area 'between the two seas' to deal with the frequent rebellions against those who are appointed to levy the King's taxes. I have gone there, and since the troops which have been sent there have been found to be weak, Monsieur de Saint-Luc and I decided that it was better not to separate them but to send them as a unit into one place. We decided not to send them into the lands in Benauge belonging to Monsieur [the duc d']Épernon,[32] from whose receivers we have had little in taxes, from fear of having too many people down on us. Events showed that we were not wrong in this, since the inhabitants of five or six parishes of the area 'between the two seas' had the audacity to go with muskets to La Seaune, where the troops were lodged, in order to kill those leaving the quarters, and steal from them. They continued this for three days, killed a soldier, wounded several cavaliers and soldiers, and took the possessions of all those they captured. I have prosecuted and hanged two leaders of these rebels. I was obliged to pass sentence at Bergerac, since I was unable to find any office-holder or advocate in Bordeaux who was willing to judge the case with me, Messieurs of the *Parlement* having made it clear that they did not want anybody to assist me. I hope that the punishment that

---

[31] The decree was dated 17 May 1656: AN E 289b, fo. 122.
[32] Formerly governor of Guyenne.

I have meted out to these rebels will serve to bring the others back to their duty. Messieurs of the *Parlement* are making a lot of noise against me, but I hope that they will calm down . . .

(Source: BL Harleian MSS 4489, fo. 180)

300. Decree of the council of finance, 28 June 1656

Certain persons who are ill-disposed towards His Majesty's service have spread rumours in various parts of the *généralité* of Alençon including a rumour that His Majesty has remitted the whole of the *taille* to his people, and prohibited the receivers, bailiffs and sergeants from taking any proceedings against them . . . These rumours are encouraged by the guile of a man [Pierre du Bois] unknown to the locality, dressed as a pedlar, who arrived at the bourg of Thiersville in the *élection* of Lisieux, where he publicly sold an alleged decree to this effect to the inhabitants . . . [The *élus* have arrested him and are empowered to carry out a prosecution].

(Source: AN E 290b, fo. 110)

301. Tallemant, intendant at Bordeaux, to Séguier, 4 September 1656

. . . The rebellion has begun to break out. Financiers, and those who act for them, are suspected of coming to establish this new tax.[33] On Friday night certain individuals discovered that the sieur Jacquier, a munitions contractor whose brother is a financier, and the sieur Sercamanen had arrived in this town. 40 or 50 armed and masked men went to their lodgings. Some guarded the door, and others mounted the stairs to find them. By good fortune they had time to escape over the roof to a neighbouring house: otherwise, they would not have escaped the fury of these people . . .

(Source: BL Harleian MSS 4489, fos. 216–17)

[33] On wine.

302. Tallemant, intendant at Bordeaux, to Séguier, 11 September 1656

... Monsieur the procurator-general[34] has let me know ... that there is no plan to establish a new tax,[35] which I have made known throughout the city. But there are plenty of discontented persons who are sorry to lose this pretext for creating an uprising in the province. They have already attempted one. Yesterday posters were placed throughout the streets in the hope that the people would rise up and start a riot: I send you a copy of one. They chose a Sunday as the best day, because the artisans have nothing to do and amuse themselves drinking, and it is in drink that resolutions to take foolish actions are made. Besides, Messieurs of the *Parlement* do not go to the hall of justice on that day, and are mostly on their country estates where they cannot speedily take action against such disorders ... The town councillors do their duty, attempting to find those responsible for the posters. I hope that the matter will not have any serious consequences ...

[Copy of the poster appended to the letter:] Messieurs. You are warned that the intendant has the commission for a levy of two *écus* on each wine cask. The letter which he has shown you is false. He must leave to deal with the ships. He has been paid 10 000 *écus* to let them pass.

(Source: BL Harleian MSS 4489, fos. 218–20)

303. Decree of the council of finance, 22 November 1656

[Concerning Mazerus, lieutenant of the seneschal of the duchy of Fronsac at the seat of Coutras, declared the 'principal author of the sedition, rebellion and murders' at Coutras in April 1656. The council has received evidence that] Mazerus was the one who did most to create the uprising, and had great intelligence in Périgord and elsewhere, where there were 3000 or 4000 men of his faction ready to take to arms. Mazerus had continued his intrigues and factions and prevented the inhabitants of Coutras and the parishes within its jurisdiction from paying His Majesty the *taille* for several years ...

(Source: AN E 295b, fo. 193)

[34] Foucquet.
[35] On wine.

304. Decree of the council of finance, 6 June 1657

[The council has seen a report of Méliand, intendant at Montauban] concerning a riot on 17, 18 and 19 May at Martres-de-Rivière, where a large number of people gathered from the plains and the mountains and conducted by a quantity of gentlemen of the province, besieged a company of the cavalry regiment of Piloy. [Despite an ordinance of the intendant, the besieging forces increased in size. Two of the intendant's servants, including his secretary, were captured by the rioters. Several people were killed.] They did not render up the prisoners or lift the siege before Martres until they were afraid of being defeated by other troops of His Majesty . . .

(Source: AN E 302a, fo. 192)

305. Decree of the council of finance, 4 October 1657

. . . For some time copies of a decree obtained by the treasurer ordinary of war have been distributed in the *élection*.[36] The inhabitants of the parishes and others of the *élection* have come to believe that they are discharged from the *taille*, and consider this view justified by copies of this decree . . . [The wording has been falsified]. Those who have spread copies of the decree have written in large letters these words 'His Majesty has remitted the arrears of their *taille*' as if it were the beginning of the command[37] of the decree. [They have also altered the wording so that it appears that coercion for the *taille* is not allowed. Tax refusal at eight named parishes has resulted.]

(Source: AN E 306a, fo. 31)

306. Decree of the council of finance, 9 May 1658

Rebellions, violence and seditions have been committed in various parishes of the *élection* of Gien [*généralité* of Orléans] since the month of March 1657 . . . over the payment which they owe for the *taille* for previous years . . . [The provost-marshal found] the inhabitants in arms, the tocsin having been sounded, and the drum beaten, which obliged

---

[36] Of Troyes.
[37] Called the *dispositif*.

236

him to withdraw . . . although he was assisted by more than sixty men. This has so increased the insolence of the people that they have continued their seditions since this time [April 1657] and are still in the same state, keeping armed guard, and visiting neighbouring parishes, obliging them to join the rebellion. There are presently more than 30 parishes in this union, which is beginning to spread to the parishes [in the *élections*] of Montargis, Clamécy and Romorantin. [They] assembled in arms on 23 April [1658 and went to] the town of St. Fargeau on the day of the fair, where they pillaged and sacked all the houses of the principal bourgeois of the said town, and announced a ban on paying the *taille* in the town and other parishes on penalty of their houses being burnt down . . .

(Source: AN E 313a, fo. 366)

307. Decree of the council of finance, 7 August 1658

Although the rebellions and seditions of the pays de Sologne have been quietened by the arrival of troops which His Majesty has sent, and most people have returned to their normal condition of obedience after a light punishment for those who have been most guilty in the rebellion . . . Nevertheless, instead of setting a good example by returning to obedience, the inhabitants of the towns, bourgs and villages of the *élections* of Gien, Montargis and Clamécy and others within the *généralité* of Orléans . . . continue in their rebellions, and form bands to oppose anybody who seeks to demand His Majesty's taxes, so that it is impossible to make any recovery of taxes, although His Majesty's troops are in the neighbourhood . . .

(Source: AN E 316a, fo. 4)

308. Decree of the council of finance, 17 May 1659

[In the *élection* of Joigny] under pretext of rumours of a peace treaty, it is said that the *taille* and particularly the winter quarter are remitted . . . [Thus there are] rebellions and riots throughout the *élection*, notably in the town of Joigny where many women and children, stirred up by ill-intentioned inhabitants . . . have assembled at the door of the receiver of the *taille* . . . and attempted to enter his house, to pillage it and murder him and his clerk . . .

(Source: AN E 324a, fo. 361)

309. Decree of the council of finance, 7 August 1659

[Recalls decree of 17 May against false rumours of remissions of taxes.] Nevertheless, several people who are ill-disposed towards His Majesty's service, including people of authority, office-holders and the principal inhabitants of towns, have scorned the decree and neglected the respect and submission . . . [they owe] because of their offices. Animated by private interests, they have written a number of seditious letters to the towns where there are *élections* and to other towns of the kingdom, which could lead to rebellion, claiming that His Majesty has remitted to his people all the taxes, that the tax-payers need not pay anything, and that the collectors need not collect any taxes due to His Majesty. These letters are written on the pretext of false rumours of the peace and His Majesty's marriage . . . [These letters have been] printed and posted up in the public places of the towns and distributed in many parishes so that it is impossible to receive any taxes, the collectors are unable to carry out their functions, and the bailiffs are unable to recover the taxes because rebellions have occurred as soon as they attempted to do so . . .

(Source: AN E 327a, fo. 282)

FURTHER READING

There are three useful introductions to the period: V-L. Tapié, *France in the age of Louis XIII and Richelieu* (trans. D. Mc.N. Lockie, 2nd ed. Cambridge, 1984); D. Parker, *The making of French absolutism* (1983); and R. J. Knecht, 'The Fronde', *Historical Association. Appreciations in history*, v (1975).

Further detail on decision-making in the central government and the organization of finance can be obtained from R. J. Bonney, *The King's Debts. Finance and politics in France, 1589–1661* (Oxford, 1981). A different interpretation is provided by J. Dent, *Crisis in finance. Crown, financiers and society in seventeenth-century France* (Newton Abbot, 1973). There are valuable comments on the ministers in O. A. Ranum, *Richelieu and the councillors of Louis XIII* . . . (Oxford, 1963), while there is now a definitive modern study of Richelieu's personal fortune by J. A. Bergin, *Cardinal Richelieu. Power and the pursuit of wealth* (New Haven and London, 1985). Additional detail on the first years of Richelieu's ministry may be gleaned from A. D. Lublinskaya, *French absolutism: the crucial phase, 1620–9* (trans. B. Pearce, Cambridge, 1968) and D. Parker, *La Rochelle and the French monarchy. Conflict and order in seventeenth-century France* (1980). An interesting perspective on Richelieu's ministry is provided by J. H. Elliott, *Richelieu and Olivares* (Cambridge, 1984). The claim that the French declaration of war in 1635 was naked aggression on Richelieu's part has been restated recently by R. A. Stradling, 'Olivares and the origins of the Franco–Spanish war, 1627–1635', *English Historical Review*, ci (1986), 68–94.

The relationship between centre and localities, particularly with regard to the introduction of the intendants, is examined in R. J. Bonney, *Political change in France under Richelieu and Mazarin, 1624–1661* (Oxford, 1978). There are several modern studies of the sovereign courts, such as A. L. Moote, *The revolt of the judges. The Parlement of Paris and the Fronde, 1643–1652* (Princeton, N.J., 1971), A. N. Hamscher, *The Parlement of Paris after the Fronde, 1653–1673* (Pittsburgh, Pa., 1976) and Sharon Kettering, *Judicial politics and urban revolt in seventeenth-century France. The Parlement of Aix, 1629–1659* (Princeton, N.J., 1978). The *pays d'états* receive full treatment in J. R. Major, *Representative government in early modern France* (New Haven and London, 1980). The structure of power in one particular province is examined by W. H. Beik, *Absolutism and society in seventeenth-century France. State power and provincial aristocracy in Languedoc* (Cambridge, 1985).

The only modern study of the great nobility in the early modern period is rather weak on the seventeenth century: R. R. Harding, *Anatomy of a power élite. The provincial governors of early modern France* (New Haven and London, 1978). Additional information may be gleaned from R. J. Bonney, 'The French civil war, 1649–53', *European Studies Review*, viii (1978), 71–100, and *idem*, 'Cardinal Mazarin and the great nobility during the Fronde', *English Historical Review*, xcvi (1981), 818–33.

Porchnev's seminal book on popular rebellions in France (cited in the printed sources) has never been translated into English, but Mousnier's riposte has appeared in *France in crisis, 1620–1675*, ed. P. J. Coveney (1977). The fundamental contributions remain in French, however. They are the works by Bercé, now reissued in shortened form as *Histoire des croquants* (1985), M. Foisil, *La révolte des Nu-Pieds et les révoltes normandes de 1639* (1970) and R. Pillorget, *Les mouvements insurrectionnels de Provence entre 1596 et 1715* (1975). There are now two general studies in English on the peasantry, which contain useful sections on peasant revolt: P. Goubert, *The French peasantry in the seventeenth century* (trans. I. Patterson, Cambridge 1986) and E. Le Roy Ladurie, *The French peasantry, 1450–1660* (trans. A. Sheridan, Aldershot, 1987).

Index